CW00828059

William Reno provides a powerful, scholarly yet shocking account of the inner workings of an African state. He focuses upon the ties between foreign firms and African rulers in Sierra Leone, where politicians and warlords use private networks that exploit relationships with international businesses to buttress their wealth and so extend their powers of patronage. This permits them to expand the reach of their governments in unorthodox ways, but in the process they undermine the bureaucracy of their own states. Dr Reno suggests that as the post-colonial state is eroded there is a return to the enclave economies and private armies that characterized the pre-colonial and colonial arrangements between European businessmen or administrators and some African political figures.

Corruption and state politics in Sierra Leone

African studies series 83

Editorial board

Professor Naomi Chazan, *The Harry S. Truman Research Institute for the Advancement of Peace, The Hebrew University of Jerusalem*
Professor Christopher Clapham, *Department of Politics and International Relations, Lancaster University*
Professor Peter Ekeh, *Department of African American Studies, State University of New York, Buffalo*
Dr John Lonsdale, *Trinity College, Cambridge*
Professor Patrick Manning, *Department of History, Northeastern University, Boston*

Published in collaboration with
THE AFRICAN STUDIES CENTRE, CAMBRIDGE

A list of books in the series will be found at the end of this volume

Corruption and state politics in Sierra Leone

William Reno

Florida International University

CAMBRIDGE
UNIVERSITY PRESS

CAMBRIDGE UNIVERSITY PRESS
Cambridge, New York, Melbourne, Madrid, Cape Town, Singapore, São Paulo, Delhi

Cambridge University Press
The Edinburgh Building, Cambridge CB2 8RU, UK

Published in the United States of America by Cambridge University Press, New York

www.cambridge.org
Information on this title: www.cambridge.org/9780521103473

© Cambridge University Press 1995

This publication is in copyright. Subject to statutory exception
and to the provisions of relevant collective licensing agreements,
no reproduction of any part may take place without the written
permission of Cambridge University Press.

First published 1995
This digitally printed version 2009

A catalogue record for this publication is available from the British Library

Library of Congress Cataloguing in Publication data

Reno, William Sampson Klock, 1962–
Corruption and state politics in Sierra Leone / William Reno.
    p.   cm. – (African studies series; 83)
ISBN 0 521 47179 6 (hardback)
1. Political corruption–Sierra Leone.   2. Business and politics–
Sierra Leone.   3. International business enterprises–Sierra Leone–
Political activity.   I. Title.   II. Series.
JQ3121.A56C6   1995
320.9664'09'04–dc20   94-12865   CIP

ISBN 978-0-521-47179-4 hardback
ISBN 978-0-521-10347-3 paperback

Contents

Maps

Tables

Acknowledgements

Many helped in the production of this work. I thank those in Sierra Leone who patiently answered my questions and directed me to what was really important. Their help shaped my decision to study informal markets instead of agricultural reform, my intended research topic when I arrived in Freetown. I also owe a debt to those people in Kono and Koindu who, for obvious reasons, are best left unnamed.

I conducted fieldwork in Sierra Leone in 1989–90 with the support of the Institute of African Studies at Fourah Bay College, Freetown. A grant from the MacArthur Foundation financed research abroad and a semester of write-up after my return. The University of Iowa's Center for International and Comparative Studies, which brought me to Iowa City as a Visiting Scholar, provided a congenial environment for the completion of my dissertation during the fall of 1991.

I owe a special debt to Crawford Young for his tireless readings of numerous drafts and his most valuable comments. Donald Emmerson and Michael Schatzberg deserve special thanks for the considerable time and effort they spent on close readings of the manuscript. Thanks also go to Dennis Dresang, Kathryn Green, Scott Christensen and numerous Sierra Leoneans for the careful attention that they have given my work. I am also grateful to Sandy Anthony for coping with editorial tasks. But for Fred Hayward's early guidance, this work would not exist. To each I am indebted. None, however, share responsibility for opinions or errors in this work.

Acronyms

ADC	Associated Development Corporation
ADMS	Alluvial Diamond Mining Scheme
AMCL	African Mining Company of Liberia
APC	All Peoples Congress
AREDOR	Association pour le Recherche et l'Exploitation du Diamant et l'Or (Guinea)
CAST	Consolidated African Selection Trust
CCM	Cooperative Contract Mining
CID	Criminal Investigation Division
CO	Colonial Office
CSO	Central Selling Organization
CSO	Colonial Secretary's Office
DC	District Commissioner (to 1964)
DC/RY	District Commissioner/Railway District
DICOR	Diamond Corporation
DO	District Officer (after 1964)
ECOMOG	ECOWAS Monitoring Group
ECOWAS	Economic Community of West African States
EP	Eastern Province
EUROFER	(European Community iron and steel producer consortium)
GDO	Government Diamond Office
GGDO	Government Gold and Diamond Office
GLB	Governor's Letter Book
IGNU	Interim Government of National Unity
IMF	International Monetary Fund
ISU	Internal Security Unit
KPM	Kono Progressive Movement
LAMCO	Liberian American Swedish Minerals Company
LIAT	(LIAT Construction and Finance – headed by Shaptai Kalmanowitch)
LPC	Liberian Peace Council

MADA	Mining Area Development Administration
MPSSL	Maritime Protection Services of Sierra Leone
NA	Native Authority (to 1964)
NDMC	National Diamond Mining Corporation
NIMCO	Nimba Mining Company
NPFL	National Patriotic Front of Liberia
NPRC	National Provisional Ruling Council
NTC	National Trading Company
PDG	Parti democratique de Guinée
PEER	Public Economic Emergency Regulation
PSEP	Provincial Secretary, Eastern Province
PWD	Public Works Department (also a society)
RAP	Rights Accumulation Programme
RUF	Revolutionary United Front
SAP	Structural Adjustment Programme
SCIPA	(Company under direction of Nir Guaz)
SDR	Special Drawing Right
SIEROMCO	Sierra Leone Ore and Metal Co.
SLPIM	Sierra Leone Peoples Independent Movement
SLPP	Sierra Leone Peoples Party
SLST	Sierra Leone Selection Trust
SSI	Specialist Services International
ULIMO	United Liberian Movement for Democracy
WAF	West African Fisheries
WB	World Bank

Introduction

"How Can Africa Survive?" asks an influential observer exploring the persistent economic crisis there.[1] Reports in the late 1980s of collapsing government administration and growing economic hardship made prospects of a year studying the economic crisis in Sierra Leone an uncertain one. But in reality, some government officials, private businessmen, and their supporters were doing quite well for themselves in a thriving informal market – that is, legally proscribed production and exchange that contributes no revenues to government. Seemingly unpredictable and destructive bribery, corruption and shortages of goods, widely lamented in the local press and development literature, provided means for these individuals to attract supplicants as they became extremely rich. Threats of informal markets to state institutional coherence and power in Sierra Leone (independent since 1961) and elsewhere in Africa are well documented. The informal market role in rulers' construction of parallel political authority in the wake of the near total decay of formal state institutions – a Shadow State – is less well known.

Writers generally either portray informal markets as barriers to development, the negation of state power, or consider how informal markets enable harassed producers to retreat from the reach of government writ and manage private resources free from the claims of predatory officials. Most stress the necessity of reviving strong state institutional capacity to control exchange as a precondition for economic development. Nearly all reject the possibility that informal markets can provide alternative material and political support for the exercise of lasting political authority.

A closer look at Sierra Leone's informal markets, particularly its lucrative illicit diamond industry, shows some politicians and a few businessmen without state office exercising significant political authority through private control of these resources. These clandestine circuits sustain powerful political and economic networks in times of crisis. Their control over informal markets significantly shapes the implementation of creditor-sponsored policies designed to undermine informal markets. They manipulate policies designed to attract foreign investors who then underwrite what emerges as an alternative Shadow State in the midst of institutional state decay. The aim of this study is to show how these men – most holding high office, mostly Sierra Leonean, a few holding no office at all, some foreigners – become rich, control diverse avenues of illicit exchange and exercise considerable political power in spite of, or, more accurately, because of the collapsing formal state's incapacity to reverse the sharp contraction of revenues.

As the debate continues over informal markets, one view attributes Africa's crisis of governance and economies to states that are alternately "weak," "soft," "vampire," and "Lame Leviathans"[2] unable to control producers. Conclusions that such states are "suspended" and "de-linked" from society propose the reclamation of state capacity to restore formal markets, tax, and deliver services to citizens.[3] An opposing view holds that state-centered analyses do not account for the multiplicity of observed forms of informal markets. These scholars explain informal market origins and logic in terms other than the reactions of autonomous producers to state failure. Recent discussion centers on the extent to which state officials pursue private interests in informal markets at the expense of the competence and credibility of the formal state in which they hold office. This inquiry shifts from the significance of state policies to the networks of informal economic exchange that cross, and sometimes shadow, the boundaries of formal state responsibilities and powers.

In keeping with this shift, this book examines the development of distinctive spheres of informal economic exchange and political power in Sierra Leone. The country's place in the global economy is a significant factor in the Shadow State's strength. Data from Sierra Leone reflects the impact of historical, social and political factors within the country. Analysis of this situation, however, raises several issues confronting students of African politics: the nature of political authority as formal state and economic structures in some African countries near collapse, and the impact of foreign investment and reform programs designed to strengthen state institutions and taxable formal economies at the expense of informal market networks.

A striking feature of the Sierra Leone case is the extent to which top politicians and businessmen pursue personal wealth and political power through informal markets. Indeed, International Monetary Fund (IMF) and World Bank-sponsored austerity programs hasten politicians' abandonment of the inherited colonial state as the strains of meeting creditor demands drain official institutions of what little capacity remains. Politicians recruit some foreign investors into their Shadow State political networks in return for advantages that power in this Shadow State offers. Collaborating investors service some minimal requirements of creditor-sponsored reform programs which promise loans that will actually further underwrite political networks. The implications for reform and the future character of state power in Sierra Leone and elsewhere in Africa are profound, but as yet have received little attention. The survival of this Shadow State founded upon informal, private control of exchange, alongside internal economic crises and international pressures for reform, indicates that the post-colonial institutional state is no longer the principal authority that many have assumed it to be since the independence of Sierra Leone, or Africa generally.

The major theme of this book is the rise of the Shadow State – the emergence of rulers drawing authority from their abilities to control markets and their material rewards. Historical experience, particularly Sierra Leone's British colonial era, brought together state officials and businessmen with stakes in informal market control. Other factors to examine include the role of ethnic, occupational and secret society networks, as well as the impact of individual initiative and choices in the parallel development of Sierra Leone's formal and informal political economies over the past century.

Chapter 1 reviews theories of the political economy of informal market–state relations. Scholars differ over whether Africa's decrepit states and growing informal markets are a consequence of societal withdrawal from illegitimate, autocratic rule, or whether informal markets are instruments of rulers' power. In Sierra Leone, officials' control over informal markets defines their domestic exercise of political power as well as their society's relations with foreigners. This situation supports analyses that conclude that informal markets are integrally linked to the exercise of political power. This observation leads to enquiries into the organization of informal markets and their roles in rulers' strategies in the Shadow State to reinterpret political power in the context of the political uncertainties of economic hardship and external challenge from creditors.

The second chapter outlines the historical and political background to the emergence of informal markets as an alternative basis of political authority. For example, British colonial officers tended to deal with their own crises of state capacity through accommodations with Africans engaged in both legitimate and illicit trade. In order to understand better the consequence of these choices, this chapter considers why colonial rulers did not choose to support a vigorous group of indigenous African businessmen responsible for a growing formal economy.

Late colonial policies, the subject of Chapter 3, widened political participation and expanded state responsibilities, yet increased informal networks of local notables active in the country's growing illicit diamond industry. Overextended officials struggled to control these individuals through the 1950s and 1960s. Ultimately, populist challengers to the first independence government catered to the interests of informal marketeers and their employees to gain political power in 1967.

Sierra Leone's populist second president, Siaka Stevens, owed much of his political strength to support from informal market networks. The fourth chapter explores President Stevens's effort to incorporate the apex of these illicit networks, especially ethnic Lebanese diamond merchants and their employees, directly into his new political organization to address popular expectations that independence placed upon state institutions and political parties. This chapter documents the changing distribution of informal market resources and opportunities as well as the fiscal value of this foundation for Stevens's growing Shadow State.

The next two chapters consider President Stevens's control over informal market networks as a strategy to gain control over grassroots political organizations. Chapter 5 documents the absorption of government-owned enterprises – through privatizations as part of a World Bank reform program – into this private political network. Chapter 6 chronicles the dramatic geographical, social and sectoral expansion of Stevens's Shadow State. Foreign creditors balked at further loans to a corrupt and bankrupt formal administration. This crisis of the Shadow State appeared to confirm many scholars' analyses that patron–client networks undermine productive investment and effective institutional state capacity, and are thus unsustainable as alternatives to the unique services and superior economic efficiency of strong formal states.

But Chapter 7 shows how Stevens's chosen successor, Major General Joseph Momoh, though facing a need for creditor support after 1986, established his own authority through informal markets. President Momoh followed IMF advice to attract foreign investors; he then used foreign investors to displace rivals in informal markets and generate income, a task made even more urgent as IMF-imposed austerity programs further starved state institutions of resources. Though deposed in 1992, Momoh's manipulations of creditor-imposed reforms set the stage for the rise of a new president-turned-warlord who devotes himself more exclusively to the subordination of markets to the political logic of the Shadow State. Private armies, a central element of this Shadow State development, are also considered here.

The final chapter considers the extent to which Shadow State rulers can maximize their power with Shadow State strategies inimical to strong formal institutions. Our attention shifts to Liberian rebel leader Charles Taylor. Though lacking the formal trappings of sovereignty, Taylor attracts both licit and illicit foreign investment. With these resources Taylor builds a private army that breaks the mold of post-colonial states in the region. He imposes effective borders where none existed. He commands a security apparatus to control economic transactions between his subjects and outsiders. This Shadow State, what Taylor calls "Greater Liberia," built upon Liberia's remains more clearly defines the possibilities and limitations of Shadow States built directly upon the foundations of the inherited colonial states in other African settings.

Before continuing, it is appropriate to give details of the study's methodology and physical setting given the difficulties of researching activities that are legally defined as clandestine.

Research method and setting

This is a study of the politics of informal markets, but it draws upon the economics, history, and sociology of informal markets. Its contribution to understanding informal market politics lies in its incorporation of these other aspects of informal markets in a holistic approach. The advantage of this eclectic approach lies in its capacity to shed light on clandestine activity in circumstances where purely quantitative data are absent or extremely difficult to obtain. The illicit nature of most of Sierra Leone's economic life makes sample surveys and quantitative techniques impossible in this setting where, as one government official commented, "if we enforced our laws, every trader would be in prison." In this situation, numerous informal interviews, direct observation and personal rapport made it possible to acquire information.

Clifford Geertz raises concerns about creating systematic knowledge of a subject from a purely observational study.[4] Geertz points to the difficulties of identifying the boundaries of significant behavior and generalizing motivations from observations of unique situations and behavior. These issues are of immediate concern given the clandestine nature of the enterprises and relationships that are the subjects of this study.

I avoided focusing on a single case, so I was able to compare a wide range of personal networks organized around informal markets. My relations with informants in Freetown, the country's ethnically diverse capital, home to 500,000 of Sierra Leone's four million inhabitants, began upon my arrival. The total absence of effective banking services and severe shortages of officially subsidized goods forced me to turn to the informal market which alone could supply them. As a white foreign pedestrian, I lacked obvious ties with the authorities or business rivals whom informants feared. My residence and participation in the daily life of a Freetown community also brought me into close contact with many individuals who operate on the margins of major business and political networks, since in them they saw their best hope for protection from the hardships of the country's disintegrating economy.

University affiliation, an official condition of my stay, brought me a measure of respect. Some officials responded positively to my requests for information when they discovered that I was writing a book on business in Sierra Leone. Many of these officials began successful political and business careers as lecturers at the national university. One such official, who has since retired, commented that he too wished to write a book about business in Sierra Leone. He then produced documents that had accompanied him into his retirement. These and other "retired documents" illustrate the extent to which officials' private interests overwhelmed definitions, and the pursuit, of formal state interests.

The geography of Sierra Leone's informal markets provided additional clues for me to define the boundaries of related political relationships. I quickly discovered that the country's (and its informal markets') main source of wealth lay in Kono District's diamond fields. This savanna region, home to about 75,000 people drawn from across Sierra Leone by the promise of gain in the illicit diamond trade, lies 200 miles northeast of the capital. Once providing nearly 70 percent of government revenues,[5] this mining centre is the setting for struggles among informal market networks and the remnants of the formal state for resources and political influence. Local government officials' almost total preoccupation with illicit mining, however, brought a corresponding decrease in officials' attention to travel restrictions. While also a symptom of the collapse of Sierra Leone's government institutions, the lack of predictable enforcement of regulations enabled me to make extended visits to local mining communities. The major barrier to direct observation lay in the assumption by some that I intended to participate in local trade rather than simply observe it.

My pursuit of the flow of goods and money, and thus of political influence in the Shadow State, also led me to the border trading town of Koindu, situated two miles from Guinea and five miles from Liberia. This town, a two-day, 300-mile journey from Freetown, is dominated by ethnic Fulani traders who also provide the community's effective civil authority. Here, political relations between this ethnic community of traders and state officials were organized almost exclusively around the division of control over, and rewards from, a vigorous commerce in smuggled consumer goods.

Political and economic conditions in Sierra Leone make it a difficult place to gather information, however. Personal insecurity, the political climate of uncertainty, and daily economic hardship confronting most people made the collection of systematic data difficult. This situation affected the availability of documentary sources. Political unrest during the mid-1980s resulted in the loss of some provincial archives to fire. Other archives have been severely damaged by insects and storage under leaky roofs.

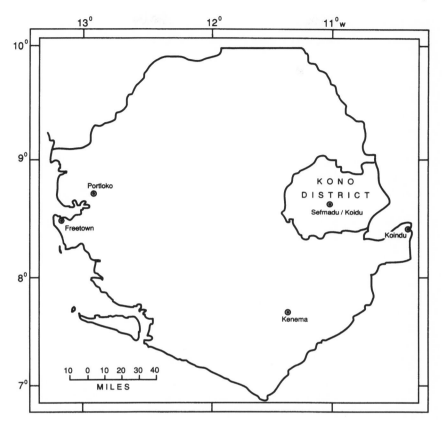

Map 1   Sierra Leone
Source: Adapted from John I. Clarke, *Sierra Leone in Maps*
(London: Hodder & Stoughton, 1969).

In addition to these problems, recent documentary sources are even more scarce. Visitors to the Government Bookstore find shelves stocked with documents from the 1950s and 1960s. Comparable reports from the 1980s are missing, or appear in much slimmer volumes. Furthermore, basic trade and production statistics and even budget expenditures from different official sources often contain widely varying figures. Lack of reliability is itself data, insofar as government officials involved in informal markets have strong incentives to obscure or omit economic data. Missing or widely varying figures often pointed to those sectors of the economy most fully absorbed into informal-market networks. Individuals' roles as state officials and informal market businessmen also provided unexpected documentary information. Records of essentially private transactions carried out by individuals in their capacity as officials were sometimes dutifully filed in ministry archives.

Freetown's half-dozen weekly newspapers provided excellent information on formal and illicit business activity. Taking advantage of relaxed press controls, these papers liberally reported rumors of politicians' private business interests and speculated upon their misuse of office. While not always of the greatest reliability, the way these newspapers attacked or praised well-known individuals was useful for discovering the boundaries of Shadow State networks linking informal business and politics. The knowledge that many of these newspapers receive financial backing from powerful patrons to attack their rivals helped to confirm the location of boundaries between informal economic and political networks. Reporters and editorial staffs also proved to be a valuable source of information about what goes on in Freetown and the provinces, and who collaborates with whom as individual fortunes rise and fall.

These details of methodology and location set the scene for an account of Sierra Leone's Shadow State – the country's informal markets and the political authority associated with them. Jean François Bayart doubts that a focus on the visible African state itself provides a basis for understanding political authority there.[6] This study takes up Bayart's identification of political authority where it is exercised in African society – his *politique du ventre*, or the juncture of economic accumulation and political authority which forms the basis of the Shadow State.

1   Informal markets and the Shadow State: Some theoretical issues

> For what is it to divide the Power of a Commonwealth, but to Dissolve it, for Powers divided mutually destroy each other.   Thomas Hobbes[1]
>
> Usai u go tie cow, e go for eat. (Wherever you tie the cow, he will eat [profit].)   Sierra Leonean proverb

Along with its creditors, Sierra Leone's citizens often remark on the abundance of the country's natural resources and potential for economic development. Yet the huge accumulation of riches by a few powerful men, a minuscule and shrinking formal economy, accelerating mass impoverishment, a crushing debt burden and the collapse of basic state institutions make Sierra Leone one of Africa's most decrepit and weak states. This chapter explores theories explaining the role of informal markets in state collapse and debates concerning the consequences of informal market growth. After considering the application of these theories to the case of state decay and informal market growth in Zaire, I provide an alternative framework to understand why informal markets survive throughout Africa, as well as in Sierra Leone, and why they attract the interests of many of the continent's politicians and businessmen. This framework also permits me to explain how increased foreign investment and creditor constraints can prompt politicians to increase their involvement in informal markets at the expense of a definition of institutional state interests.

Students of state decay quickly recognize the weak hold that formal institutions have on African societies and economies. Fixations on state institutions as both cause and remedy for informal markets, however, downplay consideration of the specific nature of informal markets. So-called society centered studies offer an alternative vantage point that reveals strategies of groups and individuals coping with political and economic uncertainty. This approach identifies groups – clan, ethnic, religious – that manage resources out of the reach of central authority. This approach often views informal market growth as a direct corollary to state decay, however. It fails to consider more broadly how informal markets serve as vehicles to organize production, distribute access to opportunity,

9

and control populations. Theories focusing on the political role of informal markets do not portray their development as a reaction to state policies. This approach notes that informal markets often grow around societal networks that predate Africa's states themselves.

These approaches raise key questions that are addressed in this work. Through what specific historical and social structures does the authority of the Shadow State become manifest? To what extent are informal channels of accumulation products of the inherited colonial state, rather than popular reactions to its predations? How is this non-institutional authority perceived and shaped by citizens, and how does this influence the way that Shadow State rulers rule? These questions have implications for understanding the relation between the actual exercise of power in Africa and the decay of formal political and economic institutions in places like Sierra Leone.

State-centered approach – informal markets as dysfunction

Recent attention to Africa's informal markets as part of a "crisis of the state" offers dichotomous views of what African states ought to be and what they in fact are. Diamond tells us that "The typical African state may be described as 'swollen' in that it is both too large and too weak."[2] Sandbrook blames declining state control of resources on "Heavy-handed regulation of civil society by suspicious autocrats ... caus[ing] people to flee to the informal sector, [and] engage in illegal activities like smuggling, or go into exile."[3] Joseph attests that widespread corruption and loss of control over markets lie in Nigerian rulers' "failure to maintain the integrity of the state in relation to the multifarious groups and organizations in civil society."[4]

These claims identify informal markets as symptoms of bad policies. How these states actually function is peripheral to this state-centered inquiry – other than to highlight practices diverging from legal norms. As the title of an examination of the crisis of Africa's governance, *How Can Africa Survive?* suggests, prescriptive measures occupy the scholar's attention.[5] From a developmentalist perspective, Sandbrook informs us that "The public sector is central to Africa's economic development." Ignoring the actual process of accumulation and exchange in African societies, he observes that "Africa needs active, developmental states capable of complementing and directing market forces."[6] Observing that the loss of control over exchange and revenues weakens African administrations, World Bank officials stress that "It is of the utmost importance for the state to establish a predictable and honest regulatory framework, to assure law and order ... "[7] Or as Nigeria's President Babangida avers, "Economic bliss cannot coexist with political decadence."[8]

Distanced from the social bases of economic and political life, state-centered views of Africa's "crisis" provide little explanation of how informal markets supplant institutional capacity. This mode of interpretation precludes observation of struggle over the contested control of exchange which it blames for the crisis of African state capacity. The use of European state development as a reference point for identifying deficiencies of African government administrations obscures the past and present of Africa's systems of production and trade. To look at markets as they exist in Africa, rather than as what critics think they should be, involves identifying what they are in that context – the forms of domination and exploitation in Africans' struggles to control, extend or resist capital.

Multilateral creditors identify bad policies as the root of poor economic performance, however. World Bank and IMF officials propose limiting state interference in the economy. Structural adjustment policies assume that an autonomy of state interests can be created sufficient to allow a leader to impose hardships upon those once favored by diversions of resources. Put differently, some argue that the reformist ruler's task is to identify and assemble a social coalition supportive of new policies.[9] But a decade of economic recession has followed the widespread adoption of IMF/World Bank managed reforms.[10] To be sure, many leaders fail to fully implement reform programs, but the problem lies in the tendency for austerity programs to cut back on what little state capacity is left as the possibility of official investment in the economy becomes more remote. Even committed reformers such as Ghana's Jerry Rawlings, fail to generate attractive gains around which to rally further support for reform.[11]

Thus bereft of even the minimal developmental capabilities that the state had earlier acquired, rulers are unlikely to attract societal or elite support for their reforms. But while popular rejection of austerity has been considered the largest danger facing reformers, there is ample evidence that rulers are willing to face the "SAP riot." More critical for rulers, however, is the tendency for austerity measures, meant to correct bad policies, to constrain political uses of state resources. Rulers are forced to seek new ways to keep intra-elite coalitions together so as to ensure the regime's stability and survival. These new strategies frequently breech the boundaries between public and private that reforms are designed to reinforce.

To preserve elite accommodations or, in Bayart's words, "hegemonic alliances,"[12] rulers extend their efforts to coopt increasingly diverse societal networks and organizations in order to continue providing benefits to loyal elites. The resources and rent-seeking opportunities present in informal markets are a powerful enticement to hard-pressed rulers. It is this struggle over control of informal markets that this book is about. The irony of structural adjustment and its assumptions of state–society dichotomies is that they strengthen the very patrimonial features of African governance that the policies are meant to address. Sure enough, many authoritarian regimes survive structural adjustment and rulers remain in power as formal economies continue their steady declines.

State-centered assumptions of the political neutrality of exchange and the primacy of economistic rationality ignore the multifarious forms of domination and control, what Achille Mbembe calls "cultures of terror" that arise from particular histories and are concerned with much more than the simple control over the allocation of resources.[13] At issue is control over elements of society associated with the production and reproduction of capital, and therefore the ability to determine the specific distribution of resources and patterns of authority.[14]

In his critique of developmentalist approaches to economic crisis on Africa, Copans notes that attention to informal markets for themselves rather than as deviations from an ideal uncovers a contested social and political terrain. Markets serve as the focal point of struggles propelled by a variety of logics that extend beyond calculations of economic benefit.[15] Copans observes in his study of Senegal's Mouride Brotherhoods' control of informal markets, that "it is impossible to separate perceptions of brotherhood in its productive, agrarian and fraternal dimensions, much less from the capitalist transformation of production and commercializa- tion."[16] Struggle for control of resources exists on several planes at once; some rulers' efforts to create formal bureaucratic structures represent only part of this struggle. Nor is state intervention over contested issues relegated to areas of legal competence. Indeed, informal pursuits of state strength may exist where institutions show signs of gross decay. In Senegal, for instance, Copans finds that Leopold Senghor merged the indigenous business and political elite that arose at the end of the colonial era and traditional elites into a ruling alliance. Senghor manipulated traditional elite control over markets to sustain and extend his own control over this elite accommodation.

Ultimately, the examination of the process of control and domination located within informal markets themselves provides a corrective to concerns limited to state "failure" alone. To undertake such an examin- ation is to observe that markets in Africa do not just put people to work. Closer examination of market organizations draws our attention to those – including state officials – who make claims on producers and traders who already experience their own forms of social control and accumulation. Abandoning functional prerequisites of state behavior as it *should* be reveals an alternative set of traits that takes into account ways in which rulers try to control (or fail to control) local societies. Attention to the impact on local struggles of local histories and the nature of ties to the global economy goes much further than references to inefficient bureaucracies and bad policies to explain the weakness of institutional state administrations.

This closer attention to the context of state–society relations in markets provides a clearer idea of what forms African states actually assume as rulers struggle to control citizens and ensure their own survival. It is the nature and logic of this contested ground, of informal markets, that offers the best vantage point for advancing a truly political analysis of the decay of formal state authority and the struggle to exercise authority in realms outside institutional state boundaries.

Society-centered approach – informal markets as survival strategies

Do state–society dichotomies exist in markets, despite officials' extensive interventions? It became increasingly obvious through the 1970s that producers were withdrawing from unproductive official economies due to the acquisitive tendencies of state officials. Studies of informal markets, focusing on societies, reveal ways that citizens produce and trade outside government reach.[17] This "exit option" spread to larger towns in the 1980s, occupying at least a portion of the energies of Ghana's government employees by the start of the decade.[18]

The notion of "exit" identifies ways that individuals avoid state regulations and revenue collections. It is also widely observed that individuals "straddle" formal and informal markets. They use powers in different spheres to seize opportunities for accumulation. Thus, "viewed from below," in Rothchild and Chazan's volume *Precarious Balance*, "the state is seen as a distributor of benefits and an intruder. It is simultaneously an oppressor and an ally, a source of much needed goods as well as of uncertainty and interference."[19] But the assumption is that, while people may believe that they too might benefit from state favors, opportunities for accumulation do exist beyond the long arm of state interference. Thus state recession allegedly results in the development of an autonomous business class.

Green observed informal markets in Uganda that have "waxed fat and powerful as the old 'legal' economic system and the state has disintegrated."[20] Public–private divides shift as patronage possibilities and rent seeking opportunities associated with state power shrivel along with the decay of state institutions.[21] Weak and irresolute governments undermine

the system of prerogatives and privilege that sustained elite accommodations, says Green. This eroding social basis of regime power is further
reflected in the rise of "non-captured" producers who enjoy autonomy
from the patrimonial tendencies that are the core logic of governance in the
decaying state.

Some are skeptical of the capacity of this new economic pluralism to
become the basis of sustained development. For this reason, extensive
inquiry into the quality of governance increasingly attracts the attention of
scholars.[22] This "Governance School" concludes that abuses of state
power can be contained with the counterweight of this emerging African
civil society. Given the diffuse nature of these societal forces, scholars and
policy-makers devote much attention to ways of organizing them that
would give them the strength to impose accountability on state officials.

Recent World Bank documents reflect this concern for governance.[23]
They propose policies to enhance indigenous individual and associational
energies. This strengthened private sector will then form the supportive
social base that will demand official accountability and support economic
reform measures. World Bank prescriptions propose that these energies,
including entrepreneurial tendencies found in informal markets, "will
reverse the breakdown over the last 10 to 15 years."[24] Coupled with roll-
backs of state involvement in the economy, this reform scenario resembles
the hopes of departing colonizers in the 1960s that strong pluralist societal
interests would emerge to turn African states into productive, efficient
primary product producers able to finance more extensive development.

But we can detect few cases where these emerging societal forces have
transformed the style of governance in Africa. Regimes have coopted or
destroyed organized groups that have emerged from civil society. Developments in Nigeria illustrate the tendency of important groups of elites to
infiltrate state efforts to guide and support private market reforms.
Furthermore, reform-minded leaders abet this process.[25] Rulers are pro-
tective of elite networks of accumulation. For example, Senegalese officials
hesitate to reduce mutually beneficial ties to a "groundnut clientele" that
enjoys numerous informal market advantages with the ruler's complicity.[26]
To the extent that austerity measures weaken the role of state resources in
elite accommodations, there is a tendency for state officials to *increase* their
interference in those market networks thought to be capable of imposing
accountability on the state. It is this alternative project – rulers' efforts to
sustain elite accommodations – emerging in part from pressures of externally imposed reform, that is at the core of the construction of the Shadow
State, and what must appear to IMF and World Bank officials as
anti-reform.

This breakdown of state–society dichotomies, especially in informal
markets, appears even in – or rather, especially in – the weakest of formal

states. "It is a manifestation of class struggle," says Janet MacGaffey; "as coping strategies for dealing with the depredations of the state and economic exigency."[27] "Smuggling," says Mukohya Vwakyanakazi in his study of Zairian traders, "appears as an act of rebellion against political and economic systems and the dominant groups."[28]MacGaffey and Vwakyanakazi depict informal markets as responses to state failure. To be sure, the collapse of state institutions in Zaire prompts enterprising individuals to seek alternative routes of social mobility. But this dichotomous view that upholds the possibility of "escape" automatically supposes communal self-sufficiency.[29] Even as state institutions fail as distribution points of privilege or benefits, individuals still live within monetary circuits. Village relatives make incessant claims on family members with jobs in the monetized economy. Schooling, health services and ceremonies all require cash.[30] Even the most remote villages are subject to officials' decisions regarding currency, credit and commerce.[31]

Informal market operators may avoid tax collectors' claims, but are subject to a multitude of other circuits of state power. In the Uganda of the 1980s, the state "decides upon the currency, fixes official exchange rates, makes many rules of commercial life, determines taxes and collects customs. As such, its economic importance is all embracing."[32] Informal markets are clearly tied to officials' decisions, especially their abilities to grant informal exemptions from currency and trading restrictions that laws create. Where MacGaffey finds an "indigenous bourgeoisie" with interests contrary to "parasites" (contrary by definition because "parasites" become "indigenous bourgeoisies" as they are "captured" by the informal market),[33] others observe a mafia-like relation between informal market businesses and officials who sell protection. Nelson Kasfir notes that in Uganda "As *magendo* operators moved into legitimate economic sectors, their involvement with state officials would necessarily have to grow more extensive. The operation of *magendo* was significantly dependent on, and continued to be related to the state."[34]

State officials may even share a common interest in abetting informal markets as part of a strategy to control political challenges or obtain essential services,[35] especially when austerity programs reduce institutional state supplies of benefits. The Sierra Leone case below illustrates how leaders have recently intensified efforts to supplement loyal followers' incomes with informal market opportunities, selling exemptions to others, and struggling to prevent rivals' access to informal markets. Similar reactions during periods of austerity and reform over the last century suggest that this may be part of a deeper historical process in Africa. Informal markets may be indistinguishable as results of state predations and as evidence of societal avoidance.[36]

Dichotomous views of state action–societal reaction downplay multi-

farious forms of state intervention, especially outside institutional channels, in informal markets. Referring to the institutions of state, MacGaffey
notes that "the political aristocracy use the state to extend their own control
over the economy, but in the process, have sometimes furthered the
interests of other classes because of administrative ineffectiveness." But she
then notes: "Regulations that are unenforceable have purposes other than
their overt one: they provide officials with additional opportunities for
harassment and extortion."[37] Oppositional state–society logics downplay
the extent to which economic and political advantages in each sphere are
connected, require accommodations, and provoke conflicts that are distant
from any notion of "disengagement." The symbiotic nature of state power
outside institutional channels and informal markets is missed where
observers see societal opposition in a context of state institutional failure.
Jean François Bayart's alternative vision of states and markets proclaims
that:

In Africa, the state *is* the prime (though not the only) channel of accumulation . . .
Even the successful businessmen in the informal sector are highly dependent on the
state because they need constantly to circumvent regulations and obtain official
permits. It is, therefore, otiose to seek to establish a conceptual difference between
the private and public sectors. Both are instruments of a dominant class striving to
establish its hegemony.[38]

The case of Zaire, briefly explored below, illustrates the extent to which this
conceptualization of the link between states and markets is more appropriate than a state versus society analysis. Zaire, an almost total "predator
state," yet hosting a vigorous informal market, is a good location to begin
expositing the theoretical foundation for an alternative conceptualization
of political power in some areas of Africa centered around the relation of
markets to the Shadow State.

Zaire: The mystery of seemingly unending "state decay"

The collapsing government institutions and the rise of informal markets in
Zaire appear to support the dichotomous state–society views of government–market relations. Zaire is called a *bula matari*, crusher of rocks, notes
Crawford Young.[39] Thomas Callaghy sees an overbearing, but "lame
Leviathan" that loses 60 percent of its revenue to the predations of its own
officials.[40] Where less than 1 percent of official expenditures go to agricultural development,[41] it is not surprising that Janet MacGaffey sees
organized informal market resistance to a state that offers few, if any,
concrete benefits.

But how should the evidence be interpreted? State-centered studies focus
on the predatory state, responsible for the economic crisis that causes

citizens to seek relief from bad policies and burdensome demands. "Corruption is the defining feature," says Young.[42] Callaghy notes that Zaire's rulers "manifest a weak sense of public purpose and collective or societal good."[43] Both authors' state-centered analyses locate the origins of "state decay" in the country's colonial legacy. Zaire's rulers inherited an authoritarian tradition of hegemony and fiscal zeal. Most importantly, they also inherited a weak legitimacy and divided population. Colonial rulers self-consciously categorized subjects, favoring some as middlemen, and emphasizing presumed differences for administrative purposes. Kinship ties and manipulations thus became dominant modes of politics – either for defensive purposes when state power would not or could not defend broad societal interests, or to gain access to state resources.

Evidence of state decay highlights the fragility of bureaucratic institutions and democratic processes in the face of this colonial legacy. Despite hastily adopted democratic reforms in the 1950s, the 1 percent who were of non-African origin and loyalties controlled 95 percent of Zaire's physical assets, 82 percent of its productive capability and 88 percent of its private savings.[44] This concentration of power and wealth permitted post-colonial rulers to dominate the distribution of resources and opportunity in society. The new rulers allocated resources to those over whom they had influence or control. They showed ingenuity in championing particular ethnic groups, often widening inherited divisions. Thus the colonial bureaucracy trained in authoritarian habits was married to a clientelism that undermined the efficiency and institutional logic of that same bureaucracy.

Politics is narrowed to those with command of, or access to state resources against the interests of those who do not, and who can be milked for resources. This dichotomy imparts what both Callaghy and Young note as Zaire's rulers' distinctive authoritarian political style and mercantilist extraction of wealth from society. As the regime has failed to develop a convincing legitimacy, both authors note that external resources provide some fiscal autonomy, but the withdrawal of an evasive society weakens the state's capacity to act.[45]

Throughout state-centered analyses, the "state bourgeoisie" or "political aristocracy" is seen as expanding with the clientelization of bureaucracies, but always searching for additional resources. Citizens resist and retreat in the face of this onslaught. The predatory state tail wags the societal dog. Officials live off their positions, using them to extort benefits from citizens. They subordinate bureaucratic interests to personal gain. These conditions make escape rational and reasonable. Young identifies a "pathology of state decay" where rulers no longer place the struggle for societal improvement at the center of their *raison d'état*, such as it is. The result "opened up new economic and societal space which is being rapidly reorganized into parallel markets ... [which] demonstrates not only the energies of civil society, but also the possibility of survival."[46]

Society-centered analyses then stress the autonomy of informal markets. Producers smuggle goods across borders in an almost universal response to discrimination by ruling groups. The volume of this evasion is very large. MacGaffey informs us that something like half of Zaire's coffee crop is smuggled.[47] This trade subsequently undermines the state's formal economic capacity, promotes a disrespect for laws and even "converts" once parasitic state officials who seek personal gain from this increasingly attractive private means of social mobility.

"Disengagement" began outside the capital in the 1970s.[48] There, MacGaffey identified the rise of a "new middle class" engaging in illicit trade. She sees this group as "significant for class formation, because some of its activities allow for considerable accumulation."[49] Is this the missing "middle strata" that colonial development failed to produce, the "civil society" that did not exist at independence to take control of state power in order to better facilitate their productive activities and accumulation of capital? Is this the core of a capitalist class that will demand accountability and a government committed to protecting their interests? Members of this "new class," MacGaffey tells us, make up 22 percent of substantial business owners in Kisangani.[50] Their political significance, she says, lies in their tendency not to look to the predatory state as protector of their rights and interests. Indeed, she sees state decay as so advanced that this private network absorbs some state officials into this alternative pursuit of wealth.

Are MacGaffey's "disengaged" entrepreneurs evidence of societal capacity to reshape society in the wake of the declining "predator state"? Opposition between state and societal authority abounds, to be sure. Group conflicts capture fundamental clashes between rulers and ruled. Yet mysteriously, Zaire's President Mobutu remains in power despite the "pathologies" of state decay and the long, sustained decline of Zaire's economy. MacGaffey's "new middle class" shows little organizational capacity, just as similar, much longer-lived networks in Latin America and India fail to provide comprehensive alternatives to weak state institutions. In Peru, Hernando DeSoto is especially skeptical of informal market operators' capacities to regulate and protect their own activities on a national scale, while he is confident of the ability of an ineffective state to disrupt accumulation.[51] Most recently in Zaire, Mobutu's announced political "reforms" have produced up to 250 political parties.[52] Opposition to the president abounds, but takes the form of kinship and commercial networks, with only the veneer of multiparty politics.[53] These political maneuvers suggest that there are other supports of the president's powers beyond the confines of the decaying state.

Explaining the duality of the Zairian state

This unexpectedly durable "lame Leviathan" and weakly organized societal opposition suggests that state power and societal networks are more intricately linked than attention to state *or* society would have us believe. Zaire's rulers do forcibly extract wealth from society as analyses of the "predator state" indicate.[54] But elite accommodations remain an important facet of political power, even as clientelized bureaucracies decline. Heads of political networks seek new resources as predatory impulses overwhelm institutional interests. Rulers of the "predator state" develop dual interests; as their power appears to recede in the formal sphere of decaying bureaucracies, they increasingly use non-formal state power, including their capacity to intervene in informal markets to seek new opportunities and resources for clients.

It is the citizens who bear the brunt of these new intrusions, while at the same time being subjected to the full impact of the collapsing formal economy. This makes accommodations with new manifestations of state power all the more imperative. Personal connection with elite privilege may protect citizens against a state that does not protect them in an institutional sense. Rulers can then sell protection and favor. Zaire's "new middle class" receives favored access to diamond, timber and consumer goods trade through ties to the president, *especially* as state institutions collapse.[55] Outside the capital, private businessmen pay armed troops to protect them; those who do not pay are attacked.[56] It is those who do curry favor that are largely responsible for the rise of divisive "multi-Mobutuisms" among the numerous new political parties that have accompanied recent political "reforms."

Interpenetrations of the non-formal state and society abound. This fluidity renders conventional public–private, urban–rural and state–society dichotomies of limited utility.[57] Assuredly, some individuals reject this elite project of absorbing and manipulating societal networks. Young notes that patriots and dissidents resist Mobutu's predations, and Michael Schatzberg observes the hard life of the honest judge in Zaire.[58] One sees the same intentions elsewhere. Nigeria's military, at times profiteers, are at other times stand-ins for the missing "national bourgeoisie" that was to accompany capitalist development. But in fact, political power in Zaire and elsewhere more often migrates to new areas as inherited colonial institutions decay and the nation-state envisioned at independence fails to appear. Halts to external aid and creditor insistence on austerity only seem to accelerate the migration of elite accommodation to new social terrain. The World Bank's release of $30 million to Zaire and the United State's "conciliatory tone"[59] reflect a growing recognition that strangling

Mobutu's government of resources might well leave the president alive and Zaire dead.

Elites not only feed upon the dwindling ruins of the state, but also upon resistance to their power. Effective predation, what Willame calls "state as bandit,"[60] along with protection rackets, draw new resources to the president's network of clients. As state power adapts to this new context, its boundaries shift. John Ayoade tells us that by 1985, only 12 percent of Zaire's roads were motorable.[61] Truly, people in rural areas are "disengaged," willing or not. But does the state need to directly control these people? Fading bureaucracies could not control them in any case, though no doubt the armed forces strike at efforts to organize armed resistance. Instead, the state, such as it exists in these areas, appears several miles above the treetops in airplanes tying together members of Mobutu's state – the army, police, remaining bureaucrats, and a shifting array of collaborators.

But even collapse provides benefits to those enjoying political favor. Hyperinflation has turned large segments of urban Kinshasa into speculators and smugglers. They then become targets of predation for soldiers and police.[62] Meanwhile, Mobutu establishes cozy ties with UNITA diamond mining operations in Angola. Mobutu incorporates UNITA and private – allegedly South African Inkatha – security forces into his illicit mining network to ensure that no pieces of this far-flung empire take advantage of distance or lack of institutional coordination to seize resources for themselves.[63]

Control over illicit exchange also operates as an effective political tool in other countries. Smuggling accounts for as much as 90 percent of the Benin's trade,[64] and benefits informal market businesses, peasants "disengaged" from the formal economy, and the country's rulers who preside over this officially illegal entrepôt trade. As in Zaire, investigation of this informal trade would reveal much about the accommodations and struggles between rulers and citizens. Did informal market trade arise from state policies, or did a preexisting, perhaps pre-colonial phenomenon make the European notion of a nation-state and single market unit within inherited colonial boundaries unlikely in the first place?

To better understand the paradoxes of simultaneous state institutional weakness and endurance it is best to look at the accommodations and struggles between rulers, elites, and citizens. Michael Schatzberg's study of Zairian politics provides such an approach. His understanding of the state as "a fluid and contextual entity whose shape and internal configurations of power are constantly changing"[65] reveals shifting patterns of accommodation and conflict. The shift in the Kimbanguist Church position from opposition to collaboration, and the Catholic Church's reverse journey illustrates changes in the boundary between state and society. As conceptions of the state change, so do peoples' understandings of what constitutes the political realm. Extensive politician involvement in informal markets may also mark a shift of the political realm, rather than simply the "exit" of state officials from state decay.

The Shadow State – informal markets and the political realm

A number of European scholars, including Bayart, offer a framework for looking at African politics through the lens of the shifting boundaries of state action. Bayart emphasizes the ambiguities and tensions between *dominants* and *dominees*. His notion of struggle – broader than class – focuses on the project of creating state control supportive of elite goals. The struggle to control society, to construct a "connective tissue" between rulers and citizens, is a focal point, not only for domination, but also for societal resistance. As institutions prove to be weakly constituted in the first place, the totality of the state offensive renders all sorts of activities, including illicit exchange, as targets of elite control. Rulers may find in these realms the resources to construct an elite accommodation. At the same time, rulers struggle to defend their authority against societal challenges, or what Bayart terms "modes of popular political action."[66] While distinctions between state and society exist, this mode of analysis sees shifting boundaries, not firm dichotomies, between state and society.

Bayart emphasizes that the character of this "state hegemonic project" is a starting point for studying political power in Africa:

The range and intensity of mechanisms of domination of the post-colonial state should not suggest that subordinated social actors remain passive or powerless. On the contrary, they resist and undermine the construction of a dominant class in all sorts of ways ... Popular modes of political action, elusive and changing, weighing on the state, limiting its range and intervention, ensuring a *revanche* of society on the state.[67]

While Bayart stresses the fragility of this hegemonic struggle, this tendency prompts rulers to seek advantage in spheres previously free from state interference.

The centrality of the ruler's hegemonic project of elite accommodation decisively shapes the terrain in which alliances with, or challenges to control develop, even though rulers cannot guarantee a particular outcome. J.L. Domenach views this struggle as "an invasion of society by politics ... not always in the form of control, but rather through the organization and mobilization of all elements of political, economic and social life under a framework oriented towards power relations."[68] That is, some African rulers claim prerogatives to recruit individuals and communities to their vision of how the country should be run, even if this is done outside the legal framework of institutional state power.

The battle for control has been difficult for African rulers. Late colonial promises of social services and democratic reform raised popular expectations. To the extent that these demands undermined state control over resources, they constituted an attack on rulers' capacities to build power-bases within diverse and often conflictual societies. Lacking widespread legitimacy, rulers tried to reclaim the apparent omnipotence of colonial state power. Patrimonial strategies provided a means to create new elite accommodations, though at the expense of declining state institutional capacity. The dangers of economic and political liberalism remain, however. They are resurfacing at precisely the time that externally imposed austerity programs further undermine any possibility that state institutions can provide the ruler with an alternative to accommodations with unruly elites.

Central to Bayart's analysis are rulers' attempts to maintain their power bases as capacities of state power shift, and groups in society flee or resist new state intrusions. This, he says, is "a project lying in a process of assimilation and fusion of pre-colonial elites and those born of the colonial and post-colonial eras. Thus current inequalities and characters of domination are solidifications of pre-colonial structures. The elites of yesterday constitute the bulk of elites today."[69]

Bayart stresses continuities in this hegemonic project. Furthermore, rulers may absorb societal networks that originally organized to resist state power. The chapters below trace just such a process, as state power shifts from suppressing informal market diamond producers to absorbing their social control and their resources in return for favors. Illicit mining and smuggling in Sierra Leone is at once "economic sabotage" and an integral part of the ruler's strategy of political survival. In turn, even Sierra Leone's British rulers became part-time accomplices of informal market operators. As early as the late nineteenth century, British rulers bought indigenous elite support through selective favor. With the discovery of diamonds in the 1930s, local officials and foreign investors busily traded a selective tolerance of elite illicit mining for assurances of social peace. Rulers became outright partners with illicit diamond producers after independence. The result is that rulers' authorities extend outside the inherited institutions of the state. This "reciprocal assimilation of elites," in Bayart's terms, became central to the exercise of power.

Seemingly non-political actions outside state control become targets of cooption or repression. In Sierra Leone we see this every time reforms threaten the omnipotence of elite alliances. The contours of the Shadow

State are found in this struggle to define and shape political power that was born with the founding of the colonial state. Bayart calls these networks of control *l'état rhisome* – or the network state defined by the ruler's effort to impose authority over elites and society as a whole. The ruler may remain vulnerable, however. Renegade elites may strike out on their own, or seek accommodations independent of the ruler. Therein lie the threats to Sierra Leone's State House from liberalization in the 1950s and 1960s, and again in the 1990s.

Bayart does not focus on these cracks in the hegemonic project, but they are central to my understanding of the extreme difficulty of reform in Africa. Numerous cracks exist in state power through which societal forces can resist, and even challenge the ruler's power. Forceful though rulers may be, they are to some extent bound by the limits of internationally recognized state sovereignty. Illicit diamond producers and traders operate in international markets. Rulers remain bound to the financial commitments incurred by decrepit institutions or earlier efforts at elite accommodation. One would imagine countries such as Sierra Leone to be the last place a foreign firm would want to do business. But the precarious nature of elite control, coupled with the demands of international creditors forces the ruler to seek ways to absorb the international linkages of illicit diamond traders. State House modifications to structural adjustment program requirements have become components of a desperate new strategy to save the hegemonic project. The Shadow State grows outside the territorial boundaries of the colonial creation. New elites are added to the accommodation, they include among them some creditor officials and a special type of foreign investor.

A new "connective tissue" develops between rulers forced to seek new methods of control and those willing to support the project in return for favors. But struggle continues as long as the promise of greater justice, more accountable government, or simply the desire to be left alone guides the actions of some. Achille Mbembe's traversal of more symbolic terrain helps us to see ways in which societal actors resist, and the tools with which they challenge the ruler's intrusions. In his analysis of Catholic Church power in Zimbabwe, Mbembe explains that clerics there confront state power on its intrusion into the spiritual realm:

This is how one explains the tendencies of clerics to undertake an *englobement* of society and surround it with their shade ... Unlike in colonial times, the secular state cannot define itself only as a regime of power, but as a system of truth. The state holds that this prerogative belongs to itself, and itself alone.[70]

Citizens possibly feel the same sort of *englobement* in African patrimonial regimes where the ruler seeks to control *all* exchange on behalf of his accommodation with elites.

Mbembe considers more broadly some African appropriations of the colonizer's religion.[71] Central to Mbembe's work is that under such conditions, Africans do not distinguish temporal and religious dichotomies of authority. After all, neither did colonial authorities when they used religion as an instrument of control and cooption. This totalization of theology can be applied to both colonial and post-colonial practice of politics. Like their colonial predecessors, African rulers often impose their own intrusive theology of rule in the service of a vision of the world that significant elements of society do not share. Yet when faced with the onslaught of state power, citizens do not hesitate to impose their own interpretations of the world to reinforce social spheres in which they have a stake. Mbembe interprets Christian revivalism as evidence of this appropriation of a theology of control for the task of resistance. These movements embody an alternative world view independent of state power.[72]

Mbembe's analysis is significant for its contextualization of the nature of the struggle over power. Leaders try to impose official fashions and hairstyles, they rename places and people; they require obedience to a cult of personality. Overbearing though these demands are, popular access to rival theologies of power provides an escape from a state-supervised universe.[73] In our Sierra Leone case, powerful informal marketeers and diamond diggers pursue their interests through contacts in the country and abroad. Their visions of their places in the world are shaped by the possibilities that the diamond trade presents, as defined both by the actions of State House – Bayart's "hegemonic alliance" – and by international diamond markets. Thus there is a constant struggle among political elites, dealers and diggers to juggle their own advantages in Sierra Leone and abroad. Sometimes, members of these groups perceive that their interests can be advanced through joining the ruler's hegemonic alliance: sometimes they may see that they have little choice; at other times, cooperation is unlikely.

Understanding these developments requires close attention to the historical evolution of the autonomy and capacity of leaders to rule. In Sierra Leone, constraints on state autonomy vis-à-vis parallel markets are profoundly influenced by the colonial rulers' struggle to balance colonial rule at low cost and the evolving legal constraints of decolonization that have undermined that authority. State decay and Shadow State construction are firmly rooted in colonial rule. Indeed, elements of the Shadow State first emerge with the actions of British colonial officials. Diamonds also shape the context of the struggle for political space. Portable and of high value, easily mined, smuggled and sold abroad, this resource offers unusual opportunities to local producers and creates obstacles to state control over production and trade. However, informal exports of peanuts in Senegal, cocoa in Ghana, coffee in Uganda, and just about everything in Benin all provide similar challenges and opportunities for rulers to impose controls over their production and exchange.

The Shadow State ruler's struggle to survive

The German jurist Carl Schmitt provides some guidance for further enquiry into rulers' responses to threats. Writing during the late twenties and early thirties, Schmitt encountered dilemmas familiar to many African rulers. Germany's Weimar regime grappled with considerable challenges from groups committed to the destruction of the foreign-imposed constitution. Schmitt believed that these threats required him, as a jurist, to depart from considering "what is state power" within the context of an airtight legal system. "How," he asked, "can an exception [challenge] be subsumed in a legal configuration when in reality the details of the exception cannot be anticipated?"[74] A key concept in Schmitt's vision of authority is that state actions are ultimately founded upon the rational pursuit of regime survival.

Regime survival, he believed, lay in liberating the concept of authority from a constraining legal order that challengers did not accept. Schmitt's sovereign slumbers within its legal order in normal times, but awakens when faced with threats. Outlining an ideal strikingly similar to the creation of Bayart's "hegemonic alliance," Schmitt observes that "As long as a state is a political entity this requirement for internal peace compels it in critical situations to decide also upon the identity of the enemy."[75]

Some subjects are dangerous; against them the state ensures physical security, peace and stability. By virtue of the state's monopoly on coercion, rulers choose who, in Schmitt's terms, is "friend" or "enemy" to this order, and prevent challenges from "negative political parties [*ohne volkerrecht*]." Such dangers demand that rulers be able to act free from rigid legal boundaries. The essence of sovereignty lies in the ruler's capacity to make these decisions about the composition of an elite alliance. Echoing the supporters of single-party states in Africa, Schmitt argues that this power is necessary due to the state's lack of organic links to the people as a whole. Democracy, he says, is more suitable to England "where the whole political machinery presupposes a people so fundamentally at one that they can afford to bicker."[76]

This rift between the facade of the institutional state, popular expectations, and the practice of rule describes Africa's crisis of governance. Lacking legitimacy, the ruler of the inherited colonial entity seeks omnipotence. It is significant that Schmitt looks to a "political theology" to fill in for the missing organic link between society and ruler. Lacking freely given popular legitimacy, extralegal powers are a logical means of preserving the regime in crisis. Sovereignty stands outside and above the political order, both to ensure its operation and to anticipate its breakdown.

Schmitt understands this project as the product of regimes under siege, in contrast to Bayart's view of the purposeful extension of authority. Rulers see dire threats and long for unchallenged authority. Like colonial officials before them, contemporary rulers in Africa find in liberalizations accompanying decolonization and the current economic crisis a denial of the ruler's right to exist independently from competing interests. The unwelcome pluralism threatens the very existence of the elite accommodations upon which his political (and physical) survival hinges. Schmitt emphasizes suppression and incorporation, a politics of balancing opposing societal forces through *ad hoc* improvisations in both the legal state and the Shadow State. The personalization of sovereign power ensures consistency in these decisions, he says. Here, true sovereignty lies in the monopoly of decision-making. Schmitt is deeply concerned that legal rigidities will undermine the ruler's project of extending and consolidating authority over diverse public opinions and elites. Such societal autonomy risks prompting challengers who can influence and eventually "colonize" state authority.

Schmitt's defensive notion of state power fits well with the context in which rulers have made choices over the past century in Sierra Leone. Schmitt's own concern over the coherence of sovereignty mirrors many African rulers' anxieties over the survival of their regimes. With the end of Cold-War recourse to powerful patrons, perhaps these anxieties may spread to concerns over the continued existence of the inherited artificial colonial entities themselves. At the same time, rulers fear societal appropriations of instruments that can be used to fend off state domination. The rationality of politics clearly overshadows rulers' concerns to protect market rationality. Looking at the pressures facing rulers across a broad front, we can see why, even with many resources at their disposal, rulers would fritter away apparent opportunities to build strong state institutions, or would oppose a growing autonomous class of entrepreneurs; actions that require a narrowly bounded definition of state interest.

Far from taking colonial state autonomy as given, this study explains how colonial rulers' insecurities contributed to shaping the methods of social control that are at the heart of the recent evolution of patrimonialism in Africa. Thus, World Bank and IMF reforms that aim to return Africa to a 1960s ideal of state–civil-society relations will not work. Rather, Shadow State adaptations to austerity take Africa back to a future that more closely resembles the 1860s. Some from a society-centered perspective may take heart in this apparent collapse of the inherited state. But it is more likely that we are seeing a return to exceedingly weak trading states at the mercy of the international economy. The rise of private armies in Sierra Leone and elsewhere in Africa is central to this recent evolution of the Shadow State. The ruler's struggle to define "enemies" and find enticements to attract "friends" takes place in an increasingly dangerous political world.

Understanding this struggle for political control in Sierra Leone entails looking at different levels where this control is contested. Well before independence, local colonial officials encountered difficulty imposing London's directives. They, and ultimately, their governor, made decisions regarding the identification of "friends" capable of aiding their efforts to rule and "enemies" likely to impose more constraints on what local British officers perceived to be already pressed colonial authority. The most interesting aspect of our story's beginning, then, is the various choices that officials made in their efforts to rule as directed that then became foundations for the Shadow State. It is to this subject that we now turn.

2 Colonial rule and the social foundations of the Shadow State

> It may be said that as Faith, Hope and Charity are to the Christian creed, so are Decentralisation, Co-operation, and Continuity to African Administration.   Lord Lugard[1]

> If I have any fears, it is that the chiefs do not fully understand their obligations. ... people hear the words of their chief, not Government's words.   Railway (Kono) District Commissioner[2]

Nostalgia for British rule grips certain quarters of Sierra Leone, notes a critic of the government, "since now we feel only the growing burdens of our own Black Colonialism."[3] Some Freetowners fondly recall British "discipline" that made trains run on time. But a closer look at the dynamic history and character of political authority reveals intimate connections between current formal governmental incapacity and the colonial past. Droughts, falling commodity prices, debt, expensive oil, and capricious leaders all contribute to the crisis of capacity plaguing most African states. This chapter, however, uncovers the colonial roots of government accommodation with Sierra Leone's vigorous informal market that emerges as the prime feature of state decay.

Colonial administration was split between informal accommodations with indigenous intermediaries and bureaucratic norms. Colonial rulers pursued a broad notion of "development" and the often incompatible local tasks of maintaining effective control over people and resources. This chapter examines this process most closely in the Kono area, long a site of informal market activity. Diamond discoveries in the 1930s in Kono added considerable energy to this struggle to control people and resources. This chapter also notes how colonial officials devised informal accommodations with powerful individuals. This will account for how local strongmen could resist colonial state initiatives. I aim to explain how, despite the powers of this seemingly formidable colonial state, local strongmen successfully opposed state directives and sometimes reached unexpected accommodations with colonial officials over informal markets. These accommodations turned British attentions away from actions that would have strengthened state capacity to rule. Developments in Kono suggest that this struggle between Freetown and informal market operators laid the social foundations for the post-colonial Shadow State.

The history of colonial rule presages contemporary Shadow State manipulations of creditor-imposed policies designed to increase formal state capacity. British Parliament and Colonial Office drives to cut expenditures prompted developments analogous to Shadow State reactions to IMF and World Bank structural adjustment programs. In both instances, state officials make rhetorical commitments to promote taxable commerce to address the seemingly continuous deficiency of state revenues. As among those who champion reform of "governance" today, their colonial counterparts assumed that a vibrant private sector would empower groups that had the most to gain from economic liberalism and administrative efficiency.

Where was economic growth to come from? As is true today, local entrepreneurs failed to lead economic development, though through no deficiency of their own. More significantly, colonial officials shared contemporary African rulers' fears that support for politically vocal local entrepreneurs would threaten an *ad hoc* administrative stability that had been built around informal accommodations with local elites. British occupants of State House continued to allow African collaborators access to state resources and informal markets in return for assurances of social peace. This system of prerogatives and privilege held together the accommodation. Meanwhile, the local population suffered the austerities and costs of "reform" designed to recoup for the state the revenues and opportunities lost to these informal accommodations. It is this manner of rule that proves destructive of formal state institutions and provides the essential elements and practice of Shadow State rule.

The colonial accommodation

Colonial officials recognized the authority of indigenous chiefs to carry out local tasks that the colonial state could not perform; an implicit admission of the incomplete domination of the colonial state. Freetown and London officials defined the relationship as tributary, to aid in administration and revenue collection. But Freetown's local collaborators did not automatically accept this interpretation of their authority. As a historian of Sierra Leone noted of British rule: "The chiefs who had signed friendly treaties were now undeceived, when they were made to realize that the administration would treat them no longer as allies but as subordinate authorities who had to obey the orders of administration whether they liked it or not."[4] Despite this risk of subordination, the costs of imposing direct rule ensured that this alternative intermediary system would not be scrapped. The dangers of noncooperation only reinforced risk-avoiding strategies among British colonial officers. An administrative manual warned: "The test of the [local officer's] work is the absence of disorder and the efficiency of the chiefs and native courts."[5] Personnel evaluations from the first decades of this century uncover positive evaluations with comments such as "well liked by the natives," or "has the trust of his chiefs."

This risk avoidance at the local level was at odds with higher-level administrators' oft-stated visions of colonial rule leading to expanding state functions and clearly defined administrative roles for chiefs. Different levels of the colonial administrative hierarchy identified diverging priorities in the establishment of state authority. As British forces extended direct control over Sierra Leone's hinterland, London worried about administrative costs and the colony's chronic fiscal shortfalls. But Freetown officials perceived that the aggressive expansion of British authority would enhance revenues from trade, enabling Freetown to promote the colony's commercial development, while also resolving longstanding concerns over French challenges to the territory's commercial hinterland. The task of managing conflicting official duties and maintaining actual control fell to local officials.

Meanwhile, Freetown's African press supported expanding commercial opportunities, but railed against "authoritarian" and "inexperienced" officials.[6] This antagonism highlighted colonial officials' fears of allowing indigenous traders to spearhead economic development of the hinterland. Colonial officials feared the disruptive demands of the group which today's supporters of liberal reform would identify as an economic and civic counterweight to abusive state power. Colonial rulers concluded that local resentment of "exploitative" traders, especially among local collaborators with colonial rule, threatened the more important task of maintaining political stability until strong state institutions could be built. Colonial officials outside of Freetown especially valued these collaborators.

The colony's reputation as the "Whiteman's Grave" did not enhance its attraction to able colonial officers.[7] Lord Lugard devoted a portion of his treatise on administration to dispelling the notion of West Africa as a "death-trap."[8] But as late as 1898, 40 percent of government soldiers were disabled with illness.[9] An earlier defender of the colony optimistically noted that only thirty-two of fifty-one missionaries died after assignment to the colony. "Attributing much of the mortality to a morbid state of mind," he nonetheless admitted that Sierra Leone was a place for Europeans to avoid.[10] Even as health standards improved, the colony remained a training ground for colonial officers who would later be transferred elsewhere; the average colonial appointee to Kono was in his mid-twenties. Kono District Commissioners (DCs) tended to be in their early thirties, no doubt eager for reappointment with a clean record away from what one Kono DC called "that malaria-infested swamp."[11] The desire for promotion probably reinforced local officials' tendencies to tolerate strongmens' informal appropriations of state resources and illegal activities in return for assurances of local peace that would please superiors. Desperation, therefore, contributes to this process of what Bayart calls "the *reciprocal assimilation of elites.*"[12]

These local collaborators were thus in a good position to influence the implementation of any expansions of state responsibilities designed to promote the colony's development. These strong local political power-bases and modifications of Indirect Rule in Sierra Leone diverged from Lugard's ideal of administrative effectiveness and control over the population. Already boundaries of state interests rigidly conceived in Freetown showed signs of breaking down at the local level. The result in Kono, and this chapter's concern, was a colonial rule that increasingly depended upon personal understandings with local strongmen not only to maintain social peace, but also to buttress expanded state institutions. Economic and administrative expansion, coupled with political reforms, gave intermediaries additional resources for extending their personal authority. The development of two spheres of authority, particularly over issues of economic control and access to revenues, became the defining characteristic of the evolution of local rule. The remainder of this chapter examines the linkages between these spheres of personal and institutional authority. These developments fundamentally reordered African polities, though certainly not in ways that colonial rulers intended.

Nineteenth-century British rule and local collaborators

British colonial officials throughout the nineteenth century consistently sought indirectly to control indigenous rulers (chiefs) of the interior. Rulers in Freetown wanted stability to minimize the risks and costs of disorder that would bring unpleasant inquiries from superiors. Freetown and European business concerns – with appointed representatives in the colony's Legislative Council – put pressure on colonial governors to guarantee social peace conducive to trade. Meanwhile, the Colonial Office in London constantly worried about the cost of colonial administration.

These diverse priorities among those concerned with colonial administration are reflected in contradictory pressures on colonial officials. Prior to 1865, London sought to discourage direct contacts with West African rulers. London's orders directly conflicted with Freetown's overall efforts to expand the colony's fiscal reach. In 1826, London forced an acting governor to renounce an area annexed to the colony several years earlier.[13]

Freetown annexed the surrounding half-mile deep coastal strip anyway "for the purpose of finding those who would defraud the revenue of the Colony by challenging the right of the government to collect customs duties in the Sierra Leone River upon the ground that no formal cession of any portion of the north bank had been made."[14]

Freetown saw a compelling need to control smuggling, since customs duties often provided up to 70 percent of nineteenth-century colonial revenues. Freetown–London clashes continued. In 1865 a Parliamentary Select Committee endorsed a policy of hinterland non-intervention and went so far as to suggest a complete British withdrawal from West Africa.[15] While Freetown officials remained convinced of the commercial desirability and security needs of bringing the hinterland under direct colonial control, battles with the Ashanti state in the Gold Coast demonstrated to London the high costs that would follow a direct imposition of colonial authority. The Colonial Office prohibited direct action, observing:

The colonies of the Gambia and Sierra Leone, with limited revenues barely sufficing for their administrative expenditure would have been unable to bear any strain in the direction of military expenditure, and the sanction of Parliament was not to be expected for the employment of Imperial resources adequate for the purpose.[16]

This statement followed popular and official criticism decrying the use of imperial resources to underwrite colonies that many saw as unfit for European settlement.

Meanwhile, Freetown continued to view relations with communities in the interior in a commercial light. Treaties with chiefs circumvented metropolitan prohibitions on formal direct intervention. By 1873, State House had signed seventy-three treaties with chiefs, an increase from eleven two decades earlier.[17] Local colonial officials and traders also expressed concern about French advances into regions previously considered within Freetown's commercial hinterland. Given London's fiscal strictures, Freetown's only immediate means of countering French moves was through military and trade contacts with chiefs, using them as intermediaries in lieu of a direct British presence. Governors reinforced allied chiefs and punished opponents through informal means such as gifts or the unauthorized recognition of collaborators' authority. "Domestic" African entrepreneurs in Freetown often clamored for punitive expeditions against recalcitrant chiefs, an action occasionally undertaken contrary to explicit instructions from London.[18]

It is in this context that the then Governor Samuel Rowe aggressively pushed Freetown's commercial orbit northeast into Kono in the 1890s. The Governor warned that "The French seek to strangle us by cutting our access to trade with this promising area."[19] Commercial opinion in

Freetown also provided governors with incentives to circumvent directives from the Colonial Office. European traders backed up their demands through the offices of their two Freetown Chamber of Commerce appointees to the colonial Legislative Council. With regard to Freetown's policy of seeking treaties, the local African-owned press observed that:

The cooperative quiet which now prevails throughout the country and the disposition for peace manifested by the various chiefdoms are indications of a brisk business ... To acquire sovereignty and secure the friendship of the chiefs in the countries of the interior reaching as far as the headwaters of the Niger would be a noble achievement.[20]

The establishment of indirect influence on affairs in the interior via cooperation from chiefs provided Freetown with a cheap and politically sound means of controling developments in the hinterland. Cooperative chiefs promised to keep trade routes open and to provide allies when action needed to be taken against recalcitrant holdouts, thus sparing London and Freetown considerable expense. For example, Freetown spent a mere forty pounds annually to fulfill its commercial treaty obligations to six Kono chiefs in 1889.[21] More valuable to these chiefs were the trade, prestige of association, and firearms the British provided. In Kono, ivory, gold, and groundnut trade came under direct chief control as traders dealt with those whom the British had deemed to be legitimate authorities in the area. Thus a precedent was established. Access to state power translated into private benefit. At the same time, hard-pressed rulers relied on these informal arrangements as an alternative to costly, but still weak formal institutions.

A visitor to Kono in 1895 remarked that the "traders sit down in the towns, but as a rule, big traders generally follow a more powerful chief, with the understanding that his natives will buy the stuff."[22] Visiting colonial officer L.J. Jeremie noted that such chiefs collected a 5 percent levy on the passage of British goods.[23] In practice, revenue from trade allowed chiefs to field standing armies and forcibly incorporate neighboring villages into their expanding realms. One Kono villager described the effects of chief–colonial collaborations as: "a day of war as the chief attacked farmers. He took them as slaves and forced them to work on the farms as his serfs without pay and with little food and clothing."[24]

Incorporated as tributaries in a growing economic network founded on privileged relations to Freetown, these villages provided food and labor to chiefs. Control of production and trade allowed chiefs to field an army, thus creating an ever-widening circle of dependent tributaries. These developments gave chiefs incentives to cooperate with British designs to choose and strengthen allies, and capitalize on their office as trade grew. However, it is important to note the fluidity with which this authority ebbed and flowed in contrast to the colonial period to follow.[25]

Invasions of the Kono area from the north, starting in the 1880s, provided the first major test of the efficacy of Freetown's reliance on its indirect influence over chiefs to maintain order without significant colonial military or fiscal commitment. Samori Touré, head of the invaders, had signed a treaty of friendship with the French. Freetown officials earlier experienced considerable friction with the French over the fiscal jurisdiction of trade routes along the northeast coast, leading to several annexations of small islands and numerous treaties with local chiefs there. Consequently, Freetown perceived France's expansion in the northwest as an extension of an external threat to trade and customs revenues.

Kono chiefs faced a dilemma. Touré's warriors sought active Kono support and attacked Kono's traditional enemies to the south, the Mendes. Touré thus delivered 3,000 captives to the Kono town of Wende. Meanwhile, Freetown emissaries sought to persuade chiefs to "keep the [trade] roads open." and promised protection to their allies against both Sofa and Mende neighbors.[26] At the same time, the French reneged on their treaty with Samori and attacked his soldiers. This brought the French military directly into Kono and the Sierra Leone hinterland. Once again contrary to London's directives, Freetown dispatched an expeditionary force to restore British influence in the area.[27] Much to London's horror, the force unintentionally clashed with French soldiers. The incident again led the Colonial Office to consider abandoning the area, as London feared the damage the incident caused to relations with France over the higher stakes of imperial competition in the Nile Valley.

Locally, the successful intervention against invaders strengthened British-allied chiefs. British strategy included providing allied chiefs with weapons, a potent source of power to people whose authority rested largely on military prowess and the provision of security to followers. One such chief was Matturi, who, once armed with British guns, quickly acquired the allegiance of other strongmen. Local opinion held that "This war greatly increased Matturi's power and influence, and made him undisputed leader of a large part of this country."[28] The British alliance provided further indirect benefits. "In revenge for past troubles the tribe had suffered, they quickly overran the Sewa valley, bringing back captives, thinking that the whiteman's war was like the blackman's – fighting for captives."[29] Putting British aid to his own uses, Matturi and his allies commanded significant authority among their own subjects when the British returned several years later to establish direct control over Sierra Leone's hinterland.

In Freetown, officials had little use for Colonial Office cautiousness and fear of provoking the French. Freetown associated security, order, trade, and revenue with influence in the interior. Therefore, friendly chiefs became natural targets of Freetown's policy, which was otherwise hobbled by rigid policy guidelines set in London. Indigenous conflicts offered opportunities to extend informal British influence and chiefs often welcomed aid to promote their own goals. For example, while British rulers considered Matturi "crafty and cruel," in 1894 Governor Frederic Cardew simply ordered Matturi's rivals banished for "bringing false complaint," even though this area was not under formal British control. In Sando, Chief Suluku attempted to install his son as successor against local wishes. When Freetown perceived that the violence represented anti-British sentiment, the uprising was quelled with Freetown's help.[30]

Almost unnoticed, the colonial preoccupation with extending influence had begun to restructure indigenous society. Chiefs built their authority with British aid but in a manner that denied colonial rulers direct control. Their positions as mediators for alien rulers while pursuing their own political objectives and economic opportunities fundamentally shaped the ways in which colonial administrators were able to exercise and extend British authority.

Strong chiefs, weak colony: To 1930

As Freetown repelled northern invasions and French influence, the Colonial Office opened a new era in West African policy under the direction of Joseph Chamberlain. Less concerned about French sensibilities and reluctant to use West Africa as collateral for territorial bargains elsewhere, Chamberlain proclaimed that in developing Britain's "tropical estate," "We have trusted entirely individual enterprise and capital ... Yet it is certain that in many cases progress has been delayed and in some cases absolutely stayed, because the only methods by which improvements could be carried out were beyond the scope of private resources."[31] This "New Colonial Policy" appeared to commit British colonial budgets to providing state assistance for building railroads, telegraphs and other infrastructure to promote private investment. Revenue collection gained a higher priority among London and Freetown officials. Recognizing fiscal restraints, Chamberlain envisioned an African colonial rule strengthened by economically and politically supportive private enterprise.

Chamberlain's activist stance also strengthened the positions of Freetown officials favoring a more active role for government outside the Freetown Colony. "All that needs to be done now," said Sir Harry Johnston in reply to the Colonial Office, "is for the Administration to act as friend to both sides and introduce the native laborer to the European capitalist."[32] Governor Cardew also welcomed the change in rhetoric coming from London. Indeed, he preferred even more direct government involvement in development. The Governor feared that state-supported private ventures, particularly among African entrepreneurs, might cause "political problems" in unregulated commercial relations among chiefs up-country.[33] Colonial field administrators also approved of the interventio-nist state role but foresaw increased responsibility. Said one soon-to-be District Commissioner: "With British law there must be employment for the people. Profitable work must take the place of raiding and fighting; but for work to be profitable, we must ensure that markets are created."[34]

With London's approval, Freetown proclaimed a Protectorate over the hinterland in August 1896. Governor Cardew found himself with growing administrative autonomy to shape the colony's future. The Protectorate was a new way to generate revenues independent of the politically vocal Freetown African community and alliances with sometimes fickle chiefs. Freetown residents had proven remarkably resistant to any form of property tax, one having been repealed in 1871. The Governor thus approved a house tax, known locally as the "Hut Tax," for the hinterland. However, some indigenous cooperation was necessary to collect the tax. The colonial legislature permitted chiefs to keep a share as "just compensa-tion" for their efforts as revenue agents. Governor Cardew made plain his conviction that the tax represented a turning point in government capabilities:

I cannot stress to you too much the importance of efficient collection of this tax. It leaves the chiefs to manage their own affairs ... but these revenues permit Local Government to preserve law and order, develop trade and communications and protect those engaged in the development of commercial interests.[35]

But the Colonial Office grew concerned about rising administrative costs, mostly related to unanticipated needs to police tax collection. Twenty percent of the colony's budget of £19,927 went to enforcing tax collection, yet massive evasion produced revenues barely equal to the costs of enforcement.[36] Cardew's and Chamberlain's views of a Sierra Leone of government-supported railways and development companies clashed with fiscal reality. Thus, tax collection proceeded "a bit strenuously" in Colonial Office eyes, and local resistance to it built in Sierra Leone.[37]

The tax posed a serious threat to existing British–chief accommodations. Some chiefs feared for their authority as they saw themselves becoming British tributors. This shift in British support for tributor-chief relations threatened the chiefs' control over their dependents. The new arrangement disrupted the clear connection between a dependent's payment of tribute and the chief's ability to provide protection by virtue of his favorable standing with the British.[38] The loss of judicial authority and the abolition of slavery particularly rankled chiefs; they feared becoming the passive intermediaries that Freetown officials meant them to be, not the local strongmen they had become with British aid. Rebellion broke out as some chiefs refused to participate in what they perceived to be the demeaning exercise of tax collection for a higher political authority.

Pacification of the revolt tested indigenous–state cooperation in Kono. The continued cooperation of chief Matturi and others proved instrumental in crushing the revolt, especially since colonial military resources were pressed into service in more sensitive areas closer to Freetown. Other Kono chiefs realized that the rebellion had little chance for success. They may also have concluded that by defeating the rebels they could enhance their own relations with the British and thus strengthen their recently elevated positions vis-à-vis rivals. The British again saw that some Kono chiefs could be relied upon to ensure stable local administration in British interests. Cooperative chiefs further realized the usefulness of British power for maintaining their positions, forestalling fears among them that they would become intolerably subordinate to Freetown. Instead, they turned their attentions to finding new ways to reassert their own interests in the new political order.

Despite increased spending on Chamberlain's "New Colonial Policy," frugality remained the watchword in Freetown. Colonial authorities concluded that, to support fiscally prudent and orderly rule, administration required further concessions of authority to collaborative elites. The first British administrator to visit Kono regularly only arrived in 1910. Until 1921, *five* resident Europeans administered more than one million inhabitants in the Protectorate.[39] Despite Colonial Office misgivings, in 1901 the Governor approved a system of chief-run police (Court Messengers) charged with preserving law and order. These forces, armed with British weapons, strengthened favored chiefs against rivals in the name of the state. The British aimed to support a stable class of intermediaries, promoting stability and efficiency and low cost. Meanwhile, chiefs were concerned with entrenching their clan's power.

Shocked by the vigorous opposition from some chiefs, the British also responded to the Hut Tax crisis with conciliatory measures directly reinforcing friendly chief authority. Forced labor was officially recognized in 1902: "Every Paramount Chief in his capacity as chief . . . shall have the same powers with respect to labor as they heretofore possessed."[40] Ostensibly conceived in Sierra Leone as a means of avoiding disruption and allowing chiefs their "customary due," chiefs used their positions as local agents of state power to translate their new legal authority into commercial advantage. Unpaid workers appeared on chiefs' farms, while colonial officials provided direct assistance to chiefs' growing commercial crops. Government recognition in 1902 of chiefdom courts responsible for "native law" gave chiefs explicit state approval to implement forced labor and impose sanctions against those challenging their chiefly authority. Other "reforms" gave chiefs broad powers to enforce their decisions with little local control or accountability.

While Freetown authorities recognized local grievances against some chiefs, their imperative was to develop hinterland trade. Enhanced trade from the region had to provide revenue to pay for administration as well as added state responsibilities such as the construction of the railroad. Forced labor by chiefs provided hope to Freetown that Sierra Leoneans could be dragged into an expanding taxable cash economy from which the state could collect greater revenues. From Freetown's perspective, political tranquility indicated that the chiefs accepted at least the veneer of the colonial state's governing techniques and Freetown's overrule. In 1905, a District Commissioner confidently wrote that "we enforce upon all the necessity of obeying their Paramount Chief,"[41] implying that chiefs derived their authority from their place in the colonial ruling hierarchy. However, the dependence that colonial officials perceived had contradictory trends. Chiefs stood to prosper under revised laws designed to strengthen Freetown's authority; they created a local rule that was not a duplicate of European social and political forms, but instead a new balance of relations with the colonial state.

For example, further reforms in 1905 placed "restrictions" on the chiefs' powers concerning trade. Designed to promote hinterland trade, the ordinance warned that "any tribal ruler ... who uses the power conferred on him so as to impede, restrain or interfere with the free course of trade, shall be liable upon conviction to deposition."[42] Believing the reform to be effective, the Colonial Secretary applauded the apparent willingness of chiefs to accept the benefits of commercial civilization. "[Chiefs] are taking to trade and beginning to understand that there are other chattel besides a multiplicity of slaves and wives which are conducive to material wealth and prosperity."[43] In Kono, chiefs were attracted to the profits of trade, but while evoking the state-sanctioned authority of their positions, they did not pursue it entirely on British terms. Thus chiefs became agents of colonial rule while exercising a parallel authority. The first DC responsible for Kono uncomfortably sensed his lack of control over his intermediaries: "I feel unsure," he said, "that I rule this place. I cannot begin to say what these chiefs tell their people about our purpose here."[44] However, the imperative to maintain order, particularly after the expensive exercise of restoring order in the wake of the 1898 rebellion, required the DC to accept this uncomfortable accommodation. Force could ensure obedience or quell opposition, but the fiscal regime that required a DC to plead with Freetown for replacement of a three-penny soap dish would not look favorably upon unplanned expenses.[45]

Table 2.1. *Official expenditures in Kono (£), 1908–23*

	1908	1913	1918	1923
Administrative	208	912	1,952	2,050
Econ. Development	806	3,180	4,630	2,972
Social Services	137	568	1,690	1,780
Debts	73	386	1,259	1,988
Unclassified	256	604	987	1,321
Total Expend.	1,480	5,650	10,518	10,111
Local Revenues	3,716	5,178	6,338	7,156

Source: N.A. Cox-George, *Finance and Development in West Africa: The Sierra Leone Experience* (London: Denis Dobson, 1961); Government of Sierra Leone, *Estimates of Revenues and Expenditures* (Freetown: Government Printer, various issues).

Most seriously for local officials, the realities of fiscal stringency clashed with London's mandate for an "innovative colonialism of the tropical estate." Official policy stressing rapid economic development coincided with a levelling off of the unpopular Hut-Tax collection after 1910, generally accounting for about 20 percent of state revenues.[46] Kono did experience significant government investment designed to facilitate economic growth after the turn of the century (Table 2.1). But infrastructure spending failed to attract outside investment, creating even more pressure on local authorities to promote chiefs' involvement in trade. The reluctance of private business to invest in an isolated area with poor links to ports and a weak colonial administration left local officials with little choice but to use development funds to underwrite chiefs' involvement in trade.[47] State-owned "model farms" were built with government development funds, then turned over to chiefs. Amidst the failure of Sir Harry Johnston's prediction of "introducing native labour to the European capitalist," promotion of chiefs' enterprises became the next best alternative.

Under the "model farm" program, Kono's administration purchased cocoa and coffee saplings and gave them to chiefs who then used forced labor to cultivate them. Freetown learned that a Kono DC told a chief "that if he provided the labour the plantation would be his." The official goal was to provide demonstrations to other farmers, but the local DC complained that under 1902 regulations allowing forced labor, chiefs often prohibited subjects from engaging in commercial agriculture on their own.[48] Freetown acquiesced in informally favoring chiefs' farms as officials recognized the need to promote exports to generate customs revenue.

Stimulation of up-country agriculture began after the first segment of the railroad, passing forty miles to the south of Kono's district headquarters, opened in 1905. High haulage fees and increased customs added to state revenues. But with investment elsewhere more attractive to Europeans, chiefs faced little price competition before the 1930s. State reliance on chiefs' commerce came at a time when other revenue sources disappeared; 1906 saw the end of direct parliamentary grants to the Freetown government for military expenditures.[49] The railroad provided some relief. By 1915, haulage fees provided 30 percent of the colonial budget. But overall expenditures rose nearly 300 percent between 1900 and 1915, due to increased recurrent costs (including the railroad), military expenses and, after the First World War, contributions to the Imperial War Fund.[50] Scarce revenues and minimal state investment ensured that Kono would not receive the large-scale state investments envisioned by Colonial Office activists. Instead, "collection of tributes and forced labour are the most fertile sources of abuse and complaint," noted a Kono official.[51] Yet no Kono chief was sanctioned for labor abuses until after reforms in the 1930s. Chiefs still had legal authority to punish absconding subjects under "native laws respecting journeys," provided the District Commissioner did not see the sanction as interfering with trade or labor markets.[52] Exit was no easy option for those facing a chief's displeasure. Colonial reluctance to enforce limits on chiefs allowed chiefs to independently levy sanctions on those who appealed to the colonial administration for their rightful due. Especially after the First World War, investigative commissions noted the growing gap between legal limits on chiefs' powers and the actual exercise of power.

These conditions foreshadowed the precarious nature of future accommodations. Chiefs competed for official patronage on their own behalf or for favored subjects. Thus they had reason to move against challengers as they exploited administrative opportunities. The less a District Commissioner demanded of chiefs by way of reform, the safer the Commissioner would be in the eyes of his superiors as the possibilities of disorder became more remote. Maintaining incumbent clans in power avoided difficulties associated with mediating local disputes. Conversely, officials trying to change the terms of cooperation in pursuit of more efficient administration faced greater difficulty in promoting continued accommodation. Colonial officials and chiefs both participated in building a parallel political authority that was separate from, but still dependent upon the formal structure of the colonial state.

These partners in accommodation were caught between two visions of colonial rule. Particularly among Kono's chiefs, passive during the 1898 rebellion, colonial rule offered opportunities. Seen in relation to their former positions as autonomous agents of British trading interests, the new security from challengers, commercialization of subject obligations, and government fiscal assistance enabled chiefs to build their profitable relationship with the colonial state. Meanwhile, Freetown and London mistakenly expected that the intensifying relationship signalled an extension of state authority that was molding African society in a European image.

Gaps between the two visions remained bridgeable as long as local officials could accommodate chiefly concerns without undercutting state revenues, and hence, institutions. As long as chiefs' "misuse" of state authority remained confined to maintaining mutually advantageous accommodations at the local level, Freetown could dictate overall state interest. Did Freetown have other options that would impose control over Sierra Leone's hinterland and relieve accommodative pressures on DCs? Were the weaknesses of colonial rule related to the incessant quest for scarce revenues inevitable? Exploring alternatives to heavy reliance on chiefs as intermediaries helps us to understand why London and Freetown officials persisted with policies that proved so destructive of state autonomy in the long run.

The threat of a productive "civil society" to the weak colony

British defense of chiefs' "customary rights" produced collaborators with considerable economic and political power, at the expense of administrative and economic efficiency. A possible alternate official strategy to promote trade and revenues would have supported Sierra Leone's Krios, descendants of freed slaves settled in Freetown. This strategy would mirror contemporary World Bank/IMF advice to weak governments to promote a "new class" of capitalists. Jennifer Whitaker declares that "Governments committed to the hard choices underlying growth could go a long way toward making entrepreneurship happen by altering the opportunity structure to make it a viable alternative."[53] Why didn't Freetown pursue this policy that would seem so supportive of Chamberlain's and Cardew's development aims?

A leading African citizen of Freetown, Samuel Lewis, argued that "British Civilization," as a commercial opportunity, represented the fastest route to achievement for the city's ethnically diverse Krio community. By the end of the nineteenth century, Krios played a significant role in the colony's economic development. High levels of education prepared Krios for administrative duties. As early as the 1840s, higher proportions of Freetown Krio children attended primary school than did children in Britain or France.[54] At the turn of the century, colonial administration included a Krio DC. In 1892, Africans, almost all Krios, held eighteen of forty senior posts. Of ninety-two such posts in existence in 1912, Africans occupied only fifteen posts.[55]

Krios also exercised considerable economic power in the nineteenth century.[56] As agents for Europeans or as independent traders, Krios conducted much of the import–export trade in kola nuts, cocoa and palm products. One Krio merchant, R.B. Blaize, donated £1,000 to found an Industrial School in Lagos, at the terminus of his extensive trading operation. J.K. Coker of Freetown operated several cocoa and maize plantations outside the Colony before the establishment of the Protectorate. Governor Rowe recognized the interdependence of Krio and British interests in 1879: "The relations of the Sierra Leone Government with its aboriginal neighbors directly affects the security of these travelling traders, and their presence in a country or their being driven away from it directly influences the sale of British manufactures and the export of African produce."[57]

As immigrants in their adopted country, Freetown Krios lacked the same power-bases of chiefs outside the government's reach. They relied directly upon the colonial state to protect their commercial interests. As we saw, until the establishment of the Protectorate, Freetown's fiscal health also demanded that officials support and help extend the reach of private traders' accumulation of wealth. But at the turn of the century, Krio economic influence abruptly declined. British policy of protecting "native rights" in the interests of maintaining order directly threatened Krio commercial interests. Freetown and Colonial Office officials also faced pressure from British commercial interests in the United Kingdom and their Freetown Chamber of Commerce representative to limit support for indigenous entrepreneurs. More importantly, colonial officials perceived other options beyond supporting a potentially politically quarrelsome indigenous business class.

While chiefs provided early *ad hoc* solutions to crises of budget and rule, Freetown and Colonial Office officials favored European investment. More oriented toward import and export, "they provide higher customs revenues than does an indigenous operation on a set volume of business."[58] The revenue advantages of favoring European businesses were already known to Freetown. Specifically, European companies presented less risk of smuggling, always a problem when Freetown was a small maritime colony.[59] After establishment of the Protectorate, Freetown and London assumed that large European firms would invest more quickly than smaller operations, a proposition implicit in Sir Harry Johnston's "marriage of native labour to European capital."

Freetown officials' responses to these pressures weakened the influence of African capital in the hinterland. Governor Cardew favored European firms because their demands on government were more easily regulated. The Freetown Chamber of Commerce and its permanent representative to the Legislative Council provided a measure of predictability in business–government contacts. The Chamber of Commerce included only the larger

European trading firms, banks and shippers. With government approval, the Chamber of Commerce began setting commodity prices in 1900. Regulated trade practices allowed Freetown greater autonomy to manage fiscal pressures. Business–state cooperation permitted firms to pass on more easily the burdens of higher tariffs and export duties to producers while allowing politically vocal urban consumers to enjoy price stability. This policy of low producer prices also undermined hoped-for hinterland investments in production and favored the few with low overheads – namely chiefs commanding forced labor working state-supported farms. But close government–European firm collaboration on fiscal matters appeared best able to generate revenues to meet increased official spending, restrain demands on government, and thus appear to preserve state autonomy of action. This policy direction addressed Freetown's fiscal troubles and relegated DCs, above all, to roles that addressed the colony's desperate need for revenues, trade and order.

The First World War and the subsequent economic downturn imposed additional fiscal burdens on Freetown. Customs receipts, stagnant after completion of the railroad, began to fall as a percentage of still growing revenues. Shortfalls were made up through a "specific duty" increase from 25 percent to 50 percent on most items. The Government also imposed a new export duty on kola and cocoa in 1915. Reduction of public and private consumption constituted the second major element of governmental fiscal policy during the war.[60] Large firms facilitated the implementation of these policies. To insulate some consumers from higher import prices, food price controls were instituted in 1915 under the supervision of a Chamber of Commerce-sponsored Food Committee, further choking off local entrepreneurial investment. This agency advised the Wartime Director of Supplies on the issuance of import licenses. A small number of collaborating firms provided greater possibilities for price and supply manipulations and macroeconomic management in support of government policy.

Firms received benefits as well. "As the international situation is quite tense," observed an agent of G.B. Ollivant, "we ought to be instructing you [government] as to the movements of all outside competition," meaning African and, increasingly, Lebanese traders.[61] The Governor's office concurred, arguing that "unnecessary middleman competition" depressed dock values of imports, consumed more local goods and promoted smuggling, thus reducing customs revenues. Equally important, the removal of a nascent "national bourgeoisie" and their replacement with chiefs and foreign intermediaries freed colonial rulers from "domestic" political pressures. This increasing apparent autonomy also allowed governors a free hand to pursue policies aimed at more intensive exploitation of revenue opportunities.

"Capacity building" with chiefs to control chief power

Freetown's reliance on managed consumption, reduced investment, and on limiting Krio demands on government helped the government weather the war with balanced budgets. However, collaborating firms failed to invest heavily in the Protectorate after the war, creating further administrative pressures on local officials. The railroad, conceived as an instrument for "the safe introduction of capital into the Protectorate," also failed to live up to revenue expectations. By 1921, the railroad's operating expenses reached 150 percent of revenues from related trade.[62] The railroad had become the colony's largest employer, and at the same time was also becoming the repository for patronage positions and less able personnel.[63] Reforms reduced losses, but the railroad remained expensive to run. Laborers' demands, particularly after a strike in 1919 (and an unwelcome inquiry from London) limited cost-cutting measures. The railroad's narrow gauge also limited haulage capacity. The lack of roads in the Protectorate until after the Second World War, while forcing use of the state-supported railroad, also limited opportunities to export goods, which along with state favoritism toward chiefs involved in production and trade, reduced local incentives to invest.

This expenditure of state resources and an unfavorable investment environment further tied chiefs to local officials. Economic pressures shaped DC attitudes toward the enforcement of law and order – ostensibly their top priority. The 1921 census shows that 10 percent of Kono people lived in servitude, mostly to chiefs. The figure was typical of conditions in the rest of Sierra Leone.[64] British officials visiting Kono in 1923 observed that "labour practices here are hair-raising . . . some chiefs exercise reason, but most remain scarcely accountable for any faults which they might commit." It was the chiefs, and not Freetown, who exercised direct control over the Protectorate's population. Recognizing Freetown's dependence on strongmen, the Provincial Commissioner replied that "with the willing cooperation of our chiefs the collection of tariffs [Hut Tax] and promotion of trade are made immeasurably less complicated."[65] Forced labor allowed chiefs alone to profit from farming despite low producer prices and high haulage fees. Such conditions limited opportunities for free labor to enter the market. Forced labor remained a common practice for decades and was a factor in disturbances in the area as late as the 1950s.

Chiefs benefited from new opportunities to maximize economic power while claiming as many "customary" privileges as possible. Chiefs claimed greater shares of state authority and translated it into private commercial advantage. This link between access to European trade and the authority of hinterland strongmen thus grew stronger. The lack of independent European traders taking advantage of Freetown's extended authority to seek their fortunes left chiefs even greater latitude to continue such practices. In the late pre-colonial period, the traveller T.S. Alldridge neatly captured strongmens' commercial interests in British authority in a manner that was recognizable a half century later:

I went out to the West Coast in 1871, and practically the lines upon which the British agent worked then are those which he works now . . . When asked why they [agents] do not pursue trade in the Protectorate, they respond "We are not here for running about the country, that is the work of the Government. Let them keep the country quiet that trade may come through to us."[66]

For chiefs, British rule, with its conditions of greater stability and the selective opportunity that accompanied official recognition, replaced war as a means of attaining wealth and status. Ten years after the establishment of the Protectorate, Chief Matturi of Nimikoro, Kono, possessed 400 wives, well above pre-colonial norms, and a sign of increasing wealth and security.[67] Chiefs used accommodations with colonial power as a means of accumulation and as a way of resisting the colonial state's hegemonic project.

These developments at the start of the century are important for understanding colonial difficulties in imposing a single vision of authority. The powerful economic positions of strongmen would become especially evident during the fiscal challenges of the Great Depression. When Lebanese traders appeared in Kono after 1930, the peculiar position of chiefs and their increasingly close relation to government would create an important role for the Lebanese in the elite accommodation as Freetown officials grew more concerned about the growing powers of chiefs. Contradictions between colonial state interests and chiefs' authority became especially evident with the discovery of diamonds in Kono. Until the discovery of diamonds, Freetown could ignore or even encourage chiefs' economic power. But as chiefs claimed resources that would eventually provide the majority of state revenues, accommodation between chiefs and the colonial state encountered new difficulties.

Diamonds and the threat of economic opportunity

The 1930s mark a watershed in the state–chief accommodation in Kono. Economic activity now evolved in a markedly different political framework. Earlier, chiefs had played a large economic role in lieu of foreign investment and in preference to local entrepreneurs. But as Freetown realized the possible fiscal benefits of diamond mining, officials seized upon an opportunity to establish more direct state control over revenue collection and economic development through collaborations with European mining companies. Since European mining companies demanded, and Freetown gladly provided, a monopoly on mineral exploitation, chiefs enjoyed only a marginal inclusion into the formal mining economy. Most Kono residents enjoyed none at all.

Colonial authorities viewed their policy decisions as being well within the framework of formally defined colonial state prerogatives. But years of collaboration with the British taught chiefs to expect direct economic gain for their political loyalty. Exclusion from diamond mining signaled to chiefs a major, unwarranted extension of state power over their authority. In any case, the past sharing of both formal and informal state authority had created a class of strongmen equipped with social networks to directly resist rearrangements in this political terrain.

Chiefs used these powers to defy colonial mining policy as Freetown faced fiscal chaos stemming from the Depression. Old accommodations became the battlefield for the struggle for influence between colonial officials and chiefs. Dissatisfied with their increasingly evident lack of direct control, Freetown officials embarked on a long process of reform to increase state capacity to directly control diamond wealth. At the same time they hoped to address Kono's increasingly vocal popular dissatisfaction with the pace of development and the chiefs' privileges. Yet "the consistent aim of the British staff to maintain and increase the prestige of the native ruler, to encourage his initiative, and to support his authority"[68] still guided reforms.

Freetown viewed chiefs' tendencies to stray from administrative norms as an administrative dilemma, not a sign of political struggle. Reforms aimed to correct "bad policies" rather than the underlying institutional weakness and lack of popular legitimacy that forced colonial officials to rely upon chiefs in the first place. Presaging late twentieth-century advice, reformers emphasized efforts to adapt to more "rational" – that is, more effective and capable – state administration. Consequently, Kono chiefs were to be denied formal authority over what they considered their rightful powers. But like later reforms, this "capacity building" exercise incorporated the very same state officials whose pursuits of private gain were also identified as part of Freetown's problem in the first place. But to local officials, the alternatives were worse.

In order to increase state institutional capacity, chiefs became everything from "health authorities" (1931), to "education officers" (1935), to enhanced "court magistrates" (1937). Crucial for their later influence over informal diamond markets, chiefs were given greater legal powers over alienation of land, control of settlement and local immigration. Meanwhile, Freetown assumed all mineral rights in 1927 after the discovery of alluvial gold deposits. While Freetown and London justified this action as "protecting native rights" from powerful foreign companies,[69] it also enabled the

Table 2.2. *Revenues and expenditures, 1928–36 (£1,000)*

			Deficit/Surplus	
	Expenditures	Revenues	No.	%
1928	815	826	+ 11	1.4
1929	871	740	− 131	17.6
1930	805	742	− 63	8.5
1931	884	883	− 1	0.1
1932	831	871	+ 40	4.4
1933	691	655	− 36	5.5
1934	603	597	− 6	1.0
1935	585	679	+ 94	13.9
1936	879	967	+ 88	9.1

Source: Compiled from Government of Sierra Leone, *Blue Book* (Freetown: Government Printer, various issues).

state to control the collection and spending of mining royalties. Freetown envisioned no significant role for Sierra Leoneans in mining apart from serving as laborers. Indigenous people, chiefs included, were excluded from decisions concerning mineral exploitation while state institutions collected revenues and directed spending. But this revamped state-led development only marginally increased state control over the economy and soon fell prey to local accommodations with chiefs, only this time with mining companies as added partners.

Following the 1927 discovery of diamonds, and eager for mining to begin during the depths of the Depression, Freetown signed a concessionary agreement with Sierra Leone Selection Trust (SLST) in 1932. This DeBeers subsidiary already mined diamonds in the Gold Coast. This agreement provided SLST with a ninety-nine-year monopoly on exploration and mining in return for a 27.5 percent tax on net profits[70] to off-set declining customs revenues during the Depression. Freetown was so eager for productive investment that in 1933 it unilaterally extended SLST's lease area to include the entire country. Governor Pollet believed that "If this company is discouraged, it might be several years before another would have the pluck to risk the capital expenditure."[71] Like reformers today, Pollet realized that the key to underwriting growing state capacity, especially during the Great Depression, lay in first achieving fiscal security with the aid of foreign firms.

Freetown's actions are best seen in the perspective of the looming fiscal constraints of the Great Depression (Table 2.2). Government rhetoric continued to adhere to the policy of balanced budgets, but the reality of periodic deficits called for emergency action. Mining revenues offered the only visible alternative. Palm products – the former leading export – dropped from 71 percent of exports in 1928 to 36.4 percent in 1936, and diamonds rose from zero in 1931 to 56 percent in 1936.[72] Revenues from SLST operations moved the colony's budget from a deficit to a persistent surplus up to the Second World War. Through diamond exports the colony also began to register a consistent trade surplus in the 1930s.[73]

Locally, one of the most important features of the arrangement concerned government efforts to limit commercial contact between SLST and Kono chiefs. Freetown was especially concerned about illicit mining. The government decision to extend the SLST lease to include the whole country was intended to provide the legal means to control illicit indigenous mining. DeBeers was adamant that the Sierra Leone Government should limit the African presence in mining areas. The company argued that discouraging any sort of African mining activity would, as in the Gold Coast, "nip in the bud" the establishment of rival illicit operations.[74] Laws after 1936 prohibiting even the possession of diamonds bear witness to official concern. Direct control over the population, especially in the mining chiefdoms, became a high priority for the revenue-hungry government.

Meanwhile, state expenditures declined as Freetown sought balanced budgets in the midst of the Depression. Again presaging later IMF and World-Bank mandated reforms, austerity and the need to exploit resources free from the informal claims of local elites prompted Freetown to use investors in its battle with powerful private interests in the face of weak state capacity to act. Freetown devolved diamond protection duties to SLST itself. After discussions in 1934, Freetown authorized SLST to field a force of twenty (later, thirty-five) armed men, deputized by the Sierra Leone Government to patrol mining areas.[75] This decision was interpreted quite negatively in Kono. The appearance of armed foreigners charged with separating Konos from the region's major resource represented an unwarranted extension of state power.

This exclusionary policy, while presented in Freetown as a logical evolution of colonial rule, clashed with local officials' accommodations with chiefs. Chiefs increasingly identified their informal involvement in the area's economic development as an additional "customary" right. This led to diverging interests between SLST, local officials and chiefs. Contradictions between official, *ad hoc*, and new policy fell especially heavily on Kono's DC. SLST's defense of lease rights also intruded on the local division of administrative powers, both at the institutional level and in informal, but *de facto*, district-level arrangements. The Kono DC complained that "a chief considers that his authority is impugned by Company Force attacks on his strangers ... I fear that this policy is spreading disruption into this area."[76] "Strangers" (tenants) often set up business, paying chiefs a "rent" in exchange for protection. The practice is an old one, dating from at least the time of nineteenth-century itinerant traders.[77] SLST was concerned that these new strangers were illicitly mining diamonds. Meanwhile, heeding Freetown and SLST demands, a superior responded that "I am impressing upon the officers concerned the urgent need to encourage the local chiefs and headmen to adhere to the new arrangements."[78]

For its part, SLST also undertook unilateral efforts to limit illicit mining and see that strangers left the area. Soon after mining commenced, the Kono DC uncovered SLST efforts to conclude private agreements with chiefs to secure compliance with official regulations. Believing that chiefs controlled the influx of illicit miners, the company made informal payments of £50 to each chief who agreed to withhold settler rights. The Kono DC demanded an end to this practice. Ignoring the basis of his own relations with chiefs, he declared that "Payments will only encourage them [chiefs] to support us if they see financial gain in it."[79] But even after local officials asserted themselves as rulers of both company and chiefs, company payoffs to chiefs continued.[80]

Even as SLST began a policy of informal payoffs, chiefs continued to permit stranger settlement. Utilizing their growing administrative capacities and considerable economic powers, chiefs played an informal intermediary role between the diamond industry and Kono residents who felt unfairly excluded from the region's wealth. Since colonial rulers already conceded that chiefs were owners of land in a socially enforceable sense and responsible for law and order, chiefs exercised great control over the terms of settlements of strangers illicitly seeking Kono's diamond wealth. As subjects' contact point between the colonial state, and now, the mining company, chiefs exercised power to regulate the entry of strangers into illicit mining and to influence the distribution of some of Kono's mineral resources. Local officials had the legal power to prohibit individuals from entering Kono. But as events would demonstrate, their accommodations with chiefs and their institutional incapacity, added to their responsibilities to SLST, would reinforce the increasing division of political authority between the institutional and the informal, or Shadow State.

Chiefs and their tenants

While state difficulties in controlling new-found resources reinforced chiefs' economic intermediary positions, these new opportunities also heightened the importance of a heretofore minor player in Kono's political economy – the stranger. Strangers were wealthier Freetown Africans or Lebanese,

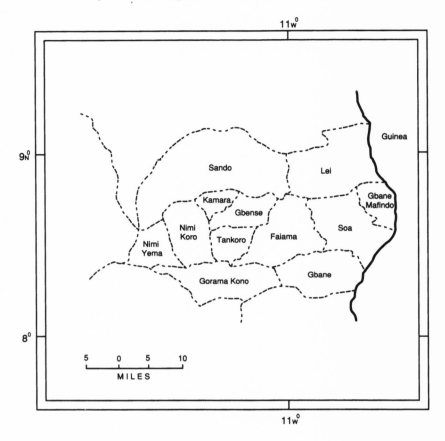

Map 2   Kono district
Source: Adapted from John I. Clarke, *Sierra Leone in Maps*
(London: Hodder & Stoughton, 1969).

increasingly squeezed out of legitimate trade by colonial policies discrimi-
nating against indigenous entrepreneurs. They were attracted to chiefs who
were access points to illicit mining. Most possessed capital sufficient to
begin illicit diamond buying operations, and as SLST feared, stimulated
local involvement in illicit diamond mining. By the late 1930s they directly
financed mining operations. These new commercial opportunities enabled
chiefs to combine their *de facto*, and increasingly *de jure* positions in the
colonial state, with their customary private duties as "landlords" to sell
protection to illicit mining operations.

In Nimikoro chiefdom in the heart of the main SLST mining area (Map 2), chiefdom authorities complained that a Chief Bona allocated plots to strangers rather than to local residents. Strangers paid a "consideration" for use of the plot. Thus a share of diamond sales went directly into the chief's pocket. Chief Kaimachende of Gbense also faced criticism for his new-found "love of strangers," usually wealthier Africans and Lebanese from outside Kono who outbid locals for now valuable land-use rights.[81] Despite efforts to directly control chiefs' behavior, SLST directors became concerned: "A gang of 300 to 500 must be mining night and day ... This represents a serious loss to us, and the loss to Government in royalties must be of no small account. The illegal miners are armed with swords and matchets and the leaders are beginning to exhort their men to resistance."[82] Chiefs' intervention into the diamond business enhanced and financed their growing personal armed forces to defend privilege. The reward of great personal wealth for successful chiefs also reinforced links between state office and private gain.

Soon the situation directly challenged colonial officers' and SLST's abilities to limit illicit mining and protect revenues and profits. But chiefs' control of wealth also awakened a powerful alternative political force available to state officials. Freetown continued to press for immediate "repatriation" of strangers, but the Kono DC outlined his own alternative understanding of the local situation:

I have no doubt that the chiefs would fear to tackle gangs. Further, we have not got the sympathy of the Chiefs and people on our side in this matter; there is a strong feeling throughout the country that Government has not given the people a fair deal and they contend that they should have greater facilities to mine in their own country. Furthermore, they [chiefs] undoubtedly make a profit from these people.[83]

Popular desire among the indigenous population for distributive justice and some freedom to mine their own land once again offered Freetown the possibility of directly mobilizing an African population independently of accommodations with strongmen. In this way, accountable state authority, or what later reformers call "governance," would accomplish the political task of reinforcing popular support for efficient policies and expanded institutional state capacity. But District Commissioners were torn between maintaining order and avoiding dreaded inquiries in the wake of disturbances due to the enforcement of unpopular policies. A tax rebellion in Kambia in 1931 demonstrated the dangers to the security of colonial rule of vigorous enforcement of measures perceived as unfair burdens.[84]

This fear of disorder, along with continuing colonial obsessions with balanced budgets – again a feature of later reformers – maintained the chiefs' roles in the Kono diamond economy. Subsequent policies both increased chiefs' involvement in illicit mining and increased the attractions

Table 2.3. *Produce marketing, 1936–56 (% market)*

		1936	1941	1946	1951	1956
European	(Palm)	69	70	79	82	83
	(Cocoa)	61	70	84	92	95
Lebanese	(Palm)	12	14	10	10	9
	(Cocoa)	4	2	3	4	2
African	(Palm)	19	16	11	8	7
	(Cocoa)	35	28	13	4	3

Source: Compiled from Government of Sierra Leone, *Blue Book* (Freetown: Government Printer, various issues); Government of Sierra Leone, *Consolidated Report SLPMB* (Freetown: Government Printer, 1959).

of illicit mining to strangers. Considering this broader colonial state response to its revenue crisis helps us to better identify these strangers who came to play a very important role in Sierra Leone's political economy and help us to see where they come into the picture and why.

As in earlier periods, the Sierra Leone government faced a serious overall reduction of revenue after 1929. Tariffs rose as a result of repeating solutions from the First World War. Some non-British consumer goods tariffs rose from 50 percent to 300 percent under the Imperial Preference Scheme of 1932. Export duties were reimposed or increased.[85] Exporters paid less for produce, passing on tariff increases to producers. Downward pressures on world commodity prices compounded this trend of rising consumer and falling producer prices. As before, large companies were better situated to weather this crisis, as collaborators in government policy-making and with their greater access to bulk shipping. Elder Dempster shipping lines now exercised significant market control along the West African coast. One Freetown newspaper detected collusion: "Healthy competition is destroyed," said an editor, "when large commercial houses circumvent and prevent supplies to arrive to smaller traders, except through them."[86]

But more importantly for Kono, these policies, along with the Depression, squeezed many agriculture-trade middlemen – the remnants of a "new class" of non-European traders – from their positions in the formal economy (Table 2.3). Some of these people turned to illicit mining, under Kono chief control. Among the Lebanese, family names prominent in produce trades such as Jaward, Salim, Shamel and Amel cropped up in references to mining, either legal (gold) or illegal (diamonds).

A similar narrowing of opportunities in French Guinea also attracted

Africans from that colony. Mandingoes and Fulas began moving into Kono in the 1930s, bringing with them small amounts of capital in the hopes of quick profits in the diamond business. Under pressure from state favor for foreign firms and biases against local producers, transborder pre-colonial migration and trade networks showed new signs of life. The restriction of formal-economy opportunities in Guinea and Sierra Leone also ensured a steady flow of diggers as the attractions of illicit mining grew in relative terms.

In the late 1930s, SLST and the government perceived a new chance to pursue the struggle to control directly all diamond revenues. These administrative reforms of 1937–the Native Authority Scheme – sought to draw chiefs more directly into the responsibilities of local government. Freetown viewed the reforms as "a progressive policy to interest African leaders in the enterprise of self-development . . . and help Government protect the interests of its subjects."[87] The Kono DC hoped that "These measures will finally force our chiefs to become *responsible* members of Government and not work against the Public Good," that is, refrain from seeking wealth through support for illicit mining.[88] Once again, reforms that were meant to force chiefs to defend a state-defined interest through administrative incentives disregarded the nature of chiefs' true interests.

These reforms followed the Gold Coast example of commuting custom-ary benefits into salaries and raising taxes to provide greater revenue for local services. Freetown officials, anxious to maintain local stability, gave chiefs the option of voluntarily joining the scheme. Hut taxes were scheduled to rise by four shillings to about twenty shillings, with all additional funds earmarked for the chiefdom's treasury. As a further incentive for chiefs to accept these changes, the Kono DC authorized chiefs' salaries, which soon compromised the bulk of treasury spending. Chiefs accepted the program as the benefits became obvious. In Nimikoro, 59 percent of the new Native Authority budget of about £4,000 in 1949 went to administrative costs. Of this amount, 94 percent went to the chief's personal use, including loans for cars, home construction, and education for his sons.[89]

The Native Authority Scheme and later reforms considerably increased chiefs' legal incomes. In general, most Kono chiefs' official incomes increased from about £500 per year as illicit mining began in the 1930s to amounts approaching £10,000 for some by the late 1940s. Overall, this development put chiefs in a much more dominant economic and political position within Kono. Many translated this windfall into concrete assets. A survey of property deed transfers in Koidu town from 1945 to 1955 indicates a growth in taxable properties from 59 in 1945 to 609 in 1955. Of the 550 properties added to the rolls during this decade, about 65 percent belonged to chiefs or locals from chiefs' clans.[90] This additional source of wealth did not end chiefs' involvement in illicit mining. Instead, it indicated the growing, and as yet, unshakable role of local officials' accommodations with chiefs in order to rule Sierra Leone.

These reforms ensured that chiefs and their strangers would play an even more important role in later state efforts to assert control over diamond revenues. The next chapter explores the chiefs' transformed role as uninvited economic intermediaries in the diamond industry. Reforms after the Second World War found the Sierra Leone government struggling to provide greater economic opportunity in response to growing political demands. All the while, Freetown officials remained anxious over budgetary shortfalls, and now, growing illicit mining. Thus the institutional state–Shadow State struggle continued. True economic and political pluralism could considerably weaken strongmen who challenged a single definition of state interests. But to do so would also overturn the fragile balance of order and privilege that underlay the quest for solvency. Again the allure of incorporating into "reform" those whose private interests were identified as the state's problem prevailed.

3   Elite hegemony and the threat of political and economic reform

New legislation was passed which will, it is hoped, give us a far tighter grip on Kono and mean that the diamond areas will at long last be not only brought under control but be kept under control.   Governor's Office[1]

The police can do little to prevent this illicit mining, as practically the entire population of the areas concerned appeared to be of the belief that the diamonds were in reality their property.   Inspector of Mines[2]

Late colonial economic and political reforms and the evolution of Sierra Leone's elite accommodation in the Shadow State contain clues for understanding problems plaguing present-day structural adjustment policies. Thomas Callaghy notes that World Bank and IMF emphases on capacity building and political conditionalities as preconditions of reform are designed to take Africa "back to the future"; back to the colonial quest for fiscal stability and state capacity to invest in infrastructure to promote private investment.[3] This solution also reflects a belief that "bad" policies are the cause of Africa's weak states and "uncaptured" economies, and that concerted efforts to build institutional state capabilities will resolve this crisis.

But these assumptions about the nature of state and society ignore the role of markets that we see accompanying the development of Sierra Leone's Shadow State under colonial rule. Contrary to common expectations in late-colonial times and now, powerful groups or individuals – foreign and indigenous – are inclined to compensate for reform through intensification of their accommodations. The result is an *increase* in elite exploitation of resources to procure support and control challenges, especially when threats of economic and political liberalism appear to undermine these accommodations. Thus "entrepreneurs" in state offices and informal markets do not respond with political support for policies that undercut their own political power through control of markets.

Yet reformers have to utilize the very members of the elite accommodation who are perceived to be obstacles to reform, but who are also officials of the state. Reformers' "capacity building" measures in both the

55

1930s and 1990s have had to face this dilemma. The cause of this dilemma lies in markets, which are at the core of accommodations in the Shadow State but seen as peripheral in dichotomous state–society analyses of Africa's malaise. To understand the functioning of elite accommodation around markets – especially diamond markets in Sierra Leone – is to understand the politics of the Shadow State. Before examining these processes in the Kono setting, this chapter looks more closely at how economic and political reforms ended up strengthening the Shadow State and the political importance of control over the informal diamond market.

Contradictions of early "capacity building" reforms

Diamonds presented Freetown with fiscal resources in the 1930s. Production climbed to over a million carats in 1942, boosting colonial revenues by 50 percent. Freetown weathered the Second World War with only one deficit year.[4] Now was the time for the state to take a more direct role in development. At the same time, the Colonial Office was offering a new vision of development. This time, the task was to bring Africans directly into the modern economy on the state's terms. Failure to do so lead the Colonial Office to worry:

The African's inexperience of all contractual relations involved in commercial transactions based on money have made him a stranger to legal methods in which a modern individualistic society has expressed its needs. How far is it possible to adjust European conceptions of law and justice to these conditions of mind? The answer does not lie in any change of the law; it depends on the extent to which administrations are determined to impress their own conceptions of behaviour on Africa.[5]

In accordance with past practice, Britain would not bear the costs of rule. Said Lord Hailey in 1938: "If African administrations are able to attain higher standards in expenditure on social improvements, the African population must pay the price necessary to earn them."[6] Planners envisioned a radical transformation of chiefs from economic intermediaries exercising power in their own right to more purely administrative intermediaries. They would serve more direct state interests, including collecting revenues and providing services on behalf of an expanded administrative apparatus. This vision of reform clashed with previous Kono chief tendencies to assume economic intermediary roles and broad social autonomy through *ad hoc* accommodations with hard-pressed local officials.

What local officials had known for decades became painfully clear to Freetown officials: control could be tenuous, and now chiefs and their allies had considerably enhanced abilities to resist. In his comments on the reorganization of the Court Messenger Force in 1939, Governor Douglas

Jardine articulated what he considered to be the most pressing state interest regarding reform. "The changing conditions of the Protectorate and the tendency toward industrialization in the mining areas," he said, "combines [sic] to demand an increased standard of efficiency in police work."[7] How could all the new tasks of administration and economic development be advanced without relying upon the only local intermediaries British officials in Sierra Leone knew? These chiefs were also identified as one of the obstacles to the more autonomous exercise of state power. Even as early as the 1930s, African public opinion was beginning to exercise a decisive impact on the government's political choices. Domestic pressures in Britain, India's independence, and home-government fears of uncontrollable nationalist agitation later added a colonial version of "political conditionalities" on Freetown. This addition of political competition clashed directly with Freetown's efforts to control diamonds and actually enhanced the power of chiefs. Vocal redistributive demands, in the name of freedom and equality, would serve only to drive chief and state official closer together.

An investigator of chiefs' abuses of power neatly summed up the government's dilemma: "The problem arises inevitably when a principal (in this case Government) uses as an agent (in this case the chief) a man whose appointment is made for other purposes and over which the principal exercises little control."[8] Yet Freetown continued to build upon the chief–government coalition. Said Senior DC Fenton of local administrative reforms in Kono in 1935: "As much as can be given without crippling Native Administration activities should be allowed to chiefs to gain their good will, which is important."[9] Of NA treasury expenditures in 1948, 58 percent went to chiefs' salaries, 3.5 percent to agricultural development and 4.5 percent to education.[10] These efforts to buy compliance undermined the legitimacy of Native Authorities in the eyes of commoners. At the same time, chiefs, and increasingly, strangers, refused to acquiesce in all state (and mining company) decisions about the distribution of resources. Where chiefs had earlier seized commercial benefits from colonial efforts to promote trade, they now found themselves increasingly in conflict with official efforts to isolate them from diamond wealth. As the state's chosen administrative and, increasingly, political intermediaries, chiefs also voiced a popular dissatisfaction with state attacks on illicit mining. The harder Freetown pushed reform, the greater the risk of upsetting the accommodations that enabled Freetown to rule the hinterland in the first place.

Officials were trapped into defending the contradictory imperatives of retaining control over the country's population and collecting revenue, and implementing reform. Particularly in Freetown, officials feared that "Increasing ease of travel and the attraction of the mines means the influx of strangers into chiefdoms, strangers who know what is done elsewhere, who criticize and despise a weak native government."[11] Again, corrective reforms offered chiefs a larger role in government. At the same time many officials recognized the integral connection between the chiefs' authority as intermediaries of the colonial state and their collaboration in illicit mining. Local officials bore the brunt of reconciling opposing pressures. Protection of diamonds and political reform both demanded a level of control which Freetown still lacked the capacity to invoke. Informal accommodations between officials and chiefs and a tolerance of limited illicit mining still maintained social order. Officials still pursued informal arrangements, usually involving an irregular distribution of state resources to chiefs or turning a blind eye to illegal practices, in exchange for limited cooperation.

While the state–chief relationship was officially defined in hierarchical administrative terms, officials began to rely on an improvised construction of cooperation with chiefs at increasingly higher levels of the Sierra Leone government hierarchy. The broad scope of colonial state interests in controlling developments in Kono, combined with the dependence on chiefs as intermediaries, ensured that opposition to domination took shape not directly *against* the state but rather *within* it. Political reform after the Second World War would open the gates to popular calls for limits to official privilege, contrary to Freetown's vision of the construction of a transformed "modern" economy and society supportive of state aims.

Bayart's analysis of the "hegemonic project" in Cameroon illuminates some difficulties that Freetown and SLST officials encountered in trying to impose a single set of rules on society:

Perhaps the greatest problem of domination lies in grasping the target, to force them into a social space in which they can be directed. The hegemonic project consists in part in the construction of such a space. However, the target produces its own social spaces in a remarkable diversity. This process remains highly autonomous. Such autonomy is itself a measure of the inadequacies of the regime's political pronouncements.[12]

Illicit mining remained exceedingly difficult for Sierra Leone officials to control. The "hegemonic project" in Sierra Leone suffered from some of the state's agents' tendencies to seek their own interests in illicit mining.

Herein lies the contradiction inherent in reform when political liberalization is added to "capacity building" measures that conflict with the elite accommodation that is the Shadow State. Political reforms ordered by London as a precondition for decolonization indeed became a tool for subjects actively resisting Freetown, SLST and chiefs' interests in Kono's resources. Consequently, to gather popular acquiescence, officials increasingly relied on informal distributions of benefits, especially after popular challenges to mining policies emerged before the first popular elections in

1957. Lacking grass-roots connections to Kono society, new state spending, mostly in the form of development funds, was, as usual, channeled
through chiefs. This provided political entrepreneurs who were taking
advantage of popular grievances and contesting elections the ability to
exploit disaffection over chiefs' privileges, the distribution of diamond
resources and the state suppression of illicit mining. Elite expressions of
dissatisfaction came from chiefs who were at the periphery of the diamond-
mining area, and hence left out of the political alliance. To their chagrin,
state officials faced illicit mining as a political issue rather than as an
administrative problem.

Non-elite challenges to the ruling party also arose. Rival parties from
outside Kono tapped popular feelings of relative deprivation and anger
toward chiefs during the 1960s. Their attack on the hegemonic alliance
mobilized illicit miners themselves, incorporating wealthier miners and
diamond dealers eager to curry favor with any potential authority in order
to protect their own access to diamonds. Thus those campaigning for office
campaigned *against* state interests. But once in power in 1968, populists
found that they now relied on illicit miners rather than on chiefs to support
them as they took control of government.

This study now turns to the government's attempts to define illicit mining
and the task of building support in administrative terms. This analysis of
the leaderships' efforts to impose more direct control over diamond-mining
areas focuses on contradictions in that effort. Strategies aimed at incorporating chiefs into this project promoted the opposite outcome. Chiefs
exercised increasing power as strongmen in their own right, claiming access
to increasing flows of state resources. These local-level compromises
proved increasingly expensive, and diverted state resources from true
economic and administrative development. Meanwhile, popular frustration over the effects of policies which appeared to favor chiefs undermined Freetown's efforts to build wide popular support for its policies and
goals.

Democratization and the strengthening Shadow State: 1948–68

How was government to stem the erosion of state revenues and SLST
profits, and increase provision of services while abiding by the restrictions
on state authority that liberal reform required? Until 1948, the Colonial
Office had envisioned constitutional reform as building upon the institutions of chiefs' powers. In 1947, however, Andrew Cohen, the head of the
Colonial Office, Africa Division, outlined policies limiting collaboration
with chiefs, "converting the system of indirect rule into an efficient,
representative and modern system of local government. The educated

people, and the rising middle class, as well as the peasants, were to be given a more effective say in local government by the use of elections."[13] Recognizing a growing popular resentment over chiefs' privileges, reformers reserved a political space for educated and politically active commoners. The British saw a need to coopt moderate nationalist movements and protect British interests, but also hoped that this new "civil society" would demand further state support for economic and administrative efficiency.[14]

For Kono, the Colonial Office decision meant elections and the formation of a local legislative council. London asked the colonial administration to shift more administrative responsibility from chiefs to a professional civil service staffed by Africans under the control of elected assemblies. For Kono and Sierra Leone's eleven other districts, voters would select a district council, an institution that would bypass chiefs and establish more direct central government connections to local society. This new policy promised a role in government for citizens expressing their social grievances in elections. The expectation of democratization, repeated in the 1990s, was that political pluralism would tap social support for further reform. But had chiefs established firm enough social and economic control to ensure a significant role in the latest reforms? More importantly, would the bonds between local officials and chiefs be so easily broken?

Because claims to represent fellow Sierra Leoneans rested on promises to increase the state's capacity to deliver services and heed popular demands, Sierra Leone's reformers could not forget the colonial imperative of protecting government access to revenues. Africans running for election shared State House's need to respond to growing popular demands for benefits from diamond revenues. Consequently, African politicians and reformist administrators found themselves relying on intermediaries to ensure the smooth flow of revenues and the maintenance of public support and order.

The costs of development, rising popular expectations and approaching independence made Kono officials even more anxious to exert state control over diamond revenue. Growing illicit mining and breakdown in public order raised the specter of chaos in the industry that provided 65 percent of state revenues by 1951.[15] Disturbances spread to Kono in 1956, and alerted officials to a popular dissatisfaction with chiefs' influence in illicit markets and their privileged access to state resources. Chiefs' privileges violated reform's promise of justice. They appeared to be inconsistent with popular interpretations of reform as an official retreat from direct control of resources and favoritism for chiefs. But for local leaders struggling to defend state authority, this critique was seen as an unacceptable interference.

The local power of chiefs continued to grow, however. Kono's average

Hut Tax rose from five shillings in 1935, before the establishment of Native Authorities, to thirty-three shillings in 1956.[16] By 1955, however, the chief-administered tax that was supposed to help finance increased state spending free of chief influence seemed to produce little public benefit. In that year, Native Authorities spent only 3 percent of revenues on education and 1.7 percent on agricultural development, while turning 30 percent over to the new district councils. Chiefs kept most of the rest.[17] Kono's district council was not known for fiscal prudence. Said a 1958 audit investigating "loans" to chiefs by the chief-dominated council, "It is clear that there is little control over the Council's finances and little or no plan to execute that control."[18]

Officials faced the familiar problem of assertively independent chiefs. A commission of inquiry into riots in 1955–6 connected chiefs' misuse of delegated authority with considerable popular discontent. "The position of chiefs," stated the report, "has been bedeviled by their trying to play a dual role. They have been chiefs *and* agents of the Central Government."[19] But riot-weary local officials saw the relationship in a different light. Said the Commissioner of Southeast Province, "It would be a mistake to allow spectacular failures to overshadow the undoubted influence which Tribal Authorities do have on the maintenance of law and order."[20] The Freetown response to London inquiries into disturbances rejected numerous suggestions for more popular involvement in local government at the expense of chiefs' power.

Recognizing his inability to rule directly, a Freetown official offered that "the chiefly cult is the only secular discipline known to the country."[21] It was a secular discipline that served the interests of the country's rulers and which illicit mining threatened. The Kono DC summed up his view of the unrest: "The atmosphere prevalent in the diamond areas, which was spread by miners with money to spend and dissolute habits, could not be other than inimical to the traditional restraints of tribal discipline and good order."[22] Freetown's rule, especially in the eyes of local officials, depended on exercising administrative control rather than addressing popular concerns about an intrusive state. This posture was fundamentally at odds with London's new strategy of building a popular base for pluralism and state-led development.

However, local unrest and continuing illicit mining forced Kono and Freetown officials to address local grievances. Officials offered two proposals to end illicit mining. One plan, the Alluvial Diamond Mining Scheme (ADMS), aimed to restore security to SLST's lease area through limited legalization of some illicit mining. The scheme would generate revenue under direct Freetown control, while addressing local concerns about the distribution of mining opportunities. The other plan, the Mining Area

Development Administration (MADA) involved government spending in Kono which would directly incorporate local administration into development projects under central government control. Officials hoped that both would generate popular support and leave the government more freedom to directly attack illicit mining. Yet again, new policies ended up putting more power in chiefs' hands. Officials manipulated policies to entice chiefs into cooperating with their superiors' aims. These strategies drew higher levels of government directly into Kono's elite accommodation of illicit mining, and an increasingly expensive local *ad hoc* arrangement, which again threatened state revenues.

ADMS – Economic pluralism and weakening state institutions

Most Kono residents believed that SLST's monopoly on diamond mining bestowed benefits upon Europeans and chiefs. In 1955, illicit miners attacked SLST security forces and a police station. "Attacks," said the Provincial Secretary, "were in complete disregard of authority which had not the means of restraining them . . . in consequence, from severe necessity, we devoted much of the year to negotiating an agreement to legalize their activities."[23] Later, SLST accepted limits on its exclusive prospecting rights to a 230-square-mile lease area in exchange for £1,570,000, providing 23 percent of Freetown's 1955 budget. Illicit miners were invited to apply for licenses to legally mine deposits outside the SLST lease. In return, they were obligated to sell diamonds to government-licensed dealers. These dealers, mining illicitly under chief control, found new legitimate uses for illegally acquired capital. One Freetown official, however, was confident that this early "liberalization" effort would restore governmental authority to impose discipline on the industry: "By the time the scheme was introduced, these characters had begun to gain control of some chiefdoms, but when the local inhabitants began to realize the advantages we offered, there was a general tendency for the occupiers and landholders to take up the mining themselves."[24] Freetown blamed illicit mining on ethnically non-Kono outsiders attracted to Kono's wealth. Posing as protectors of ethnic Konos, Freetown's paramilitary "Operation Parasite" removed 40,000 "malevolent strangers threatening the progress of our [Kono] people."[25]

Freetown's efforts to impose order on the mining industry brought radical new intrusions of state authority into miners' lives. Arrests rose 39 percent in 1956–7. By 1959, felony charges for illicit mining in Kono rose 210 percent above the figures from three years earlier.[26] More arrests and longer sentencing prompted the Governor's Office to investigate the effect of this major offensive against illicit mining, noting that "the increasing number of arrests in Kono has made the Ministry of Education and Social

Welfare still more concerned about overcrowding in prisons."[27] But Freetown sought to connect the acceptance of its authority and economic advancement by simultaneously attacking, removing, and imprisoning "malevolent" strangers, while providing legal mining opportunities to law-abiding citizens. Emphasizing his faith that economic reform would produce political support for state action, Governor Dorman said of ADMS:

Although it was not felt to be desirable to take the property of diamonds from the Crown and restore it to indigenous inhabitants, it was decided that the scheme should enable the landholders, headmen, and chiefs to exercise power which they themselves believe they hold . . . as such, the scheme will create a much healthier and more law abiding atmosphere in those chiefdoms where it is introduced.[28]

Africans would benefit from diamond resources, but only under direct government control. But again, the remedy for "bad" policies required greater reliance on chief cooperation.

Initially under DC control, officials delegated licensing to Kono chiefs. The Kono DC complained that he was overwhelmed by thousands of applications and feared "the consternation caused by direct government influence" that local residents blamed for the unfair distribution of resources in the first place. He also noted that wealthier African and Lebanese strangers already involved in illicit mining with chiefs' approval presented ready-made, easily monitored private mining operations.[29] Thus Kono chiefs approved licenses, assigned lands for mining and collected a "surface rent." In practice, this new formal authority gave chiefs additional rent-seeking opportunities. A Kono businessman complained that unofficial payments to chiefs increased 500 percent as a result of increased chief authority under the licensing scheme.[30] Prior to 1956, when all African mining was illegal, miners shared risks. A Kono resident noted that even possessing certain farm implements invited arrest at the hands of officers recruited to enforce anti-mining ordinances for SLST.[31] Now, "liberalization" increased the ability of chiefs and their favorites to sell protection to miners as Freetown shifted greater powers to chiefs to declare certain mining legal or illegal.

New regulations also favored wealthier miners, since they could afford to pay for access to better plots. These wealthy strangers offered chiefs their support, since they owed their continued presence to the chiefs' approval. Some strangers occupied positions in Native Authorities as chiefs manipulated councillor lists. A 1971 audit of Kono chiefdom lists revealed that more than half of all councillors were non-Konos.[32] This reduced ethnic Kono representation in formal political organizations and left the Konos economically dependent on outsiders. Chiefs' control of the courts also enforced this arrangement. For example, a 1961 "stranger drive" netted forty-seven miners in Nimikoro. The Native Court convicted four and the remainder were released. Three of the four had connections with rival chiefdom factions.[33]

Freetown continued to face political challenges. Strangers continued to arrive in Kono to man increasingly well-organized illicit operations.[34] Even when official prices rose and illicit mining decreased, wealth still found its way into private hands. SLST still complained of losses to illicit mining. Police forces continued to encounter threats to their authority; in 1957 an Assistant Superintendent of Police raided a mining area within the SLST lease and was held for two days by the miners because, as he said during an inquiry, "The people were annoyed and said that they had no proper area to mine and complained."[35] With political liberalization and the approach of Independence, chasing away miners would have political costs as well. In response to SLST complaints of illicit mining, officials observed that force "could have most undesirable political consequences which could only cause the company difficulty."[36]

More administrative reforms aimed at regulating African mining, coupled with stranger drives, further increased the chiefs' powers. A 1959 lease scheme sought to answer popular criticisms that SLST left idle many promising mining sites. Freetown unveiled a plan to allow cooperative African–SLST joint ventures to mine some areas within the reduced SLST lease area. The new strategy gave chiefs a stake in ensuring SLST lease security. SLST and the government retained control over marketing while the lease system provided more legal opportunities for miners. Again, private capital with chief connections was favored. Few chiefs invested on their own. Instead, wealthy outsiders, particularly Lebanese who had benefited from earlier illicit opportunities, connections with chiefs, and official recognition under ADMS, set up firms with nominal local participation and edged out potential indigenous Kono investment. By 1964, fourteen contract schemes were in operation. All were accused of irregularities, especially payoffs to chiefs whose authorization was needed for the joint venture to mine on local land.[37]

But the key to liberalization lay in attacking incentives for illicit diamond dealing. In 1959, the government Gold and Diamond Office (GDO) was established to buy all dealers' diamonds for export. The government paid prices that left little official profit margin, but some diamond sales did shift to legal channels, a performance maintained up to the mid-1960s. However, production and primary marketing stages remained in the hands of wealthy strangers, many of whom still employed illicit miners but sold diamonds through official channels. State regulation remained tenuous, while the, autonomous economic networks of chiefs and strangers remained intact.

Economic and social connections between chiefs and their strangers proved resilient to official efforts to change the organization of production and exchange. Illicit miners perceived maximization of opportunity as including friendly relations with powerful chiefs for mutual economic benefit and protection against disruption of operations.

Economic reforms also failed to eliminate SLST concerns about losses to illicit mining. Fearing lost profits and lacking the authority to legislate, SLST began making informal payments to chiefs who promised to cooperate in controlling mining. An agreement in 1954 between SLST and the colonial government already required annual payments from SLST of £10,000 for local development purposes. However, the company began making unauthorized direct payments to chiefs as private citizens for "development purposes."[38] SLST also provided electricity to chiefdom compounds and extended "loans" for the purchase of cars or building materials. SLST's private efforts to protect corporate interests further undermined Freetown's efforts to gain direct control over the mining industry in Kono. Freetown's own officials, however, soon joined SLST in pursuing further informal accommodations.

MADA – "development" that strengthens the Shadow State

Local Kono officials began making unofficial payments to chiefs under the auspices of the MADA program. Conceived after the 1955 disturbances and in response to politicians' claims that Kono did not benefit from diamond revenues, MADA was to be administered through the Kono DC and the newly elected district council. Funding for the program came directly from Freetown to provide politically visible development projects for which Freetown could take credit. Officials in Freetown also explicitly conceived of this "capacity building" program as an opportunity to use diamond revenues *without* chiefs' involvement for projects benefiting the general community. Development came to be seen as a political tool for officials in both Kono and Freetown:

The immediate commencement of work in Kono District is essential for security reasons. The opinion is that unless visible results are produced very soon, the Kono people will again become restive, particularly as the "hungry season" is approaching and very little work can be done in the alluvial mining fields.[39]

But lacking an extensive administrative or grassroots connection to Kono citizens, local officials again made chiefs local agents for policy implementation. Now that Africans were voicing political demands, local colonial officials also faced unwelcome pressures on local administration. Colonial officials sought out "MADA chiefs" and followers belonging to the "right" political party. This came to mean chiefs' support for the Sierra Leone Peoples' Party (SLPP), which opposed a more radical regional Kono party, the Kono Progressive Movement (KPM) in the 1957 and 1962 elections. The radical party attacked government restrictions on African access to diamonds in language that stressed themes of domination and oppression. Claiming that SLST was an agent of foreign imperialism and that diamonds were Kono property, the KPM challenged the very basis of Freetown's control of accumulation and, therefore, the autonomy of state power to allocate resources. Control of mining was of additional personal concern to at least some colonial officials; a 1962 SLST management roster included prominent former colonial officials.

Chiefs capitalized on officials' perceptions of threat. Kono's DC approved payments of £10,000 each to six chiefs out of MADA funds. The Minister of Mines in Freetown complained that:

No Paramount Chief has been "led" to expect any personal profit ... What they have been "allowed" to expect is a different matter. The statement made by Sir Robert Hall [Kono DC] at Koidu, which has never been publicly contradicted, certainly implied that Chiefs, Tribal Authorities, and Village Heads in Kono will receive annual payments as long as they are "helpful to Government."[40]

Concerned about order in the district, however, the Provincial Commissioner responded that impounding funds "would be regarded by Konos as dishonesty on Government's part and would cause intense ill-will."[41] In his own defense over the irregular disbursement of a total of £100,000 from MADA funds in 1958, the Kono DC stated that "payments are not tied to any inescapable commitment, but merely evidence of Government's goodwill."[42] Such "development" spending rose rapidly (Table 3.1).

Chiefs did their part to ensure that they received these funds for their service to local officials' interests. Once accustomed to informal payments, the Nimikoro chief provided a threatening rationalization for local policy:

My people and I feel that this grant is in appreciation of our effort at preventing a wild-scale illicit mining. This is to keep Government informed that unless such grants are made available from year to year, the bush owners and Tribal Authorities will gradually lose their interest in fostering the good relationship with the Company, and subsequently, it would be hard to have an effective control over the situation.[43]

Government in Freetown was not an unwilling partner: funds were used not only to buy social order, but also to buy electoral support. MADA payments become a recurrent item in the 1962/63 budget, a development that a former Kono DC notes was a reward for active chiefs' support in turning out SLPP voters and harassing KPM supporters during the 1962 election.[44] More significantly, its distribution came under discretionary

Table 3.1. *Kono development funds, 1951–8 (£)*

	Grants	Marketing Board	Contracts	Mining Fund	Total
1951	5,000	651	—	500	6,151
1952	5,080	10,602	4,806	3,000	23,488
1953	5,480	3,319	5,067	4,000	17,866
1954	9,641	2,575	9,828	2,000	24,044
1955	21,814	1,629	17,531	2,500	43,474
1956	40,000	2,246	21,713	2,500	66,459
1957	40,000	3,912	22,824	2,500	69,236
1958	100,000	2,773	25,635	2,500	130,908

Source: Government of Sierra Leone, *Blue Book* (Freetown, Government Printer, various issues); Government of Sierra Leone, *Report on the Administration of the Province* (Freetown: Government Printer, 1960); MADA correspondence.

powers, thus bypassing the Kono District Council, which as the only local elected body, would become a center of opposition to unpopular government policies.

Local officials ignored further irregularities in the use of chiefdom development funds for similar reasons. Chiefdom treasuries increasingly turned state resources over to chiefs' personal uses. Presumably this was done with local officials' acquiescence since DCs reviewed chiefdom budgets. Later reports of DC protection of chiefs' powers in defiance of 1964 reforms to centralize district administration underlines the growing tension between the pressures of popular political demands and the government's need to exercise control.[45] Chiefdom incomes from official sources now rivaled regular budgetary outlays for Kono, a process begun under British rule. Table 3.2 gives only a rough gauge of the growing importance of irregular expenditures that increasingly characterized government spending in Kono. The table does not cover local sources of chiefdom funds such as court and license fees directly attached to Native Authority administration. The scale of informal payments was considerable, however. In 1960, for example, Tankoro chiefdom revenues amounted to only 45 percent of its chief's private income.[46]

Naturally, receipt of government funds required support by rulers in Freetown. Elections after 1957 also increased high officials' needs to buy support and cooperation from strongmen. The continuing influx of strangers attracted to illicit mining, and the resulting civil disorder also placed further pressures on local, and increasingly, national-level officials to reach progressively more expensive accommodations with chiefs to keep this activity under control.

Table 3.2. *Chiefdom incomes from non-local government sources,*
1954–62 (£)

	1954	1956	1958	1960	1962
Nimikoro	7,017	5,826	13,916	14,150	14,316
Gbense	2,830	2,694	10,985	12,650	13,321
Tankoro	4,645	5,961	16,338	17,580	18,266
Total	14,492	14,481	41,239	44,380	45,903

Source: Calculated from Native Authority Estimates; MADA files; "The Facts About
Kono District Council Finances," *Daily Mail* (Freetown) 22 August 1960.

These accommodations provided short-term political control, but at the
expense of increased political distance from the illicit miners that Freetown
sought to influence. The result was that Kono chiefs became more
powerful. Expensive accommodations with chiefs deprived district councils
of funds from Freetown for meaningful development projects that could
serve as a basis for widespread popular support for the newly independent
government. Under these conditions, Kono people saw little reason to
continue paying taxes to Native Authorities that supported local administrative expenses. Gbense chiefdom receipts in 1961 were 14 percent lower
than in 1957, despite a rise in population; by 1965, they had dropped
another 18 percent.[47] Revenue was collected only by vigorous police
enforcement, and by Sierra Leone Police and SLST security-force attacks
on illicit mining. Economic pluralism alone threatened state control over
resources and spending. It was thought, however, that political pluralism
would balance these elite claims to state resources. Intended to supplement
aggressive state-led development with a popular base of support, political
reforms, or what today are called "political conditionalities," instead
reinforced elite accommodations at the core of the Shadow State.

The failures of political reform

Events in the completion of the transition to formal mass political
competition in 1957 more fully illustrate how elite accommodations shaped
politics in Kono. As Kono grievances about chiefs' privileges or distribution of resources made an electoral debut, official payoffs to political allies
further undermined the resource base available for development projects.
Despite popular rejections of privilege in the riots of the mid-1950s, these
resources encouraged individuals to support those with access to resources.
Factional politics developed around the acquisition of state resources

rather than on class politics or a societal consensus around government policies.

Chiefs' rivals seized upon grievances against this control and attempted to shift debate toward more distributive issues around which the ruling coalition had become more vulnerable. However, the regime did not command the political security, and challengers did not command the resources to address this deeper social issue. But the challenges of electoral competition prompted officials to redouble their efforts to retain control over resources and a supportive political coalition to control formal political competition. The populist KPM challenge[48] to elite privilege, begun in 1957, ultimately failed in most of its objectives. But the challenge taught the inheritors of the colonial state that rivals appealing to popular dissatisfaction with policies would increase the costs of building a secure political power base. The nature of the challenge also revealed that preexisting accommodations were crucial for dealing with threats. The KPM's leaders all came from marginalized chief families. The KPM's head, T.S. Mbriwa, was chief of diamond-poor Faiama. His capital, Ngagbwema, lay outside the diamond protection area, so neither he nor his chiefdom saw the benefits of MADA. Of the other three founders, two were sons of chiefs and the third was from a ruling family outside the mining area.

Their populist rhetoric called into question state policies that favored SLST and some chiefs over most Kono people. It is significant that chiefs' support for these calls came from the periphery of the diamond mining area – Lei, Nimi Yema, and Sando (see Map 2, p. 50). Diamond-area chiefs remained hostile to the KPM, supporting instead the ruling Sierra Leone Peoples Party (SLPP), with whom the British negotiated independence terms in 1960–1. However, the message was heard among illicit miners dissatisfied with government policies and chiefs' intrusions into their affairs.

The campaign produced a KPM victory. The party won one of two Kono Parliamentary seats in 1957. Under British rule, direct attacks on KPM supporters were barred. However, during the next general election in 1962, the rules changed. The KPM allied itself with two other opposition parties under the name of Sierra Leone Peoples Independent Movement (SLPIM). The new alliance won four out of nine Kono seats. The next year, they won seventeen out of twenty-four district council seats in local elections. The limits of state tolerance to opposition threats became more clear. With the British departure in 1961, Freetown officials moved more decisively against their opponents. The day after the 1962 alliance was announced, T.S. Mbriwa was charged with "general misbehaviour ... flouting the authority of the government,"[49] and deposed as chief. After the SLPIM victory in the

1963 election, he was banished from the district. Local SLPP officials and chiefs now directly enforced SLPP dominance. Reflecting the centrality of intermediaries, the Provincial Secretary declared that it was not the government's duty to prevent chiefs from prohibiting opposition activity.[50]

Steps also had to be taken to protect the SLPP government's capacity to control local development in the new competitive political environment. After the 1963 elections, the Kono DC recommended that more MADA grants be shifted to (richer) central diamond-area chiefdoms, depriving poorer opposition areas of funds.[51] He also recommended and approved a special £5,000 appropriation for mining-area chiefdoms from MADA funds. These actions came after MADA was removed from nominal district council control and placed under the District Commissioner and the Province Resident Minister, both central government appointees.[52]

SLPP appointees in local administration exercised greater control over development funds than did the Ministry of Internal Affairs, supposedly responsible for local direction of the expanded MADA program. This power was also used to financially isolate political rivals. After the 1963 SLPIM sweep of the Kono district council, the council enquired about the whereabouts of its £26,000 MADA grant. Of this money, £22,000 had already been disbursed directly to chiefdoms.[53] When the council pressed for the remaining £4,000, the Provincial Resident Minister directed that the money be payable directly to the Kono DC, not to the council.[54] This *ad hoc* circumvention of standard practice left honest officials unable to follow formal administrative procedures. When solicited directly for funds by pro-SLPP chiefs, an Internal Affairs secretary wrote that "This Ministry is not aware of any policy of grants to diamond chiefdoms for assisting to curb illicit mining."[55] Higher officials intercepted his reply and amended it to read that "The Ministry of Finance has now approved a supplementary expenditure of Le 20,000 to Gbense and Tankoro chiefdoms and the warrant is enclosed."[56] This was double the sum requested.

SLST also benefited from Freetown's strategy of targeting financial rewards. When informed of the decision to provide additional development funds after the 1963 election, SLST's European manager, J.P. DuCane, concurred with the government's position: "I think that you will agree with me that the attitude of these people has shown them to be worthy of favourable consideration."[57] The next day DuCane sent a letter to Nimikoro's Chief Bona informing him that SLST would not support his request for a contract mining scheme under the 1959 legislation. In a cover letter sent with a copy to the Ministry of Mines, DuCane reminded the Minister of the "substantial contribution to Government revenue from SLST" and suggested that the Ministry handle higher local requests for payoffs.[58] SLST stood to benefit from Freetown's reliance on the company to generate revenues for political purposes. The company could then shift the burdens of growing informal demands onto the government.

Outwardly, the SLPP strategy appeared to incorporate local elite support. By 1964, enticements were great enough to convince three Kono Parliamentary members to defect to the ruling party. For the first time since 1957, a Kono, S.L. Matturi, became a cabinet member with the lucrative position of Resident Minister, Eastern Province. In 1965, Mbriwa finally agreed to dissolve the SLPIM after a personal visit by Prime Minister Albert Margai. Two months later he was returned to his vacant chiefdom seat.

The gap between the SLPIM leaders and the ruling party was bridged and rival strongmen were incorporated into the ruling alliance. Government actions showed that demands for a better deal for Konos could be controlled within this elite accommodation. But those from non-chief backgrounds, and hence offering less local influence to SLPP leaders, continued their opposition. They looked elsewhere for support. Consequently, many joined SLPIM's old partner, the All Peoples Congress (APC), seeking a more egalitarian society with no special powers for chiefs. This position threatened the SLPP government's control, since it proposed changing the existing social and economic order. And since there was a large constituency that shared these aims – the illicit miners – the threat was real.

Official accommodation with chiefs also created more political space for such challenges. Freetown could control British-imposed institutions of electoral competition, but the privileged nature of this control created vulnerabilities elsewhere. In particular, the SLPP never posed an alternative ideological appeal to directly explain reasons for its actions. A British advisor to a Freetown ministry official in 1962 recorded his thoughts on the contradictory nature of buying elite political support without any efforts to seek broad popular support: "They are merely evidence of Government's good-will, which in the future must be directed to the development of the area as a whole and not to the enrichment of any particular category of persons. Otherwise in the eyes of most, good-will can no longer remain to us to give."[59] The SLPP government remained bound in the collaborative elite discourse that British colonial practice had imposed on chief–state relations. Officials inherited the deeply conservative British priority for order and state access to resources. Yet illicit miners' claims more closely paralleled the British rhetoric of political reforms in the 1950s and justifications for administrative steps taken in recognition of ethnic Kono perceptions of deprivation. These continuing illicit miner challenges would prove to be far more impervious to officials' control than the elite organized (but widely popular) KPM/SLPIM challenge. It is also in this political space that rival parties discovered the potentials of wealthy Kono strangers as alternative intermediaries, a discovery that was to catapult these strangers into positions of political prominence.

The informal diamond market as political battleground

The APC challenge stressed "radical improvements in the political, economic and social conditions of the toiling masses."[60] But party leaders had few elite contacts useful for extracting resources from the state to bolster their appeal. Kono's 1966 Youth Wing roster lists members from a diversity of ethnic backgrounds, suggesting that they, as illicit miners, also lacked significant contact with local elites. Many of the party's leaders came from outside Kono and lacked organizational bases in the region. However, Kono opposition to chiefs' privileges made mining organizations a valuable source of potential APC support. APC leaders faced the problem of building grassroots contacts outside the hegemonic alliance constructed around state control of resources. Wealthy strangers, particularly Lebanese[61] licensed dealers – most of whom also dealt in diamonds illicitly – provided resources and access to social organizations built up around illicit mining. This organizational structure was crucial for APC success. The special position that wealthy strangers occupied in Kono's diamond industry became the cornerstone of the APC's political organizing strategy.

As noted earlier, administrative reforms in the 1950s allowed licensed diamond digging and dealing, but favored those with more capital. A registry of Sierra Leone businesses in 1966 indicates that Lebanese owned 73 percent of all shops in the country,[62] a result of close family collaboration and organizational skill that allowed them to fill the Krio middleman niche between European capital and African customers after the turn of the century. As legal mining began in Kono, Lebanese dealers were in the best position vis-à-vis African competitors to purchase licenses (£500 for dealers) and afford illicit payoffs to chiefs for preferred plots since they could finance operations from the profits of other commercial activities. As the 1959 contract mining scheme got under way, these larger operations required dam building and excavation with heavy equipment. Such investments required capital outlays beyond the means of all but the wealthiest African businessmen. Consequently, Lebanese dominated these operations, though often with African partners.

Throughout the history of Kono's illicit mining, wealthier Lebanese dealers also supplied food and equipment to poorer miners, and protected them from state and SLST security forces. In exchange, miners sold

Table 3.3. *Lebanese share of*
GDO sales, 1960–7

	carats (1,000)	% non-native
1960	1,099	63
1961	1,188	74
1962	879	80
1963	517	74
1964	661	80
1965	716	81
1966	673	86
1967	687	87

Source: Government Diamond Office,
Reports (Freetown: Government Printer,
1960, 1965, 1968).

diamonds to these men. A "tributor" system arose, based upon this variable access to capital. British policy further supported these wealthier dealers as local and Freetown officials concluded that a legalized tributor system was the most efficient way of ensuring stable employment of miners and more efficient mining methods.[63] The organizers of illicit diamond production became the targets of Freetown efforts to control local production and wealth. In fact, most dealers engaged in both illicit and legal mining in order to satisfy local officials and "landlord" chiefs while still benefiting from higher official prices for diamonds.

While dealers' illegal activities remained useful to chiefs as an informal source of income, these dealers also benefited from state control of diamond revenues through occasional cooperation with regulations. As Table 3.3 shows, GDO purchases increasingly relied upon Lebanese "non-native" sales. Individual "non-native" sales to the GDO averaged five times the amount of citizens' sales through the period. Lebanese dealer license-holders increased from 32 percent of the total in 1960 to 68 percent in 1967.[64] Clearly Lebanese dealers were an important element in state access to revenues, particularly as illicit mining rose again in the mid-1960s.

A relatively small number of people organized Kono diamond production, a factor aiding them in their dealings with the authorities. In 1966, only 112 Lebanese held dealer licenses; only 334 Lebanese lived in Kono in 1963. However, they also acted as a new link in maintaining social peace as state revenues increasingly serviced elite accommodations. Below these dealers in the tribute system were approximately 2,500 licensed diggers as well as non-licensed diggers. Most had financial ties to wealthier dealers;

many were directly employed. These African strangers, mostly Fulas and Mandingos from north of Kono, employed an average of 25–30,000 laborers, making this the largest category of wage employment in the country.[65]

Yet even these additional revenues could not cover all of the government's needs. As revenue pressures became more acute in the 1960s, the government utilized the old British method of increasing extraction from the rural sector. Official producer prices fell by nearly 50 percent in the fifteen years to 1970,[66] spurring further migrations into Kono. Stranger populations again surpassed 60,000 in 1967. If estimates of illicit laborers are included, the diamond fields were employing approximately 60 percent of the money economy's workers in 1967.[67] These developments resulted in declines in food production, putting further strains on government resources. From self-sufficiency in the early 1950s, the government imported 21,000 tons of the country's staple, rice, in 1963.[68] Thus a large part of the country's economic activity, and with it, the maintenance of social peace, came to depend on strangers operating on the fringes of the legal economy. The importance of strangers, especially Lebanese businessmen, rose in the diamond trade while that of chiefs fell.

While Lebanese dealers played key roles, providing for revenue extraction and maintenance of order, they suffered the insecurity of becoming non-citizens. By a 1960 Constitutional decree, Freetown denied citizenship to those not of African parentage. Many ethnic Lebanese and Afro-Lebanese then applied for Lebanese passports. Their African associates in the "tributor" system, especially Fulas and Mandingos, also encountered official harassment, since many were suspected of illegally immigrating from Guinea. These developments formalized both groups' legal marginalization.

Having their interests defined as fundamentally illegitimate, yet serving as economic intermediaries for both chiefs and the state, Lebanese dealers and non-local associates were not seen as attractive formal political allies. They were attractive candidates for the Shadow State alliance as perceived in Freetown, however. Their non-citizen status ensured that they posed no independent electoral threat. Their ethnicity also prevented them from mounting populist campaigns like the KPM's that attacked non-Kono privilege. These insecure businessmen found that payoffs to politicians and administrators was the most effective strategy for safeguarding their interests. For example, after 1961, some were allowed to buy citizenship from the Immigration Control Committee. Of seven committee members, five were Kono politicians, all supporters of the ruling party. In 1965, the Prime Minister, Sir Albert Margai, became head of the committee. He reportedly sold eighty-seven citizenships in 1966 at a cost of Le 1,000 (£500) each.[69] The Prime Minister was also found to have demanded contributions of Le 50,000 to finance his campaign for the 1967 elections.[70]

Individual dealers also discovered rewards in political connections. One dealer, Jamil Mohamed, was expelled from Kono in 1960, accused of possessing diamonds valued at £8,000. Six years later, he returned with a dealer's license, residential permit, and naturalization papers. He was reputed to have 7,000 customers a month, a three-story house and legal sales of £100,000 a month to the Government Diamond Office (GDO).[71] Dealers' covert political accommodations also enhanced their market control. Several African dealers indicated that individual Fulas and Mandingos who dominated the diamond trade until the late 1950s increasingly worked for Lebanese dealers. By 1966, these Africans felt the challenge acutely enough to join with other African dealers to form an Association of African Diamond Dealers to demand that Lebanese dealers be driven out of Kono. The Prime Minister ordered the group disbanded despite government rhetoric calling for greater African participation, especially in commerce.[72]

Wealthy dealers were now rivalling chiefs as economic intermediaries. Their formal political isolation also became an APC asset. State officials often harassed Lebanese dealers, especially since they had gained a popular reputation for extensive illicit economic activity and had a local reputation as "exploiters." However, officials were reluctant to disrupt one of the few controls they maintained over a rival source of diamond wealth accumulation. Individual officials also had incentives to keep Lebanese dealers around, tapping vulnerable dealers for protection payoffs. Thus Lebanese dealers remained socially and economically isolated from the waning African business community, but with certain economic advantages over the African competition, albeit advantages that also required serving as officials' milchcows. Ironically, their isolation helped them develop the ability to play both sides of political competition, building personal ties to individuals in the ruling party and its rivals through the 1960s.

Dealers' access to miners' organizations was what ultimately drew APC organizers to dealers. In the 1950s, it was reported that dealers presided over "youth gangs structured like police riot units," with fifty or more members, who defended illicit mining operations.[73] These "youth gangs" were in fact miner organizations, based upon the tributor method of production. The strangers – Lebanese dealers – bought food and tools for miners, made arrangements with chiefs, and "staked" them in return for a share of the dig's finds. Many of these production units developed as societies offering social and financial support to individual miners, a survival strategy prevalent in Kono today. Societies received financial support from dealers sponsoring their production. They also became convenient vehicles for dissent.

A leader of the APC Youth League in the mid-1960s recalls party organizers' interest in Kono mining organization: "People remember the riots in the late fifties as aimless. But look at how they moved the British. That was our opponent's weakness; they did not know how to talk to the people. They had all the other Big Men wrapped up, but as long as they would call an election, the miners could say no."[74] These diamond market organizations backed APC Youth Wing officials. For example, the forerunner of Kono Tenda, a society including both legal and illicit miners (individuals often engage in both), dug diamonds for a politically astute Lebanese patron and provided a base for the political organization for an APC Youth Wing official. Outbidding African competitors, this dealer provided food, work, and credit to organization members under the "tribute" system. For his part, the dealer used threats of APC-backed violence as leverage over two of his chief "landlords." In this light, it is significant that chief and state property was most often the target of rioting in the 1950s and 1960s while dealers were little molested. Knowledge that the comparatively radical message of the APC opposition had been heard among these miners heightened local officials' fears of disorder and allowed dealers to limit politicians' claims on illicit profits. Besides, there was no harm in developing good relations with those who could be in a position to assist business in the future.[75]

This alliance of convenience provided the APC with crucial resources outside normal elite channels. If reports of 10–15 percent dealer profits on legal transactions apply to illicit transactions as well, one arrives at an estimation of total yearly profits for Kono dealers in the 1960s of around £1 million, five times the total government expenditure in the district.[76] Frozen out of the distribution of state resources, rivals found a new terrain on which to organize their struggle to break the state monopoly on the distribution of power and wealth.

The contradictions of pluralism and social control

Post-colonial assimilation of old and new elites appeared to lay the foundations for a new political order. The greater problem for political leaders in Freetown, however, lay in reaching illicit miners and controlling their activities. Scholarly attention to elite politics generally has been reluctant to include the role of non-elites in promoting or thwarting this project. Walter Barrows's analysis of local politics in Sierra Leone considers that:

The most pressing challenge in Sierra Leone ... is the problem of devising a set of symbols and ideas which can accommodate yet overcome its distinctive style of politics by tempering materialism with morality and utilitarianism with utopia. Development and integration depend ultimately upon the inventiveness of political elites.[77]

Barrows calls upon elites to continue integrating diverse social elements under a single authority. He downplays Sierra Leoneans' resistance to domination and what they did to provide an alternative vision of how the country should be run. Ideological appeals from the SLPP regime remained limited since most of Prime Minister Sir Milton Margai's and his associates' interests focused on controlling challenges among the inherited elite accommodation. This political maneuvering limited competition and produced few initiatives relevant to most peoples' daily pursuits of survival. Much of the practice of politics among elites ceased to matter to subjects, except as evidence of their rulers' betrayal of popular desires.

A strength of Prime Minister Sir Milton Margai's (and after his death in 1964, his brother Sir Albert's) strategy of accommodation among strongman chiefs was the weakening of opposition challenges in the 1957 and 1962 elections. The strategy required reconciling diverse views at the top of the political hierarchy. Thus multiparty competition posed a manageable threat to coalition-building. This control lay in Sir Milton's willingness to expand patronage to allies. Local chiefs could then be counted upon to coerce voters.

But the SLPP leadership's weakness lay in the autonomy and attractions of the illicit mining economy. Local officials seeking wealth, and a broad government bias against small-scale indigenous dealers undermined the politically active African business class. Strangers and dissatisfied miners now sought protection wherever they could find it. In coopting diverse elite interests, the SLPP leadership had also undermined its overall capacity to manage political challenge from the mining sector. As miners grew dissatisfied, remaining Lebanese and non-indigenous African dealers found some security in shifting their financial support to wherever they could find the most effective protection for their businesses.

Ironically, Freetown's unwillingness to act in concert against chiefs or illicit diamond dealers also reflected Freetown's fears of the nationalist sentiments that Andrew Cohen's liberal reforms and subsequent changes in mining policy were meant to coopt. Citizens, however, really believed that Independence in 1961 and rising development expenditures held the promise that officials would defend them against chiefs' privileges and provide them with more services. But the costs of maintaining the SLPP power-base drained state resources. Soon, official pronouncements and popular views of the practice of government bore little relation to each other. Individuals' efforts to survive free of control by chiefs, whether as illicit miners, or as dealers, translated into political acts threatening state power since they also resisted the elite control of resources. Leaders in Freetown perceived this activity as a direct threat to state control of resources and revenue. But SLPP leaders actually continued some commitment to liberal political practices even though this allowed some with grievances to publicly challenge the expanding elite hegemony. APC organizers built a political following of miners and disaffected Konos inside this political space, but most effectively with the material support of illicit diamond dealers.

Perhaps the *reciprocal* assimilation of elites under the British caused the Margais to tolerate electoral competition. Echoing what Ali Mazrui called an "Afrosaxon" perspective, Sir Milton's successor and brother, Sir Albert Margai declared "When the time comes in Sierra Leone that Government lacks opposition, that will be the time that some of us will pack up our bags and baggage and quit politics. This system of government is one of the best things we have inherited from our colonial masters."[78] But their tolerance had limits. A 1967 coup overturned the APC victory. Another coup reaffirmed the APC's victory in 1968. SLPP errors were very instructive to their APC successors. The APC leader, Siaka Stevens, concluded that efforts to gain social control must be broadened and that potential SLPP rivals, especially chiefs, must be curbed. Stevens rejected liberal reforms and instead utilized informal diamond networks. He made major steps in the construction of the Shadow State, but his patrimonial strategies were firmly rooted in the social foundations of colonial rule.

4   Reining in the informal markets: The early Stevens years, 1968–1973

> Not only as leader of the APC but as an individual citizen, I abhor and detest the One Party System of Government.
>
> Opposition Leader Stevens, 1965[1]

> The widespread belief that political parties are indispensable for the existence and maintenance of good and effective government is certainly erroneous.
>
> President Stevens, 1978[2]

Elections, at least multiparty ones, and elite hegemony do not mix well. New office holders can use their positions to build electoral power bases in defiance of their leader. Fiscal pressures and weak administrative capacity prevented President Siaka Stevens from unilaterally imposing APC control upon inherited intermediaries. Once in power, APC leaders faced choices similar to those once facing British overlords: how does a ruler establish cheap and effective control over intermediaries who do not necessarily share the interests of their superiors? State House's new resident also quickly learned that government's institutional weakness and revenue shortfalls ruled out simply refashioning collaborative rule inherited from the colonial era. Stevens had to devise new ways of building political authority. His reordering of Sierra Leone's elite alliance provides additional clues for understanding Shadow State responses to reform. Stevens's own victory demonstrated the dangers of allowing rivals to establish independent power bases. Diamonds would finance this new elite accommodation; diamond miners and dealers had arisen as new social forces along with the start of mining. Stevens now sought to manage and benefit from these forces, which the APC had mobilized to oust the colonial elite coalition, as well as to control still-powerful SLPP stalwarts.

This chapter about Stevens's new elite alliance brings us one step closer to understanding dilemmas of reform that exist today in Africa's "weak states" like Sierra Leone. Stevens's selective assimilation of some SLPP stalwarts, miners, dealers, and his own APC activists, illustrates the degree to which his maintenance of political security overrode the implementation of formal policies, without significantly changing the overall style of informal governance in Sierra Leone. Stevens's efforts to coopt leaders of Kono's Gbense chiefdom illustrate these truths. The attractions to Stevens of continuing this strategy emerge as we first observe his less successful efforts to manage Tankoro chiefdom through formal institutional channels. Ironically, Stevens's efforts to maximize his power through a "strong [formal] state" strategy actually left him exposed to threats from rivals and his own political network. But his Gbense strategies show how informal Shadow State techniques, especially interventions to control the production and exchange of diamonds, strengthened Stevens's rule even as they stripped state institutions of resources and the means to serve the country's people.

Compared to colonial or SLPP elite accommodations, the new ruling alliance made unusually heavy demands on state resources to buy collaborators' loyalties. Certainly the ultimate threat of the force of the British Empire had kept the colonial era costs of accommodation low. Intimidation of elites remained possible, though the weakening of formal state institutions and popular participation in politics made this strategy more expensive, as the Tankoro case will show. But even as inter-party rivalry diminished, political entrepreneurs from within the APC continued to emerge as rival claimants to authority as they gave voice to unresolved popular grievances over state claims to resources. As formal state capacity declined, its replacement with Shadow State sovereignty came at a higher price.

This chapter highlights the fiscal demands of elite accommodation while also exploring why the seemingly rational alternative of creating a "strong state" in this setting would actually create something quite different from the efficient and effective government, attracting popular support, that contemporary IMF and World Bank reformers envision. These dangers also explain why manipulations of markets became such a major element of Stevens's management of elites and add to our understanding of the fate of reform in this setting.

Learning from the failure of institutional control: Tankoro

APC victors confronted local leaders with deep roots in Kono society. The relatively autonomous local political networks of chiefs were underpinned by their influence in the diamond fields. By 1967, 75 percent of Kono's parliamentarians claimed chiefly lineages. Chiefs remained anxious to protect political and economic privilege upon which rested their claims to local and familial authority. Some sought private reward through defection to the APC. Most resisted Freetown's claim that the central government must reassert control over diamond revenues to finance development.

From the point of view of elites who had acquired considerable informal powers, Freetown's posture of "legality" presented the same sorts of challenges as had early colonial rule. To them, it appeared that Stevens would try to build a "strong state," a project bound to limit their personal authority.

But Kono politics remained under the control of a strong network organized around the political authority of Paul Dunbar, an SLPP stalwart, active since the advent of popular formal political competition following the electoral reforms of 1948. Family ties linked him to at least three Kono chiefdom ruling houses, which proved useful for mobilizing support for his candidates for state and chiefdom offices in the face of miners' support for the APC. Dunbar thus helped forcibly to suppress Kono's KPM in the mid-1950s, and then the rival APC organization during the 1967 election. With the support of Prime Minister Albert Margai, Dunbar built a private armed "action group" to intimidate the SLPP's rivals. By 1968, this "action group" of fifty armed men under Dunbar's personal command gave Dunbar independent means to defend his and his clients' privileged positions in Kono.[3]

The armed force enabled Dunbar and his allies to retain influence after the SLPP's electoral defeat. Freetown could not collect revenues and suppress illicit diamond mining without local cooperation. Stevens was caught in a bind. He needed to control these people, but he also needed cooperation from local leaders to control access to diamond revenues. Consequently, he sought to isolate and weaken individual rivals' political independence in Kono. Government development grants to central Kono chiefdom authorities fell from Le120,000 in 1966–7 to zero in June, 1968, following the APC restoration. Even though funds were formally allocated, Ministry of Interior officials in Freetown blocked transfers.[4] Authority to approve mining licenses remained in Freetown Ministry of Mines hands, to which it had been recently moved, depriving chiefs of another source of influence and income.[5] However, Dunbar's "action group" continued to gather resources through intimidation of diggers and dealers drawn to Kono by the lure of quick riches in the diamond fields. Threats of "action group" violence also discouraged local APC activists from confronting incumbent local leaders by demanding the larger voice in administration to which the APC victory entitled them.

These Kono strongmen neutralized APC attempts to directly mobilize constituents in support of its own goals or officials. The new APC-appointed Kono District Officer complained that "the great influence and former political authority which he [Dunbar] still assumes greatly hampers my efforts here."[6] The APC government even proved incapable of ensuring the safety of its own officials. An APC parliamentarian from Kono complained that threats of violence prevented him from visiting his constituents.[7] Similarly, a licensed diamond dealer complained to the regional police commander of "action group" harassment. He returned to find his house on fire; his case against the perpetrators was later dismissed.[8]

Despite State House orders, the APC's local administrators failed to assert political control over Kono. Like their colonial predecessors, local administrators had to weigh pressures to act against the danger to their careers that came from the violence and disruption following attacks on local political networks. Stevens himself understood that local control would not come exclusively through policy changes. Other tasks loomed first. "The priorities of the first twenty years of our state – the consolidation of independence, the unification and integration of the country ... were mainly political ... Those of the next few decades are likely to be of an economic nature but I think that the past few years have called for a bias in the direction of politics."[9] That is, if state interest was not to bend before challenges from strong societal interests, Stevens had to either banish or coopt these groups in an overall drive to assert his position as the preeminent political force in society.

The death of Tankoro's chief Gando III provided Stevens with an opportunity to use direct administrative intervention to assert APC domination over an area providing support for its rivals. This campaign would rid Kono of opponents enjoying privileged access to the area's resources. But the target, the Gando family, had deep roots in local politics, having ruled Tankoro chiefdom continuously since 1936. The presence of family members in SLPP governments attested to the Gandos' political influence. The family's significant real-estate holdings in Sefadu and Freetown also highlighted the financial rewards of chieftaincy. In return for the benefit of British, and then SLPP favor, Gando rulers helped to suppress KPM and APC campaign activity among their subjects. After 1964, Dunbar's "action group" helped his Gando kin suppress opposition political activity. Dunbar's support for claimant T.M. Quee, another relative, threatened to deny the APC access to the chiefdom's resources just when APC victory appeared to promise a wider distribution of opportunity to APC supporters.

Former KPM and APC organizer, John Kellie, emerged as the APC favorite with miner support. His campaigns among miners, particularly as an APC Youth League grassroots organizer, supported Tamba Kaimondo's failed APC "radical" challenge to Dunbar's parliamentary seat in the 1967 election. During that campaign, Kellie berated Dunbar as an "agent of SLST exploitation," contrasting Dunbar's heavy-handed interference in illicit mining with the APC's promise to back miner demands for a wider distribution of Kono's diamond resources. Kellie's candidacy also seemed poised to benefit from lax law enforcement and the attraction of riches that caused Kono's stranger population to swell by 20,000 to reach 50,000 by 1968.[10]

Kellie's candidacy presented Stevens and his associates with a serious dilemma. APC organizational weakness in the 1967 election forced party leaders to rely upon local supporters such as Kellie who addressed local grievances with little regard to overall elite interests. Kellie's support for radical miner redistributive demands, while compatible with local APC campaigns appealing to popular dissatisfaction with SLPP chiefs' privileges, undercut government efforts to keep mining in the hands of larger operators able to make significant investments and employ efficient mining methods. Continued "SLST exploitation" also preserved one of the government's few remaining means of limiting illicit mining to ensure continued formal state revenue from diamond production.

But Kellie's populist claims to advance miner interests linked the APC to promises that favored unregulated, and therefore, untaxed mining. Local APC organizational weakness and "action group" strength precluded imposing a more acceptable candidate for the chiefdom seat. Consequently, State House strategy focused on direct aid to Kellie's campaign, but in such a way as to minimize his political autonomy and bind him directly to the interests of Stevens's Freetown administration. Stevens's officials intervened directly on Kellie's behalf. Stevens sought to avoid providing Kellie with an independent means of building his own power-base, as happened among the inherited intermediaries whom State House now sought to unseat.

Stevens's bureaucratic offensive began. The Ministry of the Interior revised councillor lists (local chief electors – Tankoro has about 400) in Kellie's favor.[11] Dunbar's response was immediate. Reported a local administrator: "The candidate that Dunbar is supporting is Sahr [ruler] Quee ... and he says that if the Chiefdom Councillors do not support the candidate of his choice, when the Ex-Prime Minister, Sir Albert Margai comes back to power he will cause each and every one of them to be severely punished."[12] Despite explicit orders from Freetown, the District Officer (DO) allowed Dunbar to supervise the councillor-list revision in preparation for the election of the chief.[13] "I failed," reported the DO, "because the so-called 'majority faction' told me categorically that the list prepared by them must be accepted by Government."[14] The "majority faction" then intimidated and harassed pro-APC councillors. Yet police records note that no prosecutions resulted from charges against the harassers.[15] Miners and town officials petitioned Freetown, complaining of a lack of confidence in government ability to advance a councillor list prepared with the help of local APC supporters.[16]

State House's second direct challenge to Dunbar's influence came in orders to the DO to hear a local complaint against Quee alleging conspiracy "to use juju against other candidates for the election of Paramount Chief and to harm them and cause their death thereby."[17] The charge was serious. The 1896 Protectorate Ordinance prohibited the practice of witchcraft for political purposes.[18] Officials feared claims of supernatural assistance, since this was one way that challengers could discredit Freetown's agents in a way that was difficult for Freetown to suppress.[19] Colonial administrators had themselves used charges of witchcraft to depose defiant chiefs, or more often, to refuse an individual's claim to the position. In Tankoro, the charge was a valuable tool for the local APC faction to discredit Dunbar's candidate and justify his removal. Nevertheless, the newly appointed Secretary of the Eastern Province defied Ministry of Interior orders to hear the charge and persuaded the Kono DO to dismiss the case. The Provincial Secretary wrote that he believed that such a direct challenge to Kono's political order would provoke unrest at a time when violence had attended a by-election in neighboring Kenema and Bo Districts under his jurisdiction.[20]

Dunbar, his allies, and his "action group" encountered institutional state challenges to their capacity to impose outcomes at odds with State-House interests. But state officials ultimately failed to prevent the election of Quee as Tankoro's chief. Nor could APC leaders protect their supporters. A diamond dealer with business connections to Kellie had provided a meeting-place for pro-Kellie organizers among his "tributor" diggers. Dunbar's "action group" attacked this dealer's agents and threatened to prevent the dealer from doing business in Kono.[21] This attack made it clear that Dunbar's organization could deliver on threats to punish those transgressing rules laid down by a local strongman. Local officials felt the diverging pressures of career, constituents, and superiors. Freetown proved incapable of sponsoring a favored candidate through a mobilization of the administrative hierarchy. This signaled that political ties between APC leaders and potential new intermediaries would have to by-pass institutional channels of political control.

State House failure to manage the Tankoro succession crisis also exposed and reinforced divergent interests within the APC elite itself. As violence between factions in Tankoro escalated, the Minister of Interior, S.I. Koroma, found opportunities to strengthen his own standing in the APC hierarchy. He provided informal support to Kono miners via non-state organizations. As Minister of Interior, Koroma oversaw the activities of, and provided financial resources to private mutual aid, ethnic and "friendly" (social club) societies that previously provided grassroots support for APC candidates.[22] Koroma personally supervised distributions of patronage to these societies, including two with branches among Kono miners supporting Kellie. Society activities among these miners became the nucleus for "radical" APC demonstrations. Koroma no doubt also aimed to develop a viable counter-force to Dunbar's "action group" and intimidate pro-Quee councillors.[23] This independent strategy failed to prevent Quee's victory but showed Stevens that associates could utilize disorder to launch their own bids for influence where central authority had failed. In a short time such challenges were to develop into a severe threat to Stevens's personal authority.

Further administrative interventions did prevent Quee from assuming office until 1970. After the failed APC bid to shape the outcome of the chief's election, the Ministry of Interior conducted an investigation into Quee's activities as a government official under SLPP rule, asserting that he misappropriated state funds.[24] However, State House eventually accepted Quee's victory, and the charges were dropped. Quee's loyalties could be shaped in less formal ways; his family members found employment in government offices, some in politically isolated overseas positions in the Ministry of External Affairs. T.M. Quee himself found ample opportunities for enrichment in office. A former Kono DO recalls, however, that Quee always stood "as a maverick, an outsider never enjoying obvious favor, but someone he [Stevens] learned to live with."[25]

The challenge of plural interests to Stevens's power

Seen in the larger setting of Sierra Leone politics, the failure to decisively crush a rival political network in Kono raised questions about Stevens's authority. Deviation from State House control undercut Stevens's local control. Audits of accounts of chiefdoms under Dunbar's sway illustrate the dangers to state finances of local autonomy:

Little attempt is made to ensure regular recoveries and I have not been able to determine the authority for several of the advances, or for the use which it was envisaged should be made of them.[26]

Five advances to Government officers have been made, the amount outstanding in this respect being Le486.16, although I know of no authority for civil servants to receive advances from chiefdom funds.[27]

Advances Personal – Le2,347.28. This balance comprises two vehicle advances. I have not seen the authority for the two advances, nor any written agreements.[28]

Kono's District Council, now under APC control, also lost its capacity to collect taxes, carry out development projects or fund its own operation. Chiefdom assessments to the council, the institution that Colonial Office reforms of 1948 envisioned as above chiefs' influence, stood in arrears of

Le 100,000, equivalent to one year's recurrent council expenditure. As an auditor exclaimed, this constituted "a most grave state of affairs" for the council.[29]

Even more grave were uncooperative local attitudes toward illicit mining, a threat to the government's major source of revenues. Chiefs continued to benefit from illicit mining, reflected in the 9.4 percent drop in official alluvial (independent miner) purchases from 1968 to 1970. The drop followed a 12 percent annual increase from 1964–7, which followed earlier steady increases after the introduction of licensed mining in 1956.[30] With little prospect of receiving favors from Freetown to replace illicit diamond benefits, pro-Dunbar chiefs had no incentive to enforce Freetown's directives. Diverted revenues also permitted them to continue financing local political networks at a time when their opponents occupied State House. No longer acting as agents of Freetown, local leaders had more freedom to arrange their own accommodations with illicit diamond dealers. This local political independence blocked direct APC influence in Kono and access to local revenues, depriving Stevens of resources to build his own political support.

Local strongmen from other parts of the country also took advantage of weak state authority. This highlighted the precariousness of Stevens's political control amidst plural interests. Several ambitious government officials broke with the APC in 1970 and formed the independent United Democratic Party (UDP). Most of this party's leaders came from Sierra Leone's north, an iron-mining region close to Stevens's family home. Like Kellie in Tankoro, their support lay among voters pressing for redistributive measures and redress for social grievances through APC action. By 1970, one activist, Dr. F.N. Forna, was using his position as a government official to selectively distribute jobs and resources to local supporters through his influence over the newly created National Development Corporation – a Stevens initiative to build direct state contacts with local beneficiaries of government spending – in return for political support.

Future UDP leaders now concluded that Stevens's efforts to widen the distribution of resources to incorporate non-northerner APC party supporters and newcomers (including those in Kono) constituted an unfair bias against the UDP's core support in the north. The final break with Forna and associates occurred as Stevens moved to personally oversee the distribution of jobs in the north through parastatals. Stevens's strategy of attacking his associates' independent base of political support centered on enticing Lonrho, a British mining firm, to set up a joint venture in iron mining in the Tonkolili area of the north, an area of strong UDP sentiment.

Foreign investors offered Stevens revenue and control over the distribution of economic development free from the vulnerabilities afflicting weak state institutions. Lonrho's interest in iron was also a prelude to Stevens's plans to allow Lonrho to mine and market Kono's diamonds. But Lonrho also cultivated Forna, then still Minister of Finance. Lonrho tried to play both sides in this internal APC struggle. During Forna's eventual downfall, the President's Office brought negotiations to a quick end.[31] Episodes like this showed firms such as Lonrho that profitable business operations in patrimonial economies such as Sierra Leone's must also consider political factors influencing return on investments.[32]

Unable to control political rivals through weak formal institutions, Stevens declared a State of Emergency in 1971 and invited Guinean troops to protect his government. But failure to secure voluntary discipline among elites also brought a doubling of acknowledged security-related expenditures as state revenues stagnated.[33] Development spending halted its previous rapid expansion. By 1971/72, deficits reached 21 percent of revenues.[34] But the task of heading off challenges took precedence over building strong state institutions. State House priorities focused on ensuring that rivals (or coup plotters) did not use state resources and independent connections with supporters to threaten State House control, making it even more unlikely that spending would produce anything resembling greater state "capacity."

While the 1967–8 APC victory destroyed political connections linking some local strongmen to the capital, Stevens struggled to build a political organization capable of replacing the authority he wished to destroy. Forcible exclusion of rivals from formal political competition alone could not bring strongmen under the control of State House. The benefits of collaboration with State House did bring aboard many ambitious external and intra-party rivals.[35] But as these expensive accommodations conflicted with redistributive promises, the APC faced a rapid loss of loyalty among individual Sierra Leoneans. Political entrepreneurs exploiting these long-standing grievances complicated Stevens's rebuilding of political authority in a state possessing diminishing administrative capacity and access to resources. If his power was not to succumb to these rival interests, Stevens would have to develop innovative solutions to build his personal authority amidst political challenge. The need to control resources, long the foundation of political authority in Sierra Leone, attracted Stevens's attentions to Kono's diamond fields. Above all, restoring his authority required eliminating strongmen's unregulated access to wealth, a consequence of the divisions of political power following the electoral reforms and coalition-building after 1948. The frustration of his efforts to create a "strong state" made a renewal and strengthening of the Shadow State elite accommodation all the more attractive to Stevens.

Diamonds and Shadow State accommodation

Several years after coming to power, Stevens and his associates still faced disobedience and unauthorized diversions of resources at the local level in Kono. Stevens also encountered problems in retaining state access to diamond resources through either the "exploitative" SLST, Lonrho or some other means while formal allies such as Kellie campaigned for greater popular access to diamonds. From Freetown's perspective, large-scale independent mining encouraged avoidance of taxes and prompted local chiefs to informally regulate mining for their own personal gain. Meanwhile, APC populist rhetoric also raised questions in the minds of investors about the sincerity of government support for foreign capital in Sierra Leone. Crises of popular legitimacy, weakness vis-à-vis local leaders, and the need for reliable revenues required quick action. But first, to control Kellie's and others' mobilizational appeals, Stevens had to establish greater control over diamonds.

While APC campaign literature focused on popular themes such as "seizing our own destiny from SLST,"[36] Stevens never objected to private enterprise or foreign investment on ideological grounds. "When I look back on what I used to say about nationalization," he remarked in 1968, "I realize that I was talking nonsense."[37] Stevens's cabinet also recognized that precipitous nationalization would jeopardize US and British foreign aid. Through the past decade, 34 percent of development capital spending came from this source.[38] At the same time, Stevens needed to do something that would remove mining from rival officials' control in order to influence the distribution of diamond wealth among strongmen.

Recalling his interest in SLST, Stevens claimed that "[i]t was not our intention to do anything which would jeopardize the life of the goose which lays the golden eggs."[39] State House came to an accommodation with SLST in which a new state-owned mining company – NDMC, or National Diamond Mining Company – would mine and market diamonds. The new company retained SLST marketing agreements with DeBeers, European managers, SLST security detachments, and investment agreements with Consolidated African Selection Trust's remaining 49 percent share in NDMC.[40] Thus "nationalization" was not intended to signal to investors any drastic change in the formal operation of legal large-scale mining in Sierra Leone. From Freetown's perspective, the enclave mining economy provided a safe source of revenues paid directly to the central government and out of the reach of both APC and rival local political entrepreneurs.[41] Official diamond production and purchases continued to fall, however, confirming foreign investors' conclusions that Freetown could not control local developments in Kono.[42] By the early 1970s, it appeared that Freetown's problem of political control was spreading to its diamond industry.

Official diamond production dropped 25 percent from the highs achieved in 1968, to 1.4 million carats in 1973. The largest decrease came in alluvial production, signalling a rise in this low-overhead, often illicit activity.[43] Inadequate security against illicit mining precipitated a decline in foreign capital investment in new equipment for NDMC operations, further undercutting the government's capacity to profit in the formal mining economy.[44] Stevens now focused on limiting the autonomy of the illicit mining sector, the base of independent political support in Kono. Breaking mutually beneficial "landlord–tenant" relationships between local officials offering protection and profitable illicit digging operations through non-institutional means would deprive rivals of a major source of revenue and influence, and would also disrupt the social basis for strongmen's personal accumulation of wealth independent of State House consent. State House's expanded control over formal diamond mining targeted Lebanese dealers in particular, since these outsiders and, in some cases, non-citizens, remained the most vulnerable to threats of legal sanctions. State power could also offer protection from harassment or prosecution. Legality and the capacity to determine its bounds remained a potent tool in the hands of an impoverished and institutionally weak government.

Since dealers now relied on the Ministry of Mines in Freetown to issue licenses, and NDMC controlled the richest territory in which much additional illicit mining took place, Stevens encouraged dealers to consider State House and NDMC, rather than local chiefs as their "landlords" providing protection. Constitutional and popular prohibitions against ethnic non-African involvement in politics ensured that these new "tenants" could not mount an independent political challenge to the leader's interests. Meanwhile, perpetually dependent Lebanese dealers, as major financers of legal and illicit private mining operations, would also allow Stevens to control the organization of local African diggers. The prospect of sharing in the payoffs that local officials had enjoyed no doubt added to the attractiveness of this policy for Freetown officials.

On the other hand, African dealers illustrated to Stevens the dangers inherent in the development of an independent indigenous business class. Many of them had appealed to local chiefs – in some cases, their kin – for local political support that their Lebanese competitors could not claim. The Ministry of Mines actively discriminated against the issuance of licenses to African dealers. Instead, Lebanese or Afro-Lebanese dealers received the bulk of new licenses (Table 4.1), laying the basis for a new government–

Table 4.1. *Licensed diamond dealers, 1968–73*

	Lebanese (heritage)		African	
	No.	%	No.	%
1968	28	15	151	85
1969	27	16	143	84
1970	60	36	104	64
1971	42	33	86	67
1972	90	55	73	45
1973	107	78	30	22

Source: Compiled from Ministry of Mines reports, in Government of Sierra Leone, *Sierra Leone Gazette* (Freetown: Government Printer, 1968–73).

dealer collaboration in both the legal and illicit diamond industry. This strategy of control led to the consolidation of the private diamond industry under Lebanese operation and its recognition by state officials.[45]

The new intermediaries were dependent upon Stevens for favorable treatment and exemption from harassment. This breaking of the link between old intermediaries and the diamond trade weakened local strongmen, thus allowing Stevens to insert Lebanese deprived of the lucrative and unregulated "landlord–tenant" relationship, which no longer served as a mutual benefit to intermediaries and the state as in the first half of the colonial era. But rulers' aims remained similar. In Arthur Abraham's analysis of colonial efforts to exert control:

It was in the interests of the Freetown administration with its colonial ambitions to prevent large aggregates either from asserting and exerting themselves or, in the case of a declining polity, from seeking to recuperate. The handful of colonial officials, in order to carry out the functions which were grossly disproportionate to their numerical strength, had to depend largely on their ability to secure local allies.[46]

Stevens, however, faced the burden of retaining popular support while serving growing numbers of clients holding state office. Stevens still had to balance cost with control. Since his regime's survival depended on maintaining at least the appearance of control, Stevens had to find cheaper strategies of control and/or new sources of revenue.

Incorporating diamonds into the accommodation: Gbense

At the geographical and political heart of Kono, Gbense was the seat of another close Dunbar relative, Chief Kaimachende. Gbense's succession crisis began with a 1970 investigation into Kaimachende's "corrupt practices," and his suspension from administrative office. The investigation of Kaimachende came as part of a broader State House strategy of attacking supporters of the old regime through commissions of inquiry. Past accommodations between Freetown and intermediaries ensured that there would be much to investigate. Locally, the campaign against Kaimachende exploited his ethnic distinction as a Koranko "outsider," despite his having held office since 1936 and his long family history linked to Kono's warrior hero, Matturi. Kaimachende family members were thus ruled ineligible to succeed their deposed kinsman.[47]

While not supporting Kaimachende, miners feared that their interests were being ignored in the succession struggle. A delegation of miners petitioned the Minister of Interior to "enquire whether there was truth in the allegation that the 'Big Men' in the party had decided to put up a particular candidate to the exclusion of others ... We morally support Your Excellency ... We must warn You that some invoke Your Name in the service of individual favour."[48] However, the favored candidate, Yafenneh Toli, was clearly Stevens's personal choice but not the radical miners'. Toli had been Stevens's bodyguard since 1964. His main ties to Kono were as a guard for the despised SLST security force. A former Kono official also noted that Toli used his exceptional physical strength – local stories attest to his unusual ability to lift his Mercedes Benz while his driver changed the tire – to intimidate rivals to the APC in the 1967 election. He was thus rewarded with the Gbense chieftainship for "services rendered."[49]

Appointed local officials rushed to support Toli, the "official" candidate. Miners were left with no radical candidate to protect their interests. Meanwhile, Dunbar's political network mobilized around Tamba Bona, a man with many ties to Dunbar and Kaimachende. In contrast to the case of the Tankoro succession, Stevens did not depend upon unreliable Sierra Leone police detachments drawn among local people to protect his favored candidate. Dunbar's and now the miner's campaigns were both limited by the presence of police officers from Freetown to maintain "public order." Preventative detention decrees associated with the 1970 State of Emergency decree also facilitated the process of intimidating campaigning for the rival candidate.

Still, a majority of chiefdom councillors cast votes for Bona, the miners' candidate. But then the election proceedings were disrupted. A local APC organizer removed Bona from the voting place. Some observers of the election hold that Toli had hired a mob to remove his rival from the building. Meanwhile, the Provincial Secretary – rather than his subordinate, the Kono District Officer – continued the election without Bona, claiming that he left of his own free will. Since many of Bona's supporters followed him (or were chased) out of the building, they were not present when the Provincial Secretary held a new vote. Sixty-eight percent of the remaining councillors supported Toli's successful election bid.[50]

Toli took his position without the access to illicit mining wealth that Kaimachende had possessed through his influence in local accommodations with illicit dealers, diggers and chiefdom administration. However, Toli still attracted some limited local support from those defecting from the periphery of the old political network. Toli's attractiveness as a well-placed local patron lay not in autonomous access to resources. Instead, Toli received a State House appointment to an NDMC management position. Government majority ownership of NDMC permitted Stevens to selectively award benefits of mining, but in such a way as to bind the recipient more closely to official favor – and partly at foreign investors' expense. Toli masterfully utilized his informal market opportunities to their fullest extent; behavior which magnified on a national scale, soon created major fiscal dilemmas for the formal state. In return, Toli raised money and campaigned for "official" APC candidates and supporters, and rooted out subordinates supportive of his predecessor.

Toli's forceful manner drove a wedge between himself and Gbense society, however. Section chiefs, normally recipients of chiefly largesse, customarily warn their patron of behavior that is unacceptable. In the past, if these warnings were ignored, Freetown encouraged section chiefs to appeal to state officials to help settle issues. But Toli's habit of summarily dismissing subordinates, together with administrative indifference to their complaints, raised considerable alarm among some local state officials that growing popular dissatisfaction with Toli could lead to disorder.[51] Toli also interfered in other chiefdoms' affairs. Toli allegedly threatened "old SLPPs" such as his neighbor, T.M. Quee of Tankoro, with violence sufficient to cause Quee to leave Kono for a time.[52] Popular dissatisfaction eventually required that police and paramilitary forces repeatedly intervene to protect Toli from threats of disorder.

Toli's high costs, or why Stevens needed the diamond trade

New allies such as Toli helped Stevens to impose more direct political control in Kono and isolate recalcitrant strongmen. But political ties to these new allies did not solve the problem of paying for the rising fiscal costs of political security. Nor did it effectively suppress political entrepreneurs from within the APC who mobilized constituents with populist appeals and gained independent access to diamond wealth in the process of furthering their own political goals. But Toli's task of reinforcing State House authority demonstrated the continuing relevance of intermediaries to Sierra Leone politics. Toli was one of three Kono chiefs installed under APC direction from 1969 to 1972, a rate of intervention much higher than under SLPP or British rule. These chiefs needed periodic police presences to enforce their elections, further underlining these allies' dependence on State House for the security of their positions. As Freetown ministries usurped the former administrative powers of chiefs over mining (advertised as "bringing power to the people"), Kono chiefs lost their major source of wealth and influence. Lacking his own local political network, Toli was cut off from seeking an independent accommodation with miners or dealers.

The near-total collapse of government development investment in Kono after 1968 colored local perceptions of recently imposed chiefs. The sudden disappearance of popular distribution of state resources heightened local feelings of alienation from new intermediaries. Freetown budgets also strained to meet other obligations inherited from the past governments. In 1970, the Central Bank still owed a Le 8.4 million debt to foreign produce-buyers after the state-owned marketing board failed to deliver contracted supplies of produce after the 1967 coup. The railroad continued consuming an annual Le 1.5 million in operating losses until it closed in the late 1970s.[53] Indirect subsidies to urban consumers and rising civil-service salary payments also deprived State House of resources to devote to building a patrimonial base of support. These demands combined to push budgets permanently into the red after 1970. Negotiations with the IMF for a loan in 1970 signalled the scarcity of state resources. Loan disbursements were also contingent upon IMF certification of efforts to limit unbudgeted expenditures.[54] Stevens also faced a politically vocal Freetown Chamber of Commerce, Jaycees and Rotary International representing the vigorous remnants of an African (especially Krio) business class concerned about the economic efficiency of formal state policies.

Stevens had to find a new strategy for generating resources under state control to distribute to loyal allies. We saw that the decision to impose more direct state control over SLST was undertaken with this goal in mind. The new NDMC provided Stevens with administrative positions that could be filled with State House approval as a reward for loyal service. But NDMC's formal exploitation of diamond resources, itself suffering from the depreda-tions of local illicit mining and subsequent foreign-investor disapproval did not increase formal state revenues. A new strategy was needed to provide allies such as Toli with wealth while reinforcing their dependence on State House. Closer examination of the sources of Toli's rent-seeking benefits

Table 4.2. *Toli's patrimonial resources, 1971–6*

NDMC sources:	(Total: Le213,992)
1972 NDMC boundary dispute compensation diverted from Chiefdom Treasury[55]	Le14,000
Diverted NDMC royalties:	
surface rents, 1972–6	Le49,742
tenancy leases	Le28,368
compensation for cash-crop damage	Le81,785
compensation for sacred bush[56]	
NDMC ground rents[57]	Le12,097
Chiefdom Cooperative Mining Scheme funds to purchase used Mercedes auto	Le28,000
Local government sources:	(Total: Le32,100)
Diverted from self-help project to extend government hospital[58]	Le1,500
Fandu–Koakor road construction "shake hand"	Le600
Misappropriated loan to Koidu/New Sembehun Town Council (Toli is a member)[59]	Le30,000
Chiefdom sources:	(Total: Le19,594)
Additional market license levy[60]	Le4,800
Illegal Levy to fund pilgrimage to Mecca	Le4,000
Unapproved court fees	Le230
Cash shortage, Chiefdom Treasury[61] (1976 only)	Le8,800
Local tax shortage (1976 only)	Le1,764
Total	Le265,686
	(approximately $375,000)

(Table 4.2) reveals significant changes in the relationship between Stevens, his allies, and their Kono subjects. Toli's loyalty took an increasing toll on formal state revenues and resulted in increased direct exploitation of "customary" claims on subjects. While Table 4.2's tally is tentative, particularly with regard to "customary" extractions, it nonetheless points to a shift in the sources of patrimonial rewards. More wealth was generated locally, either directly from subjects or from the mining company, bypassing the national treasury. Toli's relationship with NDMC was by no means unique. By 1981, at least ten of Kono's twelve chiefs enjoyed NDMC management positions.

Chiefs' relations with the mining company underwent drastic changes in these first years of APC rule. Under British, then SLPP rule, mining-company compensations to chiefs consisted mainly of damage awards for property lost to mining operations or informal gestures designed to gain local support such as electrification of chief compounds at SLST expense.[62]

Prior to the APC victory, the bulk of patrimonial rewards came via official development expenditures. These funds were diverted mainly from taxes and royalties, but only after they had first passed through institutional state channels. Most directly appropriated benefits had come from local sources. A study conducted in 1960 concluded that chiefs claimed 30–35 percent of local tax and development expenditures as patrimonial benefits,[63] a finding similar to that of an investigation undertaken after anti-chief riots in 1955–6.[64] These figures indicate that the yearly income of the chief of Gbense would have approached Le 35,000 (about $50,000) from official sources. These figures do not include benefits from control over illicit mining derived from authorities that chiefs no longer possessed after 1968.

Thus, after 1968, the installation of Stevens's allies and the closer NDMC–chief connection represented an informal "nationalization" of distributions of patrimonial resources. These demands seriously undermined formal state revenue collection. The reported "cash shortage" in Table 4.2 for 1976 represented over 60 percent of that year's estimated collection.[65] While in the past, programs such as MADA provided some popular development expenditure, declining NDMC revenues and increased extractions by chiefs from the company deprived Kono residents of returns from the area's mineral resources. Local residents were even further deprived of opportunity as former accommodations with chiefs over illicit mining were absorbed into this new network. Chiefs concentrated more on their lucrative relationships with NDMC and the opportunities to extract wealth from subjects while enjoying police protection. Toli's private interests in gathering wealth now depended more on his favorable relationship with Siaka Stevens than on the strength of his local accommodations or political networks. Stevens pursued control in Kono through more direct ties to intermediaries. By "sub-contracting" collections of reward to them, Stevens also expanded the sources and amount of resources available to his political network beyond institutional state resources.

NDMC played an increasingly important role in the distribution of wealth to Stevens's favorites. Suddenly, chiefs found a powerful incentive to cooperate with government efforts to regulate the organization of mining, both illicit and legal, in order to increase the volume of resources available for distribution to elites under State-House control. Cooperative chiefs imposed a market structure on the diamond trade that diverted resources from local accommodations and instead forced dealers to rely on arrangements with Freetown. Chiefs themselves favored strangers – particularly Lebanese dealers – and resident Konos more amenable to Freetown. While chiefs received some payoffs from their resident "strangers," the more important payoff lay in the assurance of a place on the board of

NDMC or access to NDMC resources for the compliant chief. Police and paramilitary protection provided by a friendly State House also allowed chiefs such as Toli to supplement their larger "formal sector" NDMC prebends with local extractions at little political risk.

These growing extractions by chiefs from local subjects served to reinforce their dependence on State House for protection from angry subjects. But the costs of additional patrimonial resources locally fell squarely on the shoulders of chiefdom residents. Just as state-funded development projects became more scarce, alternative means of survival, such as illicit mining, or the acquisition of a small-business license became more difficult as they became increasingly subject to chief depredations. The APC government's purchase of short-term political control in Kono came at the cost of public disillusionment as the redistributive and participatory promises of the APC and their predecessors receded farther behind the high costs of elite accommodation.

Rising patrimonial costs crippled Freetown's direct mobilizational capability, even as it increased Stevens's political network. Toli's claims on public resources in the mid 1970s alone were (at least) equal to 80 percent of the 1971/72 budgeted expenditure for hospitals and clinics throughout Sierra Leone.[66] Kono has eleven and Sierra Leone has 145 other chiefdoms, many with chiefs making significant demands on state resources. While draining resources from the formal state, Stevens's installation of some new chiefs and cutting-off of independent sources of wealth appeared to offer him some increased political security. The construction of the new political network, however, eroded APC recourse to popular appeals. APC leaders earlier promised that the "feudal remnant" of chieftaincy, against which the Kono KPM railed in the 1950s, would not stand in the way of a broader distribution of the regions' resources and a higher standard of living.[67] Yet obvious government favor for chiefs such as Toli reinforced Kono's social grievances against chiefs. These were the same sentiments which prompted Colonial Office policy-makers to propose liberal political and economic reforms that promised a more equitable distribution of wealth and political power.

But Toli's installation clearly clashed with earlier APC promises of "a welfare state based upon a socialist pattern of society, based upon a high degree of industrialization and agricultural productivity."[68] While the government never clarified the meaning of "socialist pattern of society," the bulk of APC rank-and-file took this promise to signal a more equitable distribution of resources and continued increases in development efforts following the lead of schemes such as MADA, inherited from the last years of colonial rule. Some Gbense residents appealed directly to State House, asking that Stevens "discipline" the wayward Toli who prevented the party from delivering on its extensive promises. "We solicit Your Excellency's fatherly indulgence," wrote local Gbense APC organizers, "so as to avert the mounting tension building up in the chiefdom."[69] Control over more immediately threatening local political networks undermined Stevens's institutional, and now ideological, capacities to seek direct support from subjects. Yet because of this weakness, political pluralism would be even more threatening to Stevens's rule. The unmet desires of large numbers of supporters found other avenues of expression, but still posed a crisis of legitimacy that threatened Stevens's security.

The shifting battle for political power

Individual APC organizers discovered that unmet social demands and central government incapacity could be exploited for personal gain. Stevens's initial strategy of extending party and government control over formal political and administrative institutions and major resources limited rivals' uses of customary channels of political competition. But now rivals came from within the APC. As noted earlier, some of Kono's radical APC factions found voices from among Stevens's Freetown associates. Many of these politicians rose in the APC due to their links to grassroots organizations and their willingness to mobilize them on behalf of Stevens's election. Most retained personal links to organizations after assuming office in 1968. We saw that Stevens's second-in-command, S.I. Koroma, even assumed legal responsibility for government management of mutual-aid societies upon which he based much of his personal influence within the party and among constituents. As head of the Ministry of Interior, Koroma found himself in a position to personally define groups as "friendly" or "an enemy" to state interests as he determined them.

One of Koroma's client organizations, a young men's mutual-aid society named Civilian Rule (now PWD and Terminator),[70] draws members from poor under- and unemployed men in Freetown's West I ward. Civilian Rule boasts links to Kono's Santo and Kono Spark societies. Both Kono societies provide social and financial support for Freetowners seeking their fortune in the Kono diamond fields. Primarily, they help Civilian Rule members in Kono find illicit "tributor" operations that will provide food and tools and organize digging operations for these workers in return for access to the rewards of their labors. As we saw above, Koroma earlier tried to channel support to these groups as part of a strategy of boosting Kellie's "pro-miner" Tankoro candidacy which many of Koroma's clients backed.

While the early effort failed, growing popular concern over unaddressed social grievances offered Koroma opportunities to support candidates attacking elite privilege. Another "radical" APC associate, F.M. Minah, also used his influence over the Ministry of Mines and armed Central Investigation Division (CID) to provide immunity from official and chief harassment for the operations of some of these miners and their "tributor" dealer financiers. A local official contended that this "outside interference" undercut long-term administrative efforts to end illicit mining and threatened social peace. Fearful of disruptions from APC factional rivalry's disregard for administration's proper role as neutral arbiter in the upcoming 1973 elections, he said that "this sabotage causes an anarchy which leads some to believe that to live under laws imposes only burdens . . . They believe that Government is the cause of their misfortunes . . . Others in affected areas take advantage of disorder in ways that undermine the confidence of their neighbors."[71]

With competition now outside formal multiparty competitive channels, political entrepreneurs pursued their interests within the state and societal terrain which Stevens and his associates claimed for themselves. New independent accommodations between illicit miners and renegade state officials provided the means to fund local political organizations.[72]

These political links between miners and Freetown officials illustrate the entrepreneurial opportunities for politicians exploiting continuing social divisions in mining areas. By the mid-1970s, many miners pressed their demands on government through mutual-aid societies, and in some cases, protests. In 1973, S.I. Koroma discovered that these demands could be directed toward the support of Tamba Kaimondo, a "pro-miner" Kellie associate and populist candidate not enjoying Stevens's favor in the upcoming single-party (multicandidate) election. Kono APC organizers – many of whom also led miner societies – oversaw the local selection of Kaimondo over Alhaji Gborie, Stevens's choice for the APC banner.

Another populist political movement, this one in Kenema to the south of Kono, illustrates the use of informal politician ties to societies in building political support. A Kono diamond dealer, M. Jaward, donated land and a building next to his Kenema office to the local miner branch of the APC. This faction supported M.M. Koroma, an APC activist with broad appeal among Jaward's employees, but without Stevens's or local elite support. Once Koroma was in office, Jaward would be in a position to promote the economic interests of his supporters through his influence over Koroma's enforcement of illicit mining and smuggling regulations. A local dealer explained Jaward's motivations: "finding one's friends is a cost of doing business here."[73] The "official" claimant to the party label, however, was seen locally as favoring tighter controls on illicit poaching of NDMC diamonds, a position allegedly derived from his close association with recently installed chiefs holding positions in NDMC.

Consequently, local miner societies campaigned for M.M. Koroma. CID and Sierra Leone Police forces under Minah's control protected society members demonstrating for their candidate. S.I. Koroma, as Minister of the Interior, gave these societies permits for demonstrations and processions in which they displayed their preference for M.M. Koroma. Society links also facilitated M.M. Koroma's search for campaign funds from among local diamond dealers. As a prominent Kono dealer remarked in regard to his contributions to diverse campaigns, "I am not a politician. I have been with all the regimes which have existed in the country and have been in the good books of all of them."[74] Coaptation of diamond dealers into autonomous political networks underlined the dangers Stevens faced from political rivals amidst weakening state administrative control. Political entrepreneurs found independent local support while diamond dealers at least temporarily operated more free of state power. Miners perhaps enjoyed greater illicit opportunity. Throughout, Stevens risked losing control of resources, the foundation of political power and influence in Sierra Leone.

These developments posed direct organizational threats to Stevens. S.I. Koroma and another Freetown associate, Chernor Maju, explored organizing society activity on an institutional basis to support other populist candidates. Since societies registered themselves with the Ministry of Interior for official recognition, S.I. Koroma was well placed to control patronage and encourage alliances among societies for political purposes. Members of Kono societies themselves recognize that joint action may have once provided them with an opportunity for a greater voice in pressuring government to pursue popular redistributive demands. Society members point to the past political strength of Freemasons among the former Krio elite of Freetown as evidence of the benefits of group action.[75]

These developments in Kenema and Kono threatened to produce social unity against state support for elite privilege. Given a more forceful leadership, or one more independent of Freetown patronage, these societal demands may have found a voice in class terms organized around an independent political challenge.[76] Stevens himself understood the mobilizational potential of organizations cutting across ethnic and regional interests. As a labor leader in the 1940s, Stevens had founded the APC Youth League, uniting youth members from urban and rural areas in support of APC goals. It was in this search for grassroots support for the APC Youth League that S.I. Koroma and Minah first made contact with societies to spread the APC populist message.

By the mid-1970s, the APC faced a more difficult task in retaining popular legitimacy. The party leadership as a whole needed support among young men and miners to generate public displays in the form of friendly society parades on behalf of the APC. At the same time, the potential of these groups for playing a role in organized challenges to Stevens's leadership was significant, especially as government performance diverged from the APC's own populist rhetoric. Meanwhile, the excessive demands of imposing patrimonial control over elites depleted the government's resources, denying them the option of attracting support to the APC banner by meeting social demands with concrete action.

Could Stevens have simply removed potential rivals within the APC by force and placed societies under his own patronage? First, the growing shortage of revenues limited large additions to Stevens's political network. Fiscal burdens were not the last of Stevens's worries. Two coup attempts in 1971 caused Stevens to appeal to Guinea's leader, Sekou Touré, for military assistance to suppress rivals within the army or among former associates. Touré reportedly favored aid to the "fraternal APC" because he approved of the populist stance of Koroma and other politicians, including several not in Stevens's good graces.[77] Consequently, Stevens could not risk serious moves against the party's radical wing without angering his own external patron. It is significant in this light that Stevens listed "Sierra Leone–Guinea relations" as a separate prerogative of his office, independent of the Ministry of External Affairs.[78] Meanwhile, radical faction leaders such as S.I. Koroma busily invoked the image of Touré's Parti democratique de Guinée (PDG) in justifying their own populist stance.[79]

While S.I. Koroma admired the PDG's efficiency at intimidating and violently disposing of political rivals,[80] the notion of effective single-party rule threatened Stevens. A truly societal force (unlike Touré's) lacking a network of associates dependent upon the leader's favor would give force to popular claims on the resources that Stevens now claimed as his own to distribute to allies. The potential for an alternative center of power organized around the APC's appeals instead of around himself posed especially grave dangers to Stevens while foreign troops tolerant of such a project remained on Sierra Leone soil. Instead, Stevens preferred a more secure "no-party" system of individuals dependent upon him for favor. But Stevens's dependence on Touré's troops forced him to reconcile himself to senior party officials' populist tactics and search for new ways to bring them under control. Meanwhile, the 1973 elections marked an effort to rid the party of more junior radical faction supporters, a move that was generally successful in the Freetown area where Stevens exercised more direct personal influence, but one which attracted the Guinea leader's criticism.[81]

The impact of the radical challenge

Stevens's exclusive claims on resources for political distribution imposed discipline on associates and at the same time garnered new resources for his renovated Shadow State. But now the competitive struggle between elites, and popular acceptance of the legitimacy of political competition, changed the rules of informal political control. Stevens could not simply rule as a colonial proconsul over relatively passive elites with the security that comes from representing the power of the British Empire. Stevens had to build a power-base capable of allowing him to control the interests of a more diverse group of intermediaries to protect his regime. But as among his predecessors, his weakness lay in the limits to his financial resources.

We saw in Toli's case a partial solution to the crises of control and finance. Stevens's willingness to further "sub-contract" some state functions to Toli and NDMC-linked trade and political authority was in a manner that resembled colonial strategies of political management in areas outside direct European control. Impressed with these favored intermediaries' power, John Mathews, an eighteenth-century trader, noted that "On the arrival at the place of trade they [traders] immediately apply to the headman, inform him of their business, and request his protection; desiring he will either be himself their landlord."[82] As the formal state was breaking down, Sierra Leone's past loomed larger in its future. The "officially appointed landlord" benefits to the extent that his client's business activities provide him with resources which he can translate into instruments to extend his power.[83] Stevens's delegation of this power to Toli provided Toli with the authority to force diamond dealers to appeal to this political network for favor.

But this strategy was fraught with danger for Stevens. How could Stevens ensure that strongmen would not strike out on their own to control market networks? Equally dangerous was the attraction to Kono miners of the liberal promise of political competition. Political reform in the 1950s had appeared to offer miners solutions to long-held social grievances. But from the perspective of the insecure leader in State House, competition to voice these concerns threatened the elite accommodation upon which Stevens based his power to rule.

Stevens's insecurity and lack of direct control over the population contrast sharply with inherited colonial notions of a sovereign state power easily distinguishable from the society it was supposed to rule and transform. Stevens noted, not disapprovingly, that in colonial times:

The choice was between joining the white man's "party," ie the administration, or opposing it. Moreover, opposition in the colonial regime could express itself only in violence and destructive or disruptive activities ... This resulted in political militancy or opposition to the government becoming identified in the minds of many people with riotous behavior and strong-arm tactics.[84]

In contrast to colonial rule, Stevens aimed to create a firm link between himself and local political interests. Not able to rule over society, Stevens had to rule society itself. Political competition was inimical to this mission. "An opposition party," said Stevens, "can also be a destructive and useless force for a party committed to the good of the country – and the interests of my country must always come first with me."[85]

Stevens's alternative Shadow State had required the selective marginalization of some groups through officially sanctioned "disengagement." Other groups were permitted rent-seeking informal market opportunities not necessarily totally outside state control. Overall, Shadow State power superseded the limits enumerated in liberal constitutions or envisioned in formal bureaucratic structures. Stevens exercised control through setting criteria which benefited some while banishing others from political life. Political challenge also required that he devise new strategies of gaining extensive powers to prevent the opposition from "causing a massive breakdown in law and order in the hope that the confusion [would] give them an opportunity to seize power."[86] It remained impossible for Stevens to pinpoint from what quarter challenge would arise, particularly given state institutional weakness, vulnerability to political entrepreneurs, and his regime's dependence on foreign troops for protection. Therefore, limits on his actions would not be found within the legal bounds of state power. Instead, limits would be found in the boundaries of the political system he constructed. The measures necessary for confronting his challenges increasingly extended beyond the legal bounds of power which the departing colonial rulers had incorrectly believed to be their legacy to their African successors.

Elite accommodations, not laws, guided State House. Collaborative relations with intermediaries that survived the 1948 Colonial Office reforms offered Stevens a framework for installing his own allies as local intermediaries who would enforce his directives. But the intensification of politics across a broad front, particularly in the diamond industry and among dealers and miners, called for stronger measures to bring these groups and activities under tighter State House control.

Stark choices faced the leader. His political strategies were set not only by the over-arching environment of a need to control the distribution of resources, but also by a need to generate them. This is why control of diamond mining became a cornerstone of Stevens's political strategy. More extensive control could not be achieved through the force of state institutional power alone. Instead, political authority came with control of diamond markets, particularly informal markets where political challenge was most likely. Stevens also had to deal realistically with the need to continue generating revenues for at least minimal state functions, even as revenue-generating institutions grew weaker. This need to control, not destroy, the organization of production, gave the objects of Stevens's attention – miners and dealers, and their overseas market contacts – certain strengths. But Stevens's survival required incorporating elements of both the formal and informal diamond industry, rather than engaging in a "state–society struggle" with each side defined by clear boundaries and capabilities. It is this story to which the next chapter is addressed.

5   An exchange of services: State power and the diamond business

We vividly recall Your Excellency's promises, but now we find ourselves surrounded by fanatics in APC clothing . . . in these anxious days the old ways are trampled . . . we are peaceful, law-abiding citizens who crave security . . .   Kono petition against local corruption[1]

Sure, there are problems, but these politicians and business men maintain an equilibrium. It shows prudence to keep out those who might use our diamond wealth against the welfare of our people.
                                                   A former government official[2]

Unruly elites gaining independent access to wealth threatened Stevens's rule in the mid-1970s. Like his British predecessors, Stevens faced a crisis of rule and searched for alternative methods to establish stable political domination. However, political reform had led citizens to expect that they would have a voice in state decisions. Popular claims on political space grew more visible as the distribution of diamond resources occupied a central position in Sierra Leone's political life. Rival political networks and independent organizations sprang up around popular dissatisfaction and were financed with diamond wealth. Weak central control and the growing revenue crisis precluded strengthening control through strong state or APC institutions, which themselves could become vehicles for independent challenges to Stevens's leadership.

Stevens focused his search for greater central control on areas of the economy that had played a role in unapproved official accommodations under British rule, and had financed Stevens's challengers – the illicit diamond market. In doing this, he risked aggravating Kono feelings of relative deprivation, the foundation of the area's populist challenges to Freetown's authority. But where resources proved lacking, the leader's capacity to intervene lay in his ability to impose decisions which denied benefits to one and conferred them upon another. This chapter explores the strategies that Stevens adopted to control Kono's resources and reimpose political order. Informal accommodations with diamond dealers form the core of these strategies. But they also extend to shape markets themselves, including commercial networks in other sectors of the economy. Bureaucratic state institutions were decaying rapidly. Stevens's Shadow State, however, was colonizing diverse areas of societal activity, redefining the entire terrain of politics and society in Sierra Leone.

Financing elite accommodation

In December 1973, Stevens announced that the government would allow private mining operations on rich diamond deposits within the NDMC lease area. This Cooperative Contract Mining (CCM) scheme aimed to "increase the living standards of our citizens through further Africanisation of our economy."[3] The intention of the announcement was clear to many Konos. Freetown finally appeared to accept a more equitable distribution of mining opportunities. Residents saw the CCM announcement as part of a larger trend toward greater tolerance of private mining ventures, begun in a limited fashion with the 1956 legalization of alluvial mining outside the lease area. Many also hoped that nationalist rhetoric accompanying the policy's announcement signalled that the Ministry of Mines would halt its official favoritism of Lebanese dealers in the issuance of mining and dealing licenses.[4] The Freetown press proclaimed that recent government policy signaled the end of European control over the vital diamond sector of Sierra Leone's economy, a promise of the APC before the 1967 and 1973 elections.[5]

Foreign investors and creditors concluded, however, that the announcement was a response to the decline of foreign investment in NDMC. Foreign investment fell as the Stevens government proved unable to sufficiently curb illicit mining, lowering returns on SLST capital investment. One negotiator arranging the government buy-out concluded that the government wished to run the mining company directly, so that it would be better able to forcibly control illicit mining without suffering the political fall-out associated with protecting a foreign firm. The assurances of security would then encourage foreign investors to participate in the new company.[6] Earlier, a British investor had pointed to deep investor concerns in his accusation that Freetown tolerated illicit mining. "Unless discipline is reestablished, we shall all risk a substantial and inevitable loss of control over diamond production," he said.[7]

Most Konos did not benefit from this "privatization" of mining. High financial hurdles suggested that small-scale miners were not invited to transfer their operations from the informal market into the formal economy. The small scale of the initial implementation disappointed many Kono residents. Only twenty mining plots had been distributed one year after the policy's announcement. This limited start only reinforced the selective nature of CCM's implementation.

The Ministry of Mines, responsible since 1968 for administering local mining regulations after that task was removed from local officials, oversaw the CCM policy. New plot assignments followed purely political criteria. Each Kono chief with an NDMC sinecure, at least six in 1974, received a plot. Already occupying positions within the state-owned NDMC, these chiefs found little difficulty in appropriating, but not paying for, NDMC heavy machinery to mine their private plots. A second favored group included government officials from outside Kono, at least two of whom were previously identified as radical APC faction supporters. One such politician gained access through a plot assignment to his brother-in-law. His wife later obtained a dealer's license in 1978. There is no evidence that any of the local candidates associated with the "pro-miner" platform in the 1973 campaign received access to plots in 1973–4.

The list of beneficiaries expanded with 1974 and 1975 announcements of new private mining schemes in the NDMC lease area. The 1975 announcement included another rich mining area around the NDMC No. 6 treatment plant, long an area of illicit mining. Several plots went to government officials who had previously benefited from a 1969 "nationalization" of non-citizen commercial enterprises under the aegis of the National Trading Company. Beneficiaries included a Vice President and a Minister of Mines. It appeared that Freetown was continuing a policy of distributing state property in return for loyalty, and extending it to the mining industry. CCM was not merely aimed at gaining support for Stevens among local legal and illicit diamond producers. Instead, through the Ministry of Mines, Stevens directly interfered with the organization of illicit diamond production to support or promote loyal political allies. The strategy of distributing privatized plots directly through the Ministry of Mines allowed the President to exercise direct personal control over the award of economic favors. Commercial calculations involving private diamond production now had to assign higher priority to the political requirements for access to plots or protection from harassment.

The new measures had an immediate radical impact on the formal mining economy (Table 5.1). Production shifted away from the mining company, the source of more than 50 percent of state revenues over the past three decades. NDMC output fell from 856,000 carats in 1973 to only 168,000 carats in 1980, amid a slow decline in legal exports of stones. By 1980, NDMC produced only 29 percent of legal non-alluvial output, a sharp decrease from the 94 percent figure in 1973.[8] These developments indicated that a considerable quantity of Sierra Leone's resources now flowed through private hands, reaching a legal trade of close to $60–70 million per

Table 5.1. *Shifting diamond production, 1975–84*

	NDMC output (1,000 carats)	Official Purchases (1,000 carats)
1975	731	539
1976	652	602
1977	368	349
1978	380	465
1979	198	654
1980	168	424
1981	166	145
1982	150	153
1983	92	239
1984	236	82
1985	74	248

Source: Compiled from Bank of Sierra Leone, *Economic Trends* and *Economic Review* (Freetown: Government Printer, various issues).

year by 1980.[9] However, much of the economic impact of direct participation by politicians in mining lies in unrecorded mining operations, an issue which we will examine below in greater detail. While CCM eroded the role of state enterprises, it allowed the creation of a "private" diamond economy organized around the ruler's strategy of political control.

The local administration's involvement with CCM illustrates Freetown's intentions regarding the policy. Despite popular expectations of more liberal official attitudes toward private mining, the Kono DO received orders commanding continued vigilance against illicit mining. "Following the unsettled conditions of the past year," wrote the Provincial Secretary, "... you must be well aware of the need for strict vigilance in enforcing permit and residence regulations."[10] Economic rewards requiring loyalty from potential political entrepreneurs enabled Freetown to suppress more vigorously small-scale illicit mining without fear of miners' grievances finding a ready political voice. At least from 1975 onward, the newly created paramilitary Internal Security Unit (ISU – or locally, "I Shoot You") conducted stranger drives on behalf of private CCM operations. Local miners complained that private CCM operations employed members of the widely hated NDMC security force to suppress diamond poaching.[11] Stevens then ordered some areas which had been open to private alluvial mining since 1956 to be closed. One such closure in 1975 turned over to cooperative operations a 570-square-mile area formerly open to small-scale mining.[12]

Clearly the exclusivity of plot distribution and officially sanctioned paramilitary efforts to suppress illicit mining dashed hopes for a wider distribution of the benefits of Kono's resources. As a Kono small business-man bitterly observed of the politician-entrepreneurs, "The policy of Government has gotten worse since the colonial days. Then, we received nothing and we gave little in return. Mostly they left us alone. Now the Big Men come and carry off to share among themselves what they take ... Now the place is spoiled."[13] The selective nature of policy implementation also reinforced perceptions in some chiefdoms, Gbense, for example, that participating chiefs utilized the prerogatives of state office to accumulate more private wealth. A local health-care worker in Koidu complained that clinic construction there had ground to a halt "as all heavy machinery is now engaged in mining."[14] Public Works Department machinery allocated for Kono development projects also found its way onto the plot of a minister's relative.[15]

In some respects, the 1973 CCM scheme and subsequent plot distribu-tions were not major departures from previous Freetown strategies of building loyalty through selective allocation of state benefits to politicians. But this intensification of Stevens's political network into Kono mining appropriated both a source of economic opportunity for Konos and a basis for political challenge centered on the resources and organization of a private mining economy. While force played a significant role in suppress-ing unsanctioned mining, Stevens's political network came to control access to Kono's diamond fields. With it disappeared a primary popular means of resisting state efforts to monopolize Kono's resources through informal arrangements between officials, residents and dealers. This exclu-sivity required the cooperation of illicit diamond dealers, not only to prevent them from seeking independent accommodations with local officials, but also to provide valuable services necessary for the private exploitation and sale of diamonds, tasks which the bureaucratically feeble Sierra Leone government found itself unable to perform.

Enlisting the dealers to finance the Shadow State

Soon after the CCM announcement in March 1974, the Minister of Finance indicated that Freetown intended to end DeBeers' monopoly over overseas marketing of Sierra Leone diamonds. Upon legalization of private alluvial mining in 1956, DeBeers had established the Diamond Corporation (DICOR) to direct all private diamond sales through its Central Selling Organization (CSO). DeBeers remained interested in Sierra Leone in order to regulate the world supply of diamonds, however. DICOR stood at the center of Freetown's and DeBeers's formal anti-smuggling strategy. With massive DeBeers financial backing, DICOR offered high prices for diamonds. The government further benefited from a 7.5 percent levy on DICOR's private purchases. In return for rights to the Sierra Leone market, DICOR was obligated to buy every stone offered. During periodically depressed markets, DICOR made little profit on these purchases.[16] Thus, up to the 1970s, DeBeers and DICOR were essential to the government's formal strategy of extracting revenues from a politically compliant and dependable enclave economy. While providing Freetown with foreign exchange, DeBeers also absorbed the expenses of enticing a portion of the independent mining traffic into formal channels in pursuit of its global marketing interests. Freetown benefited from higher returns in the formal sector, while still being able to selectively tolerate smuggling by its own officials and favored dealers.

But Freetown quickly ended what appeared to be a favorable arrangement. In 1974, the Ministry of Mines announced that it was granting private export licenses to five individuals to export 20 percent of Sierra Leone's diamonds. With this announcement, Freetown unilaterally ended DICOR's commitment to purchase all diamonds. The nature of resource allocations reveals the changing interests of Freetown with respect to DeBeers and diamonds. DeBeers offered Freetown the capacity to produce and manage diamond resources, but it offered little control over distribution. DeBeers tried to use market incentives to manage Sierra Leone's informal diamond market. Its purchasing office in Monrovia, Liberia, paid dollars to anyone bringing diamonds out of Sierra Leone. This policy enabled DeBeers to compete with Stevens's efforts to use informal diamond markets to reward political allies in ways that undercut DeBeers's market control. In response, Stevens gave a more compliant foreign operation, Jack Lunzar's Industrial Diamond Corporation, an 8 percent quota of the country's production. Lunzar already marketed Guinea's AREDOR diamonds (Association pour la Recherche et l'Exploitation du Diamant et l'Or) outside CSO channels.[17] A well-known Afro-Lebanese dealer active in Kono's market, Jamil Said Mohamed ("Jamil"), and three associates received the remaining 12 percent.

These five exporters took politicians as partners as "political insurance" to assure favor, said one NDMC official.[18] Officially, the private exporters paid a 7.5 percent levy on diamonds. The end of DICOR's purchasing monopoly, however, offered new commercial opportunities for private exporters, some of whom had illicitly competed against DeBeers for years. With DICOR no longer committed to buying all stones, dealers found that they could offer lower prices to diggers. Freetown also gained greater access to foreign exchange through the creation of the Government Diamond Office (GDO). This office valued all privately marketed diamonds and assessed the official levy, a task formerly performed by DICOR. The GDO then required that the proceeds from sales abroad be deposited in the Bank of Sierra Leone.[19] However, with both Stevens and Jamil as board members from 1976, the GDO allowed favored exporters to undervalue diamonds with the difference going into private pockets. Some favored dealers and private plot holders were also not required to repatriate all foreign-exchange earnings from the overseas sales of diamonds. Thus dealer–state official collaborations received a competitive advantage in exemption from laws and regulations which were selectively enforced.

Private dealers acting as exporters enabled Stevens to gain personal access to foreign exchange and control diamond sales. Already active in the informal market, dealers had overseas connections to obtain capital for purchases in Sierra Leone and access to diamond markets independent of closely regulated CSO channels, an asset state institutions did not possess. Lebanese connections abroad, which politicians lacked, provided a business network to market diamonds and raise capital in the Middle East and Europe. For example, Nabih Berri, Lebanon's Amal militia leader, hailed from Port Loko, Jamil's birthplace.[20] Large diamond dealers like Jamil Mohamed and associates, Tony Yazbeck, and Mohammed Jaward all had long-term contacts with Beirut's Byblos Bank, giving them and their partners access to credit backed by diamonds at a time when foreign investors were shying away from Sierra Leone. Incorporating these contacts freed Stevens from the political bonds of maintaining legal predictability or protecting foreign investors.

These five exporters, non-African Sierra Leone residents legally prohibited from holding office, provided Stevens with a safe means of underwriting his political network's extension to Kono's diamond fields. This was achieved without incurring the financial expense or political dangers of building a bureaucratic edifice to administer an expanding state sector, which political entrepreneurs might use to arrive at independent accommodations with Kono miners. As both private mining and export operations depended upon official favor to survive, these "clients" depended upon Stevens's personal favor. Stevens found additional security in the tendency of most Sierra Leoneans to identify those of Lebanese or Afro-Lebanese descent as outsiders. Collaboration with reliable, but politically emasculated dealers advanced Stevens's efforts to monopolize diamond digging and remove a resource base from the reach of potential rivals. For dealers, Stevens's favor was one of the only ways to protect their access to diamonds.

In this context, to weaken formal bureaucratic state institutions would deprive Stevens's new political network of resources, but to build up those institutions would also bring the danger of challenge from within his own government. The "exchange of services" between dealers and Freetown indicated the extent to which informal accommodations seemed to be a rational political response for Stevens when he was faced with unruly inherited elite alliances. Stevens resolved the dilemmas of political challenge and declining revenues by replacing true political competition with a struggle for his favor, financed through his control of the private diamond market, since state institutions could not safely provide sufficient resources to finance his new elite accommodation. Stevens also discovered that ties to politically vulnerable non-African informal diamond market traders helped him to solidify his personal control over this new arrangement. Lebanese dealers had few local social networks from which they could challenge Stevens, but they did have access to international diamond-market and credit networks to help make collaborative private ventures a success.

This strategy considerably blurred the boundaries between "state" and "private" enterprise and profit. Rigid dichotomies between state and society make little sense amidst the informal links between the two. As during the colonial era, the ruler's political task centered on curbing the fundamentally dangerous tendencies for the development of autonomous interests within the newly incorporated network. The incorporation ideally produced an exchange of services on a wider scale similar to the joint pursuit of private–state interests in Freetown's early colonial efforts to influence hinterland chiefs through control of trade.

Unfortunately for Kono's people, Stevens's informal strategies weakened bureaucratic state capacity to engage in what most people understood as development, or to allow greater popular access to Kono's resources that would enable people to improve their own conditions. Economic opportunity in Kono, both legal and illicit, became progressively more dependent upon one's position in Stevens's political network. Popular opportunities in formal and informal markets declined as favored dealers and officials increasingly dominated the accumulation of wealth and the organization of commerce in Kono. Accordingly, Stevens still faced popular challenges. Stevens's response with naked force uncovered the extent to which coercion was a vital component of this elite accommodation. This collaborative "rule through subcontractors" produced a significant change in the distribution of opportunity and resulted in a more intensive exploitation of Kono's diamond resources, primarily for the benefit of favored non-Konos.

Table 5.2. *Distribution of dealer licenses, 1973–82*

	Lebanese (heritage)		African		Shared addresses	
	No.	%	No.	%	No.	%
1973	107	78	30	22	—	—
1974	152	75	52	25	—	—
1975	134	79	36	21	—	—
1976	110	65	57	35	22	13
1977	88	64	49	36	22	17
1978	99	70	42	30	37	26
1979	139	66	72	34	96	46
1980	102	56	79	44	92	51
1981	104	62	63	38	74	44
1982	96	73	36	27	90	68

Source: Compiled from Ministry of Mines, "Government Notices – List of Alluvial Diamond Dealer Licences."

Stevens's political invasion of Kono's popular economy

The new economic collaboration disrupted Kono's commercial and political life. Favored chiefs and larger dealers quickly utilized their positions to extend their control over the local diamond market, depriving considerable numbers of people of an economic opportunity that had previously offered them a means of resisting overbearing state power. The most immediate impact of the collaboration came in the distribution of opportunity in the diamond industry itself. Dealer licenses have long served as the most visible indicator of the industry's social make-up. Since the legalization of private mining in 1956, all dealers have required licenses. Even primarily illicit operators obtained licenses. As one miner intoned, "the license is the charm that protects the bearer from harm." That is, the license protects the bearer from being singled out for prosecution.[21] Before 1968, award of a license signalled the dealer's accommodation with the old elite alliance, usually after the payment of a bribe in addition to the license fee. After 1968, when license operations moved to Freetown, the accommodation was with Stevens's Ministry of Mines. Licenses now cost much more. License fees stood at Le 1,000 in 1974, but rose to $5,000 (payable in dollars only) by 1990.[22] Closer examination of the allocation of dealer licenses provides considerable additional information concerning the nature of the Shadow State's extension in Kono.

By late 1974, the largest dealers who had become exporters no longer appeared on Ministry of Mines license rosters. However, increasing numbers of smaller operators listed addresses connected with these private exporters (Table 5.2). In 1979, 46 percent of all license applications had shared addresses. The concentration of license holding reached a height in 1982, when in February of that year (the start of the mining season), the Ministry of Mines issued eighty licenses to just ten addresses. African dealers exhibited even greater exporter connections, with 80 percent of all Africans listing a single Sefadu address connected with Jamil. Listed addresses represent a legal commercial collaboration, but are also a guide to illicit marketing arrangements. These figures can be taken as an estimation of the new network's influence over Kono's diamond industry.

It appears that these dealers used contacts with private export-license holders as a "postbox" to market diamonds overseas.[23] This ensured that larger percentages of Sierra Leone's stones passed through the Lebanese-run marketing arrangement. In turn, Stevens had access to proportionally larger amounts of foreign exchange generated from these sales through the joint government–dealer administered GDO. Official production declined, dropping to about 20 percent of 1974 levels by 1983. Meanwhile, GDO purchases of private production constituted a growing proportion of official exports,[24] suggesting that far more than the initial 20 percent quota of diamonds left the country through informal channels. The dealer licenses remained vital for official sanctions to do business in the diamond industry, however. The rising costs of licenses, about four times more expensive in real terms in 1990 than in 1974, further ensured that dealers would become dependent upon a commercial patron to pay the ever-increasing fee to ensure access to diamonds. This partly explains why African dealers more often tended to become financially dependent upon a wealthy sponsor than their better-off Lebanese competitors.

These cooperative dealers carried out much of the actual mining of private plots through their tributor operations. That is, dealers provided tools and food to workers in return for access to the recovered stones. However, smaller dealers now had to sell to commercial patrons who provided access to licensing and perhaps also paid the license fee and obtained resident permits, a requirement for all non-Konos living in the area. This dealer hierarchy, regulating production and sales, released plot-holders, many of whom were non-resident politicians, from the task of overseeing their own mining operations. Consequently, smaller-scale dealers became dependent upon the political favor of both their commercial patron and their politician "landlord."

Dealer-license records also illustrate the increasingly parallel interests of local politicians and cooperative dealers regulating the lucrative "priva-tized" diamond market. Dealer licenses themselves became a source of benefits for local politicians. Larger dealers had to accept these new middlemen. Most new middlemen simply sold their purchases to the exporter who had previously marketed the diamonds directly from diggers working on the politician's plot to buyers abroad. Official favor in the form of dealer licenses ensured that these officials got another cut from the marketing of diamonds. By 1982, at least twelve of Kono's fourteen chiefs held dealer licenses along with their plots. Some held multiple licenses, as was the case with Nimi Yema's Chief Torto.[25] In 1981, Stevens waived the Le3,000 license fees for some chiefs, further facilitating their entry into the diamond market. Some of these chiefs also enjoyed additional opportunities to encroach on NDMC land, since, by 1979 at least six chiefs who held dealer licenses sat on the NDMC board of directors.[26] By the 1982 election, all six (later, eight) of Kono's Members of Parliament held licenses or plots. Indeed, licensed dealer (and one-time radical APC candidate) John Kamanda, a parliamentary member from Kono Central, became Managing Director of NDMC in 1985.

Access to NDMC land and equipment and private marketing channels permitted favored state officials to share in considerable benefits. An outside observer concluded that the average licensed dealer grossed about $0.5 million in one mining season (January to June).[27] This figure accords with the approximately $70 million *recorded* private yearly trade in diamonds by the early 1980s. Declining official exports, along with continued intensive mining activity, indicate that illicit activity may have added an additional $100–120 million in export values. Of this amount, dealers reportedly earn an 8–10 percent profit on diamond purchases, as many sellers have become quite expert valuers themselves.

But more importantly, the diamond trade gave local chiefs and politicians access to foreign exchange. If they held dealer licenses, they could buy diamonds with the leones collected from their exploitation of their official positions. They could then sell the diamonds abroad for hard currency and deposit the proceeds in foreign accounts. Under the old rules for diamond sales to DICOR, they would have received payment in non-convertible leones. Of course, transfers of money abroad required the approval of "gatekeepers." That is, the GDO (with Stevens and Jamil as heads) had to turn a blind eye to the non-repatriation of foreign exchange from reported sales. The holding of foreign bank accounts protected collaborators from having their money confiscated should they fall into disfavor, but it also dissuaded politicians and chiefs from using the financial rewards of political success for local productive investment or for projects that might attract an independent popular following.

Large dealer-exporters also shared directly in the management of the state-controlled diamond industry. Jamil and an associate, dealer and Freetown businessman Tony Yazbeck, both occupied NDMC management positions from 1977. While Jamil was one of the largest private exporters of diamonds in the country, he acted as managing director of

NDMC from 1979 to 1985. This dealer also joined President Stevens as co-director of GDO; he valued private diamond exports and oversaw the repatriation of hard currency from overseas sales. Thus private exporters exercised considerable control over informal NDMC cooperation with "private" plot production as well as providing private export financing and laborers.

Favored non-African dealers also found greater social acceptance among Kono's elite. One group, a "Hunting Society" organization claiming many local APC leaders and local officials as members, included a growing non-African contingent in its yearly photographs. This group contained no non-Africans in 1968. By 1989, a portrait of the membership, which includes local chiefs, reveals that about 25 percent of the membership was of non-African origin.[28] These social clubs, drawing membership from the local leadership, parallel well-defined lines of political authority.[29] Accordingly, they increasingly claim members from all aspects of the new collaborative relationship, both wealthy non-African businessmen and politicians. Such societies presented far less threat to the government's claim of unique authority than did miner societies organized around dealers who resisted official efforts to suppress illicit mining.

Miners were the immediate victims of these changes. After dealers sought direct accommodation with Freetown, the miners lost powerful business allies who had previously defended autonomous economic interests against state intrusion. Still worse for miners, both private plot-holders and Freetown were still anxious to limit mining that undermined collaborative market control or poached diamonds from newly privatized plots. Stevens continued to threaten non-Konos and uncooperative dealers with expulsion and deportation. Paramilitary forces from outside Kono enforced informal-market discipline; Jamil reputedly outfitted and maintained an "official" ISU detachment near Yengema, a mining area near the district capital.[30] A former Sefadu dealer noted that these men punished dealers and diggers operating outside the new network. He recalled that one such neighbor suffered a robbery. The "robbers" carried government-issued automatic weapons and used NDMC dynamite to blow open the metal shutters that dealers use to close up their houses at night.[31] As both diamond-buyers and politicians demanded greater dealer loyalty, miners would also lose opportunities to set up digging operations outside the control of the growing patrimonial network.[32]

Changes in the organization of the diamond market made it more apparent to Kono residents that powerful members of Kono society received expanding benefits from the new arrangements. This process also brought these members of Kono society into more direct dependence on Stevens's personal favor for individual gain. On the whole, Stevens's political network absorbed new members from the rival informal-market network that challenged the state monopoly over diamonds. These changes did not create any significant new opportunity for those customarily deprived of legal access to Kono's resources. The CCM scheme and the subsequent restructuring of the diamond market considerably disrupted the local commercial economy as well, resulting in a concentration of opportunity in the hands of commercial networks emanating from diamond-dealer collaborators at the expense of African entrepreneurs.

Fading political boundaries between formal and informal markets

Kono's district headquarters, Koidu/Sefadu is a regional market center. Both legal and illicit mining opportunities create demand for supplies and opportunities for local residents to participate in a cash economy. Retail businesses and services have long provided a legal outlet for the local investment of illicit mining proceeds, especially since commercial agriculture has remained the province of chiefs since the colonial era. Decaying roads, the closing of the railroad in 1976, and the halving of official producer prices for cocoa and coffee in the 1970s,[33] further reinforced local perceptions that retail trade offered one of the few commercial opportunities open to enterprising individuals.

While commercial opportunities initially attracted local entrepreneurs, this group felt the effects of increased commercial competition from relatives of favored Lebanese dealers. Said one African merchant of his experience of doing business in Koidu:

I came to Kono in 1966 from Kabala [in the north] after my brother. At first, I was unemployed, but my brother found work for me in Koquima [a mining village]. I was lucky and got enough money to begin trading, which I did from this shop from 1970. To do trading in this place is to really make money . . . I know that with the help of my brother, we could sell hardware and provisions.

Now, the biggest problem is credit. These big Lebanese guys go into the bank and get money for their friends. But a black man walks in there, nothing! After my mother's people came out here [in the 1970s], they help us with money they get from digging. The problem with us Sierra Leoneans is that we discriminate against ourselves. Anytime an outsider comes in, we immediately give everything to him.[34]

Other merchants have complained of similar reliance on informal credit arrangements and lack of access to banking services. As one former NDMC official pointed out, the prevalence of large customers at Koidu's banks results in irregular fees for services, reinforcing local perceptions of discrimination.[35]

African merchants complain that they are the victims of petty, but constant, "customary contributions" imposed by chiefdom administration from which non-Africans are by law immune. Gbense traders complained of organized irregular extortions. "Such 'courts,'" complained local traders, "operate in the big market areas and diamond mining areas as well, and pay Le 4.00 each daily to the Paramount Chief. We are at a loss to this gross violation of the rule of law and blatant misuse of power."[36] As CCM operations bound chiefs more closely to Freetown for favor, chiefs such as Toli translated the changing foundation for local authority into additional financial gain. This process undermined the formal legal limits that earlier colonial and SLPP governments had attempted to impose on chiefs to constrain their domination of local society. Other Gbense merchants complained:

Contrary to the Local Courts Act, 1963, the Paramount Chief maintains and runs separate "STAR CHAMBER COURTS" where he appoints relatives to adjudicate and impose fines on litigants without valid receipts, thereby depriving the legally constituted courts of much needed revenue. One of these courts in the Chief's compound pays Le600.00 to the Paramount chief monthly.[37]

The Freetown–chief accommodation fostered a steady erosion of direct control over rules governing Kono society. In a manner reminiscent of their capacity to build personal authority while acting as agents of the state under Indirect Rule policies to the 1930s and as participants in the bureaucratic expansion thereafter, chiefs claimed more "traditional" authority to interpret Freetown's rule over local society. These developments harmed African businessmen much more than non-Africans, since non-Africans enjoyed privileged access to the benefits of Stevens's Shadow State, while African entrepreneurs lost what little protection the bureaucratic institutions of the formal state had provided.

"Lebanese" (a Kono term for peoples of the Levant) entrepreneurs quickly translated their success in the diamond business into wider economic gains. Many African retailers suspect that Lebanese entrepreneurs receive better treatment since they can pay bribes when applying for licenses or undergoing any other of the multitude of bureaucratic procedures plaguing businesses in Sierra Leone. "Their people always pay for their own to get what they want," complained one African shop owner.[38] While accusations of payoffs often appear in explanations of rivals' business successes, Kono's tax records indicate that Lebanese-owned businesses contribute a large proportion of receipts. Lebanese entrepreneurs paid approximately 90 percent of Koidu/Sefadu tax receipts in 1987.[39] Lebanese businesses no doubt do bribe local officials, but they also provide virtually the only source of revenue to finance even minimal local government operations. Chiefs appropriate for themselves the revenue collected from chiefdom subjects. Ironically, this lack of social power to evade tax collection ensures that Lebanese traders remain far more "honest" in their dealings with local government – that is, they abide by formal regulations – than most Sierra Leoneans suppose.

Lebanese merchants also have incentives to cultivate local officials, especially since the existence of many Lebanese businesses directly violate popular expectations that government should support African enterprise. In any case, these non-African businesses represent a valuable source of personal benefits for local officials.[40] African merchants also suspect that Lebanese competitors cultivate official favor through connections with diamond-dealer relatives who provide additional payoffs for official tolerance of their kin's businesses. In this way, local officials receive additional indirect benefits from dealer–official collaboration in the diamond industry and therefore favor non-African businessmen over African businessmen, who do not offer the same benefits from accommodations with local officials.

The link between favor in Stevens's political network and commercial advantage becomes clearer as we look at the character of Lebanese enterprise in Kono and its connection to the diamond industry. As a young wholesaler of Lebanese origin explained:

When my brothers and cousins and I reached an age, we were given a considerable sum of money. It is ours to do with as we wish, but I began my business right here next to my cousin who helps me . . . It is difficult for these Africans because any time they get money, their relatives appear, asking for their own. But we help each other.[41]

He noted that his family's access to foreign exchange and business contacts outside the country greatly aided him in importing cloth dyes from a German firm and selling them at a price that no African competitor could match. Others note that this family cooperation and access to foreign exchange are crucial elements of Lebanese business success in Sierra Leone, especially the tradition of family support for young entrepreneurs.[42]

Combined with the new Lebanese position in Stevens's political hierarchy, this custom shaped Kono's business class. Stevens's intrusion into diamond mining coincided with the start of the Lebanese civil war, which brought large-scale Lebanese immigration to Sierra Leonean relatives. The country's Lebanese population had risen by 230 percent to 13,000 by the early 1980s,[43] providing Freetown officials with additional income from the sale of visas. Kono's Lebanese community grew by about the same percentage from 1967 to 1985, indicating the high level of opportunity for Lebanese residents there. Many of these new immigrants entered Kono's retail trades with the help of family financial support.

By the mid-1980s, Lebanese dealers' prosperity and immigration had substantially altered the distribution of non-mining commercial oppor-

Table 5.3. *Ethnic representation in fixed location Kono business establishments, 1966 and 1989*

	1966		1989	
	Afr. %	non-Afr.	Afr. %	non-Afr.
Tailors	176 (95)	9	162 (100)	0
Furniture mfg.	1 (50)	1	3 (100)	0
Furniture sales	1 (100)	0	1 (33)	2
Electric repair	2 (100)	0	3 (100)	0
Mechanics	4 (100)	0	4 (80)	1
Barber/Beauty	3 (100)	0	3 (75)	1
Restaurant	1 (100)	0	10 (92)	2
Wholesale	1 (20)	4	1 (7)	15
Grocery	0 (0)	1	0 (0)	5
Pharmacy	0 (0)	1	1 (50)	2
Dry goods	11 (35)	20	4 (11)	35
Hardware	1 (50)	1	0 (0)	5
Photo Studio	3 (75)	1	0 (0)	3

Source: Data for 1966 are from Central Statistics Office, *A Survey of Sierra Leone Businesses* (Freetown: Government Printer, 1967). Data for 1989 are from informant tallies. Figures for tailors for 1989 supplied in a survey by United Indigenous Commercial and Petty Traders Association, Freetown.

tunity in Kono (Table 5.3). Despite official pronouncements promising business opportunities for Africans, Kono's Lebanese community dominated commerce at the same time that Lebanese dealers enjoyed a more favored position in the diamond industry. Indeed, official prohibitions against "stranger" ownership of Kono land may have further directed Lebanese tendencies to trade rather than invest in property.

The sectoral distribution of Lebanese enterprise in Kono also indicates that these businesses took advantage of their greater access to capital and understandings with officials. The largest increases in Lebanese ownership occurred in businesses requiring foreign exchange for imports, while African ownership remained strongest in services. Data in Table 5.3 no doubt underestimate the segregation of Africans to low-capital enterprises, since much African business activity takes place outside the recorded formal sector. Much of this involves "petty trading," or the resale of inexpensive goods. Most of these traders are totally reliant upon local Lebanese wholesalers and larger retailers for supplies and credit, further reinforcing Lebanese commercial and, by extension, Stevens's personal influence in Kono.

The distribution of opportunity following the start of systematic state–

dealer cooperation in the diamond industry disproportionately favored collaborating officials and the largest diamond dealers. The distribution of the benefits of cooperation outside the diamond industry itself also drew new groups and activities into the expanded elite accommodation. For the local Kono resident, cooperation between Lebanese and state officials at all levels confirms suspicions that, in the words of one NDMC employee, "Our leaders are not interested in this place as a country. Look at the Pajeros.* How can we survive when everything is given to the Lebanese to run while these blatant frauds live off the proceeds?"[44] Auto registration in Kono supports this perception. As of 1988, 71 percent of all cars in Kono were registered under Lebanese names.[45] Autos remain a potent symbol of social divisions – interpreted in ethnic terms – in Kono. As one businessman explained, "I only drive this small Japanese car because you see after the football matches that it is the Mercedes Benz that they burn."[46] These perceptions of social divisions continue to shape Kono politics.

Local officials in the new elite accommodation

Patrimonial cooperation effectively tied formal and informal diamond production to State House interests. Economic competition still shaped local factional politics in both the succession of chiefs and single-party/ multicandidate elections. However, these events now served as "gateways" of access to Kono's resources under the control of Stevens and Lebanese exporters.[47] Membership, or the promise of membership in Stevens's network quelled political entrepreneur challenges, even as some candidates still used populist rhetoric to appeal to voters. Even for those without privileged access, the scarcity of opportunities outside Stevens's network forced the less privileged to scramble for favor.

Enlarging the elite accommodation's grip on resources did not resolve social grievances. Popular resentment and resistance to state intrusion confronted elected local officials. Quite low incumbency return rates subjected client politicians to considerable insecurity. But Stevens's preference for a single-party framework ensured that no candidates totally unacceptable to State House would stand for election, though voters were still presented with choices. Voters in Kono's 1973 parliamentary elections returned no incumbents; 1977 saw a 50 percent return rate. Again in 1982, no incumbents were reelected, and the last elections in 1986 returned 42 percent.[48] Consequently, local political competition for state-regulated access to newly "privatized" resources incorporated factional struggles into

* Four-wheel-drive Mitsubishi Pajeros are replacing Mercedes Benzes in Sierra Leone as prestige cars due to deteriorating road conditions.

the political network, rendering political competition less threatening to the regime's survival. Stevens used factional struggle to gain popular support to control his clients' activities; rival factions sought his favor as gatekeeper of resources. Use of both parliamentary and chieftain elections (by councillors) as access points to the resources of state office gave Stevens both the appearance of promoting public accountability and the benefit of a level of insecurity for incumbents that limited opportunities for them to establish autonomous political bases among constituents. This control flowed from Stevens's monopoly over access to resources and his supplicants' dearth of alternatives. A second look at Kono's factional struggles shows how former rivals' appeals came to reinforce the patrimonial network rather than undermine it.

Tankoro's politics illustrate the transformation of Kono's factional politics in the new context of Shadow State domination of economic opportunity. Recall that Tankoro was the scene of Stevens's earlier retreat and acceptance of a locally popular chief in 1971. Upon this chief's death in 1981, his younger brother stood before chiefdom electors. As a member of Sierra Leone's diplomatic corps, this claimant, F.J. Quee, had established considerable contacts within the APC government. Indeed, by 1981, he ran an export enterprise in partnership with the Secretary of the Eastern Province. This associate conducted the election. If victorious, Quee stood to inherit his brother's mining operations as well as dealer licenses. No doubt Quee's business associate stood to benefit from his friend's probable access to Kono's diamonds, and hence, foreign exchange.

Quee needed the Provincial Secretary to head off his prosecution in the politically motivated "Vouchergate" corruption investigation directed against Stevens's rivals and wayward clients.[49] Despite Quee's legal troubles, the Provincial Secretary held the election, which his associate Quee won. The Provincial Secretary pointed out to State House that "recognizing him as the present Natural Ruler of Tankoro Chiefdom will in my view help to minimize the serious nature of the charges he is now facing."[50] Meanwhile, the incumbent parliamentary representative and APC activist, S.H.O. Gborie, also under the shadow of a "Vouchergate" investigation, desperately needed local allies to aid his campaign. He thus sponsored the Kono Central APC Chair, a man eligible for Tankoro's chiefdom succession, in an effort to "forestall what our Party's supporters can only view with disgust!"[51] Quee, who was popularly perceived as unpretentious and "sticking up for the common man" had already made known his intention to support John Kamanda, a populist campaigner seeking Gborie's parliamentary seat.

State House's response to the Provincial Secretary's unauthorized action in Quee's support in this local factional battle led to the nullification of

Quee's election.[52] Stevens ordered that another APC organizer from outside Kono serve as regent chief, instead of Gborie's choice. Stevens appears to have used this appointment to reward the relative of an APC organizer in Kenema District with access to Tankoro's diamonds. This man wasted no time in applying for a dealer's license. The Ministry of Mines obliged, and he had a license in hand ten days after assuming office. The Provincial Secretary (now also under "Vouchergate" investigation) reheld the election. His business partner, Quee, was again elected. Now Stevens himself traveled to Kono to personally manage the situation. The former Provincial Secretary claims that Stevens intended to depose Quee again.[53] But in the words of one resident, "before he could say a word, we said 'we want our own chief' and from that time Stevens recognized him as chief."[54] Stevens turned his inability to eliminate Quee into the act of a benevolent patron, recognizing Quee to underline his leading role in dispensing munificent favor. For those believing that Stevens exercised control over the situation, the victory of the "maverick" warned other politicians of the insecurity of their own positions, including that of the government official who supported the initial State-House choice. In this way, the leader appeared as a defender of popular interests and underlined his position as ultimate arbiter of state intrusion into local affairs.

Even though the "populist" Quee assumed his brother's mining operation and currently serves on the board of directors of NDMC, he maintains wide popularity for his avoidance of excessive displays of wealth and apparent efforts to control irregular extractions from subjects. But unlike a decade earlier, this "populist" chief poses little threat of undermining Freetown's control in Kono. While Quee's private accommodation with the Provincial Secretary annoyed Stevens, it did not threaten his overall political security. Politics, while still played on a public stage, gained an order defined by access to informal market opportunities under the firm control of the leader. But this arrangement did not extend the same security to Stevens's clients. Quee's victory was far more menacing for Gborie – a Kono parliamentary representative backing the "wrong" candidate and, by extension, his own access to state resources.

Gborie thereafter looked to other quarters to gain local support crucial for his own continued access to wealth. Being under investigation for corruption (along with three other Kono MPs), Gborie sought the support of Gbense Chief Toli, Stevens's favorite, against "those new A.P.C. members whose association with the Party can best be measured with a yard stick,"[55] that is, newcomers to the APC coalition. Clearly Kono's APC "old guard" felt threatened. This factional struggle threatened Toli as well. Gborie's challenger was John Kamanda, the grandson of Toli's deposed predecessor, Kaimachende. Kamanda's campaign focused on Toli's abuses of power under Gborie's protection, and recalled easier illicit miner access to diamonds under his grandfather.[56] Kamanda's campaign adopted a populist rhetoric that had characterized challengers in the past. Even for political challengers, the APC label and loyalty to Stevens offered financial reward in an environment of scarce opportunity. But from Toli's perspective, a victory by the "rival faction" would limit his access to resources. Toli took matters into his own hands: he shot three of Kamanda's supporters, including Kaimachende, the deposed strongman whom Toli had replaced in 1970.[57] The shooting angered "pro-miner" forces who were opposed to Toli because of his abuses of power and great wealth; to these objections were now added his attacks on a candidate who was voicing popular dissatisfaction over dwindling economic opportunities. Organized mobs looted and burned the chief's two houses and fields after his arrest, and ensured that Gborie lost in the election. Meanwhile, "in the interests of peace and security" Freetown recommended one of Toli's associates for the regency.[58] The Provincial Secretary again moved to install his own choice, this time the "pro-miner" nephew of the deposed Kaimachende, a move that did not now threaten State House.[59]

S.H. Gborie's reaction was considerably less sanguine:

The purport of my letter concerns ... the appointment of the arch traitor Sahr Manyi Gborie as the Regent Chief. Of the fourteen chiefs of Kono, only P.C. Thorlie [Toli] gave me his unflinching support during and after Elections in Kono Central Constituency. Long before said election, there had in fact been a clandestine move to get P.C. Thorlie out of power. On the return of the tyrannic Resident Minister, who totally hates anything A.P.C .... all my supporters were rounded up in a determined effort to rid me of victory at the polls.[60]

The "old-line APC" faction's defeat had additional local implications. Toli was attacked on his way to court and continuing violence required army intervention. While in his prison cell, local police subjected Toli to tear-gassing, and looters continued attacking his ill-gotten property.[61] Stevens pardoned his old ally six months later and returned him to office. Thus while Kamanda occupied the parliamentary seat, a leader of a rival faction continued as head of the chiefdom.

Did Kamanda's victory threaten Stevens's strategy of central control through new intermediaries? Initially, Kono residents presumed that Kamanda favored greater popular access to Kono's resources. However, Kamanda's position in the mining industry vied with constituent service for his attentions. As a member of NDMC's board of directors, Kamanda obliged when Jamil and CCM operators demanded evictions of illicit miners in 1984–5. "Kamanda was our favourite," recalls a Kono student, "but with all these attacks while in office, he lost the confidence of miners."[62] Kamanda's loyalty to NDMC found its own rewards, however.

He became Managing Director of NDMC upon Jamil's departure in 1985. But having lost voter support, Kamanda was defeated in the 1986 election and Gborie regained his seat, while Kamanda retained his NDMC seat. Such was the Shadow State's economic domination of Kono that Stevens could tie political competition to support this new political formation.

Resistance to the Shadow State

Meanwhile, the APC's turn from its populism inflamed Kono sentiments. Stevens's accommodations excluded most people as he regulated unofficial accommodations between those illicit diamond dealers and state officials who had in the past resisted state intervention in mining. Stevens's control was effective enough to render the grandson of former APC foe Kaima-chende dependent upon Stevens's favor to compete in the 1982 election. John Kamanda's populist campaign rhetoric became a tool for gaining access to the resources of office and the private benefits of the political network. Popular acceptance of competitive elections appeared to force candidates to be accountable. Defeat of the unpopular incumbent appeared to permit access to privileged circles. Elections also provided Stevens with leverage over local collaborators. Nominations within the framework of the APC, selective prosecutions of officials for corruption, and finally, elections attracting numerous contenders for each office allowed Stevens to exercise even greater control over the "gateway" of access to benefits. At the same time, a voter turnout of 78 percent in the 1986 election indicated that elections were widely accepted as a means of punishing wayward incumbents.

But growing popular inaccessibility to wealth also drove people to search for alternative means of survival, which sometimes confronted constraints that state officials and the informal political network imposed upon them. John Kamanda's "defection" from his promise to defend local interests against Freetown's intrusions enraged many miners. Kamanda's NDMC position and acquiescence to renewed "stranger drives" against illicit miners highlighted to many Kono voters his collaboration with elites. Popular dissatisfaction led to riots in 1984 and 1985, resulting in the destruction of property belonging to Kamanda, other politicians, and the state.

Said a former miner, "disturbances provided an opportunity for the people to educate their leaders."[63] Kamanda's reliance on Jamil's local paramilitary force for protection also provided a visible display of the close collaboration between politicians and the seemingly more powerful non-African dealers. This violence, however, reinforced the political network's control over political competition. Kamanda's opponent in 1986, the APC stalwart Gborie, campaigned against Kamanda's close relations with non-Kono "stranger" miners intent on looting Kono of its riches. In the words of a retired administrator:

Gborie could not attack that "sacred cow" of politicians in business as the cause of Kono's problems. Instead, he pointed to what everyone can see – these wealthy outsiders who come in and take diamonds away from our people. By shifting attention outward, he avoided directing anger in an unhappy direction ... We are lucky to be in a position of such political openness. It is only by speaking our minds in this way that tensions are reduced.[64]

Indeed, Gborie's appeals left him relatively immune from riots in 1988 which destroyed several dealers' cars. Disturbances again in 1989 forced these junior beneficiaries of collaboration to retreat behind metal shutters. This later incident also demonstrated that the network could manage even spontaneous violence. After the 1989 riots, a Freetown newspaper owned by Jamil and a business associate, the current Speaker of Parliament, attributed much of Kono's economic difficulties to "Gambian traders who come to our country to take away our products which are all in great demand abroad."[65]

State officials and dealers could not regulate all violence, however. For example, 1989 agricultural development funds were to be "pumped through District Councils," but in reality went to the chiefs; District Councils had been dismantled in 1972 by a State House fearing the programs of grassroots APC organizers in some areas. (As potential sites of criticism, District Councils were incompatible with Stevens's strategy of political control founded upon controlled competition.) Popular reaction to this latest chief appropriation of money resulted in the burning of two chiefs' farms. Explained one Kono resident, "during this dry season, his farm will be very flammable."[66] However, security forces limited this spontaneous violence.

Even the intrusion of security forces offer common people an opportunity for collaboration. Membership on a dealer's or the NDMC force is a coveted position. This job offers the usual benefits of extractions from roadblocks or checks for the identity papers that all non-Konos must carry as proof of official residency in the diamond-mining area. But more significant for security personnel is the opportunity to engage in illicit mining. Diggers' pits ring the NDMC security force compound near the village of Koquima to the extent that they are undermining the buildings. Local villagers complain that the pits are so numerous that they pose a serious health hazard as mosquito breeding-grounds. Residents also resent mining syndicates' invasion of farmland and village sites for the private pursuit of minerals.

Even continued illicit mining outside the regulated framework of CCM and large-dealer control reinforces selective dependence on the patrimonial network. Disgruntled Kono residents, and even security forces, find that they must sell diamonds to available dealers, lest they suffer the more vigorous anti-smuggling efforts directed toward those who attempt to operate outside the network of the controlled private market. Stevens's expansion of his political network even required that legal–illegal distinctions should become contingent upon the network's need for resources. Inherited colonial institutional boundaries of legality become one more manipulable resource – and one that makes few demands on the shrinking treasury – that the leader, as head of state, possesses by virtue of his office. The network's sales of diamonds abroad generate even greater access to foreign exchange for the network's leaders. Meanwhile, illicit miners are paid in leones.

The monopoly of opportunity also shapes the context of customary forms of resistance, limiting mobility and constraining exit. This lack of alternatives creates an explosive situation in which subjects occasionally assert what they perceive to be their just access to resources. As long as the monopoly of resources exists, in the long-term all seek meager collaborations with elite networks for subsistence. Most of these activities put people in a position of obligation to some aspect of the network's authority.[67] As all seek access, even while they recognize and condemn elite privilege, independent political activity remains difficult to organize. Social categories such as illicit miner, security officer, rich merchant, or frustrated entrepreneur become defined in terms of one's level of access to the Shadow State.

Widening social divisions, however, pose growing dangers of creating a political space of resistance over which rulers have little control. Some activities remain immune from direct government control. For example, an APC organizer disappeared at the start of the 1991 election campaign in Lower Bambara chiefdom. Local residents explain to officials such happenings as the result of sorcery aimed at bad individuals.[68] But this campaign activity "from below" allows local residents to remove unwanted intruders in a manner that outsiders find quite threatening. Defendants in such cases often admit that the ritual activities are meant to influence the choice of successors to government posts.[69] Freetown answers this challenge with a vigor and publicity not given to other criminal charges, but often the perpetrators are exceedingly difficult to find.

Despite the progressive loss of opportunity, exit short of physical departure remains virtually impossible. Some unemployed youths organize "alternative societies" in the wooded hills surrounding Kono's diamond-mining area. Named after popular films (e.g. "Delta Force," "Terminator"), societies protect members' illicit activities, raid politicians' private plots, and occasionally sell protection to smaller dealers. However, even "Delta Force" members market their ill-gotten diamonds through the regulated dealer network. Even these "resisters" contribute to politicians' access to the foreign exchange derived from sales of diamonds abroad. Meanwhile, they dig illicitly without large scale dealer logistical support and suffer private plot owners' efforts to limit poaching.

To the extent that Kono residents believe that they share the illicit miners' troubles (or suffer from disruptive network interventions), this further highlights the perceived privilege of non-African dealers. These dealers remain immune from state sanctions on Africans in elections or factional struggles, and apparently even benefit from the politicians' struggles to retain access. To most Sierra Leoneans, favored non-Africans who form the basis of state incorporation of the informal market receive the network's protection while reaping the rewards of association. This perception of blatant favoritism has proved to be most difficult for Freetown to control, particularly as people associate it with their own lack of opportunity.

This breakdown of institutional barriers to massive state intrusion into society ensured Stevens's control over access to opportunity. Alterations of popularly accepted colonial inheritances such as elections had appeared to dispense justice to venal officials. At the same time, the patrimonial uses of elections and the material wealth available to its victors and their offices became potent reference points for factional strife and popular demands for justice. A more rigid and controlled hierarchy has emerged, able at least to appear to institutionalize its own personalistic vision of authority on society.[70] Stevens's rational pursuit of political control and regime survival did *not* cause him to strengthen bureaucratic institutions indicative of a "strong state," even though diamond wealth and a potentially dynamic entrepreneur class made this option possible in a purely fiscal context. Increases in wealth where no broad consensus exists over the appropriate contours of the political authority, or even over the definition of the boundaries of political community, did not lead to a "strong state" in this case. In fact, it further undermined the hand-me-down colonial state.

Violence and the Shadow State

Stevens's construction of a Shadow State draws attention to the particular nature of state–society relations upon which his authority in Sierra Leone rested. The monopoly of opportunity incorporated non-African-dealer access to the world market for diamonds and foreign exchange. This accommodation between private enterprise and political authority in order to exert political control resembled officials' informal pre-colonial and colonial accommodations with "strangers." First pre-colonial war chiefs, then colonial officials and collaborative chiefs sought outsiders' help in gaining access to the benefits of trade with the wider world economy in order to meet local challenges to their political authority. Local authorities then translated the rewards of trade into political power through regulating subjects' access to its benefits.

A Kono resident's recent criticism of politicians reveals much about the popular interpretation of the contemporary form of this relationship: "It is too easy for any outsider to come to our country and do as he pleases. Politicians always assume that the outsider has something for them, and that their own people have nothing that they can offer . . . They believe that they can make money with the foreigner and nobody else."[71] Conversations during long distance car travel in Sierra Leone produce similar lamentations. Many people point to their leaders' "lack of trust," or "hatred of anything Sierra Leonean" to explain the country's economic crisis and politicians' pursuit of their own interests within the political hierarchy. These complaints recall earlier criticisms of a "landlord–tenant" relation between chiefs and traders: "You have stopped us from coming ourselves to the factories of the whiteman . . . Large sums of money are lent to you, but, through your persuasions, we are thought unworthy to be trusted. In fact, by a combination between you and the white people, the whole trade of the country is driven into your hands."[72]

Persisting popular critiques of privilege point to the patrimonial network's primary weakness. Rulers long benefited from outsiders' abilities to exploit links between the world economy and the local economy in return for official favor. But official control over access to the fruits of collaboration does not leave these elite alliances with many defenses against popular approbation over the naked preference rulers show for strangers. Since Lebanese dealers were not limited by the same insecurities of politician clients, they pursued their economic interests in a more stable setting. Like their British predecessors, rulers gave up some of their claim to completely control society in return for collaboration in the search for resources necessary to rule. Accordingly, rulers risk creating strongmen, whether indigenous or stranger, who are capable of pursuing independent interests and are not bound by the same rules as local society.

Yet rulers still pursue their project of dominating access to resources as a means of maintaining social control as cheaply and efficiently as possible. But there is a danger that, as the network becomes more dependent upon their services, "official" business partners will identify a commercial interest above the concerns of maintaining their network positions. This possibility creates major challenges to the Shadow State's exclusive control of access to wealth. These potentially unruly associates, the network's growing costs, popular unrest, and demands for basic amenities create pressures to turn to foreign creditors for additional resources. But creditors will demand reforms designed to dismantle the Shadow State as a requirement for loans, introducing once again the "strong state" option.

Ironically, creditor demands caused Stevens to intensify his dependence on Lebanese dealers in order to attract creditor support while at the same time weathering their demands. Again external insistence on a bureaucratic "strong state" devised outside the context of Stevens's struggle for authority promoted the opposite outcome. As the next chapter shows, Stevens instead further institutionalized his alternative Shadow State with the help of Lebanese and creditor resources and connections.

6   The Shadow State and international commerce

> Why do we prosper? In this place, government and traders work as a team.
>
> Government official, Koindu, on the Guinea border[1]

> Those traders who live here can play politics . . . Those traders support all aspirants. They have great respect for authority and get rich by it.
>
> Koindu trader[2]

Stevens exploited divisions in Kono society to selectively incorporate individuals. This meant that many suffered from the uneven enforcement of laws and the weakening of state institutions that did not serve the leader's interests.[3] Social and market organizations remained precariously tied to Stevens's favor in this uncertain environment. In the Kono case, we saw how Stevens used control over resources and local officials to build and maintain control over Kono society. Stevens pursued control and survival amidst conditions of scarcity and political challenge, which pushed him to move farther from "legal-rational" notions of rigid boundaries of state and society power.

Stevens's elite coalition dominance created the context in which subjects found themselves as patrons, clients, members of the presidential clique, or as collaborators. As the network expanded, where one sat politically increasingly determined one's economic status. This *englobement* also absorbed social relations and interests that were partly an inheritance of membership within previously incorporated social groups. The role of Lebanese dealers in Stevens's network reflected this joining of market and social networks to the service of his elite accommodation. But control over private diamond mining was not sufficient to finance the expanding needs of the elite accommodation. Not only were informal market activities earlier "unexploited" from a State-House perspective, but the formal state of Sierra Leone faced external pressures to fulfill official obligations, especially to service loans.

This chapter investigates Stevens's Shadow State strategies for overcoming these internal, and growing external challenges. Through Lebanese dealer mediation, Stevens linked his Shadow State political network and the still significant sovereign powers of the decaying institutional state. Stevens affected a commitment to market reforms to secure grants and loans that further freed him from dependence on bureaucratic institutions. He also discovered that he could manipulate creditors' conditions to produce more Shadow State resources.[4] While it was not their intention, creditors provided resources that permitted Stevens to move father from the "strong state" project of creating effective bureaucracies and an efficient, taxable economy to finance them. Creditor conditions for loans also introduced Stevens to foreign firms that could provide even more resources in return for services that Stevens's flexible application of law and force could provide.

Stevens's political challenges were formidable, however. Bureaucratic collapse left the formal state incapable of protecting citizens and reigning in predatory elites. Local politics therefore focused more on citizens' efforts to find personal security. Given these conditions, political entrepreneurs with access to diamond wealth could possibly align themselves with disgruntled Kono residents and with disaffected losers from past local power struggles at the expense of Stevens's authority.[5] Thus Stevens faced his own revenue imperative of finding resources to maintain his political network in a manner that allowed him to remain as sole arbiter of their distribution. Ironically, Stevens addressed these pressures with greater reliance on Lebanese middlemen and reluctant creditors who became new financial sources. Yet creditors – who were vital for avoiding total reliance on Lebanese businessmen – demanded a minimally functioning formal economy, the suppression of informal markets, and a state capacity to collect and deliver arrears payments.

This apparent contradiction in fact prompted Stevens to choose intentionally to further weaken bureaucratic state capacity. Stevens concluded that he needed new allies for his elite alliance to raise more revenues in the Shadow State so as to meet formal state obligations to creditors. Creditors condemned what they viewed as irresponsible behavior. On the other hand, as the legally recognized government of Sierra Leone came to mean less and less in the exercise of power in the country, creditors anxious to collect arrears payments found themselves forced to decide how they would deal with the network that was engulfing the old colonial state. From below, this struggle brought an acceleration of the Shadow State's invasion of everyday life. Citizens bore the brunt of creditors' austerity plans as well as the humiliation of seeing more foreigners join Stevens in the exploitation of what, at independence, had almost appeared to be their country. It is little wonder that Konos began referring to these developments as "Black Colonialism."

The crisis of Shadow State capacity

Lebanese dealers protected the Shadow State's resource base from domestic competition and kept wealth out of the hands of political entrepreneurs who could have used it to give voice to popular anger. Yazbeck and particularly Jamil, provided Stevens with extensive business contacts in Lebanon and elsewhere which dated from unsanctioned illicit trading before 1973, when they had sought overseas banking services to finance their illegal activities. These existing contacts proved useful to politician partners after 1973 as they searched for ways to finance private diamond exports outside DeBeers' CSO. Barclays Bank's Freetown office, a major underwriter of diamond exports, refused credit to dealers or politicians who circumvented the government's contracts with DeBeers's Sierra Leone subsidiary. State House also recognized that as other foreign bankers became aware of the extent of officials' involvement in private mining, they too would shy away from these operations. Stevens and his advisors also believed that the decline of available credits was linked to DeBeers's pressure to frustrate their private mining operations.[6]

Jamil procured credit through Beirut's Byblos Bank to finance private buying and export operations for his politician partners. As head of the pre-1973 hierarchy of dealers, he was already using the services of Lebanese banks to finance illicit exports. By 1976, he held a 12 percent share in Byblos Bank. He also held a 15 percent share in the Jammal Bank, also of Lebanon. Beirut's Intra Bank established a Freetown branch in 1977 through diamond dealers Nabil Bamieh and Edward Aboud, but the Lebanon office closed the branch when it suspected that their Freetown managers were siphoning off profits. In 1984, Jamil established his own banking operation in Freetown, International Bank of Trade and Industry, in cooperation with Byblos Bank and Bank of Credit and Commerce International to directly handle private export financing. These banking houses on the periphery of international financial markets took advantage of opportunities where other banks hesitated to disobey industry norms prohibiting lending to operations considered to be illicit.[7] Sierra Leone's diamond dealers were the crucial link bringing together capital willing to finance patrimonial expenditures, necessary collateral, and a leadership seeking to bring additional resources under its control.

Lebanese business intermediation enabled Stevens to monopolize more thoroughly the diamond trade and control the distribution of opportunity to his favorites. The president's centrality in the state and the Shadow State network was reflected in Stevens's tendency to rotate administrative assignments. Ministerial rosters in 1967 showed that the average cabinet member had held his job for just under three years. By 1973, average office tenure had fallen to twenty-five months. In 1983, it stood at nineteen months. One fairly typical political ally served as Minister of Transport (twice), Works (twice), Trade, Information, and as Attorney General. Favored officials could use state offices to gain access to Shadow State benefits, an opportunity they owed to Stevens. But job insecurity ensured that they became neither effective in their jobs nor politically tied to some grateful constituency. Above all, tenure required loyalty. Under such conditions, bureaucratic institutions became even less likely to serve as agents of development or as generators of revenue.

Frequent widely publicized corruption investigations ensured that clients understood that the president could take away what he gave. Once out of office, politicians struggled to convince their patron of their loyalty. One disgraced official wrote while undergoing interrogation during an investigation into corruption: "I cannot reduce to writing my sincere gratitude to You and beg that You continue the manifest interest that You have always exhibited towards me in particular."[8] Stevens did exhibit munificence. The official returned to high office and became a prosperous Kono diamond dealer. In this manner, state power and bureaucratic hierarchies were absorbed into a personal network emanating from the person of the president. The rules of this relationship did not allow officials to develop institutional perspectives that led to effective policy implementation.

Yet obedience to Stevens depended upon his ability to bind elements of his political power-base together by bonds stronger than simple offers of reward. Since state institutions produced little of the opportunity or stability that citizens expected, politics in the old manner of mass mobilization was not an attractive option. Stevens thus needed expensive security forces to enforce presidential edicts, a basic level of services to keep quiescent the overwhelming majority of subjects not receiving direct benefits, and to convince clients of his capacity to enforce discipline. This last imperative was important, since only a monopoly over the use of force permitted Stevens to continue labeling unsanctioned economic activity as "crime." Failure here would court disaster, since unruly clients would otherwise raise private armies and recruit followers along the lines of economic and social conflict on which Stevens's network was built.

But while weakened state institutions served Stevens's political network, privatized mining by politicians sapped formal state revenue capacity. Providing up to 70 percent of revenues in 1970, private diamond sales to government fell by 50 percent and NDMC production fell 90 percent in the decade up to 1984.[9] More production took place outside the formal economy. Despite this revenue drain, the president still needed state resources to sustain a loyal following and incorporate new clients. Diverse

Table 6.1. *Budget deficits, 1976/77–1985/86*

	revenue (million Le)	expenditure (million Le)	deficit (% rev)
1976/77	118.6	169.9	43.3
1977/78	160.7	249.1	55.0
1978/79	171.5	308.2	79.7
1979/80	193.3	327.7	69.5
1980/81	220.6	351.6	59.4
1981/82	266.3	407.9	53.2
1982/83	181.5	352.5	71.5
1983/84	155.7	415.8	167.7
1984/85	228.9	450.9	97.4
1985/86	286.2	578.2	98.0

Source: International Monetary Fund, *Balance of Payments Statistics Yearbook* (Washington, DC: IMF, 1990).

clients relied upon Stevens's discretionary, non-budgeted spending. These expenditures reached 60 percent of operating budgets by 1979 and climbed even higher in the 1980s. Discretionary spending reached ten times planned capital spending by the late 1970s.[10] Consequently, Freetown faced severe revenue shortfalls (Table 6.1). In real terms, 1985/86 domestic revenue collection stood at 18 percent of 1977/78 figures. Real revenues fell through the 1970s. Illicit diamond profits supported other non-taxed activities such as smuggling, which further diminished state revenues. Income-tax collections virtually ceased. In 1980, the Minister of Finance complained that the country's businesses had paid only Le 1.7 million out of over Le 100 million in assessed taxes since 1971.[11] The collapse of state services accelerated. By 1984, development outlays stood at only 3 percent of the overall budget.

At first, Stevens made little effort to accommodate foreign firms that had earlier provided such a large portion of state revenues. Collapsing services and competition from the "official" private economy caused direct foreign investment to drop from $102.7 million in 1974/78 to $-26.9 million in 1979/83.[12] Old European agricultural marketing firms such as CFAO and P&Z left Freetown. New investors in light industry such as Bata Shoes departed as the infrastructure decayed and official corruption ate up profits. By 1983 with the export sector of the formal economy in full retreat, Freetown still depended on vulnerable customs tariffs for 55 percent of its revenues.[13]

Even though departing foreign companies had removed foreign competition from the economy, Stevens's threats of prosecution and confiscations prevented most politicians from setting up their own businesses. Indigenous businessmen without political connections especially felt economic uncertainty and official harassment. Wealth remaining in the country often ended up in "safe" real-estate investments.[14] City tax records indicate a nearly 300 percent increase in the real assessed value of real estate from 1977 to 1987 in Freetown's exclusive West III constituency, home to many among the country's elite.[15]

International commerce and Shadow State resources

Amidst horrendous budget deficits and collapsing revenue capacity, cooperation with Lebanese businessmen in areas beyond the diamond industry offered Stevens the most promising way of sustaining his political network. Lebanese businessmen-dealers, particularly the two most prominent, Jamil and Yazbeck, offered Stevens a solution. Utilizing overseas contacts, these men procured private loans for Freetown. When this source of revenue proved insufficient by 1979, these Lebanese businessmen provided crucial services in adapting IMF demands for economic and administrative reform to the requirements of his elite accommodation. We can clearly see outlines of the "landlord–tenant" politics of the pre-colonial era, superimposed on Stevens's claim to a monopoly of authority. But within the intensifying symbiotic relation of politicians and businessmen, could wealthier Lebanese businessmen and politician partners become powerful enough to challenge or influence Stevens's political authority for their own benefit?

Lebanese businessmen-dealers procured "supplier" loans to cover revenue shortfalls that allowed the president to continue massive discretionary spending. These private creditors, among them the Beirut Banks who were financing diamond exports, accepted illicit diamond exports as collateral. These loans carried no apparent conditions regarding their use, so formal state-guaranteed loans could then be utilized for political purposes. These creditors also charged high interest rates: 9.2 percent in 1979, a rate considerably above the 1.2 percent that Sierra Leone paid for concessionary loans.[16] These loans covered a considerable portion of the growing gap between official revenues and expenditures. Yearly private credits increased from SDR 9.2 million in 1976 to SDR 80.5 million in 1980 and financed about half of the budget deficit through the latter half of the 1970s.[17]

Loan procurement tied the Lebanese business network and the Shadow State more closely to one another (Table 6.2). Private dealers' management of the diamond industry, coupled with their overseas contacts, enabled them to negotiate, and in some cases, provide collateral for official loans. These loans enabled Stevens to continue his discretionary spending of the new state resources unhindered. This spending drew Lebanese dealers further into Stevens's network as they not only arranged the finance for patrimonial projects, but also for projects under contract – including

Table 6.2. *Some supplier loans to Sierra Leone*

MF 18/21 (1977)	"Request for a £1.5m loan from Byblos Bank, Beirut, Lebanon." Jamil held a 12% share of this bank.
MF 5/82 (1977)	"Proposal of Financial Group in Gazimagusa (North Cyprus) Regarding a Loan of US $25 m to GSL." (Connections with Jamil via Byblos Bank.)
MF 1/3/22 (1978)	"Proposed Long-term Loan from Rachid I. Saghyeh & Co., Beirut, Lebanon (£2.5m)."
MF 5/90 (1978)	"Offer of Loan by Assad Yazbeck & Sons, Ltd., US $3m." (Local Lebanese businessmen.)

Source: All from Ministry of Finance, "Closed File" folder 5.

providing armed security for Shadow State enterprises – as formal institutions continued to decay.

Lebanese businessmen from this financial network also organized joint ventures with foreigners to the advantage of themselves and foreign contractors. Politicians acted as partners in these deals, partly as political insurance for dealers, extending the resource base of Stevens's political network. Lebanese mediation and "supplier" loans underwrote these politically motivated, but largely non-productive projects. For example, Yazbeck secured financing, imported materials and enlisted contractors to build a $17 million police barracks in the late 1970s. He made similar arrangements to build a $20 million resort hotel. Jamil arranged for a $7.5 million loan to purchase vehicles from Fiat for officials and a $10 million Fokker 614 aircraft for Sierra Leone Airways (of which he would soon become Managing Director).[18]

Supplier loans installed Lebanese businessmen and the flow of diamond resources at the heart of the operation of the elite accommodation. Disbursements of "supplier" loans rose 870 percent from 1976 to SDR 80.5 million in 1980.[19] But private loans offered no long-term solution to the president's revenue problem. Freetown faced an SDR 36.7 million finance and arrears charge to the World Bank in 1980. Fewer proposals for private loans reached Ministry of Finance files, indicating private-creditor reluctance to loan to a sovereign debtor experiencing drastic declines in revenues with dwindling prospects for repayment. The country's debt crunch worsened as the extent of independently contracted loans to ministries and parastatals became known.[20] Creditors' legal action abroad to seize Sierra Leonean parastatal assets and formal economy exports further reduced state revenue capacity.[21]

This revenue crunch also threatened payments on obligations to the IMF and the World Bank. Freetown needed to make regular payments to multilateral creditors in order to become eligible for a 1979 Paris Club debt re-scheduling of $120m in obligations coming due over the next five years. An agreement with the IMF was also badly needed to maintain access to concessionary loans, particularly in the wake of declining private credits. President Stevens found himself facing two apparently contradictory interests. An IMF economic stabilization program negotiated in 1979 included conditions designed to improve state budget performance that threatened to hinder the president's discretionary distribution of state resources. Stevens's dilemma was especially acute, since he planned to host the 1980 Organisation for African Unity conference, a $200 million extravaganza of state spending, constituting half of budgeted outlays amidst further cutbacks to development programs and social services.[22]

The OAU conference, however, played a major role in extending both the size and scope of Stevens's Shadow State, while speeding formal economic decline. Lebanese businessmen and politicians became even more important as procurers of foreign exchange. Lungi airport needed a new "Presidential Lounge" to comfort visiting OAU presidents. Three new ferries would whisk delegates from the airport across the Sierra Leone River to Freetown. Bright street lights and widened roads led delegates to any of the sixty Moorish-style chalets, each built at a cost of $250,000. Later, the residences became housing for politicians.

Money was also needed to refurbish three Freetown hotels and build two luxury hotels at Lumley Beach. Project costs doubled over the original $30 million estimate. Money was needed to build a conference hall and a bridge to connect it to the mainland. All of these projects provided more lucrative government contracts to Lebanese businessmen, especially Yazbeck, now involved in construction, and their politician associates. Foreign construction materials and equipment also generated a brisk trade in import licenses.[23] The projects' high costs were not lost on citizens, however. "OAU today, IOU tomorrow" became the unofficial conference slogan. State House, however, tolerated no organized opposition. The Bank of Sierra Leone Governor, Sam Bangurah, was murdered shortly before the conference, allegedly because of his critical attitude toward contract arrangements, his first-hand knowledge of financial dealings to prepare for the meeting, and his refusal to authorize foreign-exchange allocations upon demand from State House.[24]

"Reforms" and the strengthened Shadow State

Stevens explored other ways to raise money for his political network and creditors. A Colorado firm emerged as a possible source of much-needed foreign exchange. The company, the first of several waste-disposal firms to come to Freetown, allegedly promised Sierra Leone's government $25 million in return for receiving toxic wastes from metal-processing plants in the United States. The proposed agreement collapsed after criticism from other African governments on the eve of the OAU summit.[25]

The IMF and the World Bank offered the Sierra Leone government one of its only certain sources of revenue outside the diminishing formal economy and free of the international scrutiny and local concerns that enterprises such as toxic-waste dumping attracted. But access to these resources required an agreement with the IMF. Consultations with the IMF in 1979 produced a stand-by arrangement for SDR 17 million. That agreement culminated in a 1981 extended facility for SDR 186 million. In return, IMF negotiators required that Freetown privatize many state-run enterprises, especially agricultural-produce marketing and light manufacturing. Both World Bank and IMF officials recognized that Stevens used parastatal positions to reward the political loyalty of non-productive clients, and as a source of personal fortune. Creditors directly linked government borrowing and appropriation of state resources for private distribution to Sierra Leone's growing revenue crisis, inflationary pressures, and external indebtedness.[26]

In general, multilateral creditors rejected state intervention in the economy, which they identified as vulnerable to politically motivated and inefficient uses of resources. As an alternative, creditors envisioned "capitaliz[ing] on the indigenous trading system, a proven asset, and let[ting] it play a bigger role in the distribution system. The private sector, with its small-scale, decentralized and flexible structure, is particularly well suited for this task."[27] Consequently, Freetown sold thirteen of twenty-four major state-owned enterprises to private investors or joint state–private ventures.[28]

While creditors stressed the virtues of liberalizing competition, Stevens placed his imprint on reforms. Many privatized parastatals were sold (or given) to Lebanese businessmen and their politician partners. Given the weakness of an indigenous business class, Lebanese access to capital meant that they were the most likely to buy enterprises. Initially, IMF field-negotiators accepted the participation of Lebanese businessmen in the privatization program. Both IMF and World Bank agendas presumed the existence of a border between state and private enterprise that would insulate the entrepreneurial energies of businessmen from politicians' interests in order to generate greater taxable economic activity. The World Bank staked $53.9m on this presumption in the five years to 1987 for the rehabilitation and upgrading of enterprises slated for privatization.[29]

But as the organization and production of Kono's diamonds increasingly underwrote Stevens's Shadow State power after 1973, releasing the energies of this "private" economy would come at the expense of remaining formal state institutions. Rather than tempering passions aggravated by Shadow State intrusion into people's daily lives, the intensified scramble for resources would aggravate growing social conflicts. Neat state–private enterprise boundaries that IMF and World Bank officials supposed to exist were not clear in the Sierra Leone case.

Yet just as many citizens concluded that political authority as it existed in Sierra Leone offered them little of value, creditors saw that the health of the "private" economy required a strengthening of bureaucratic state capacities. For the IMF and World Bank in particular this entailed government capital investments, but this was geared toward paying arrears to creditors.[30] Creditors' demands recalled colonial imperatives of "preventing exit" and imposing a "(re)engagement" of state and society. Like London's fiscal conservatives, the country's creditors encountered a local revenue imperative whatever the policy choice. Creditors proposed that needed spending would come from a growing private economy. Instead, the unification of state and informal-market power enabled leaders of both to accept creditor policies, while shifting the costs of this strategy onto those who did not occupy high positions in the elite accommodation.

State House and its Lebanese collaborators immediately took advantage of the new opportunities that reform offered. Part of the IMF reform package allowed currency-exchange restrictions designed to increase the government's access to foreign-exchange revenue and direct investment into high-priority sectors of the economy. Stevens used these "reforms" to allow his clients easier access to foreign exchange than their non-favored competitors. Stevens also retained many of the regulations giving former state-owned enterprises exclusive import and trading rights. These new managers used exemptions from the harsh effects of stabilization without challenge from non-favored business competitors. Lebanese businessmen and their politician partners received the rewards of privilege. Stevens punished those defying the new arrangements, including those of his own officials who criticized the government for the negative social impact and fiscal irresponsibility of political arrangements.[31]

A sudden surge in the visible trade deficit following "privatization" of agricultural-marketing and light-manufacturing parastatals reflected the extent to which economic activity deserted the formal sector after 1979. The visible trade deficit rose rapidly from 164 percent of exports in 1979 to 270 percent in 1982.[32] Unrecorded were the uses to which newly patrimonialized resources were put. A foreign financial expert reckons that about 70 percent of the country's trade flowed through non-formal channels in the 1980s.[33] Declining formal trade further reduced government revenues, as Sierra Leone's tax system continued to rely on customs receipts. As late as 1979, together with excise taxes, import and export duties accounted for 70 percent of tax revenues,[34] pointing to the continued vulnerability of state revenues to the Shadow-Statization of Sierra Leone's trade.

Amidst a shrinking formal economy and declining state revenues following "reform," Stevens used his position as head of a legally recognized state to seek more multilateral credits. Despite the growing reservations of IMF field-negotiator about state officials' participation in the informal economy, arrangements were concluded for loans of SDR 20.7 million in February 1983 and SDR 50.2 million in February 1984. An agreement was reached despite an early termination of the 1981 arrangement due to the Sierra Leone government's noncompliance with conditions, in particular, its failure to adhere to an arrears payment schedule. Other multilateral and bilateral credits followed agreement on IMF programs. As before, very little of this lending enhanced local revenue collection. Budget deficits worsened as Freetown continued to finance deficits through non-payment of arrears to official and private creditors.

Ironically, Sierra Leone's non-performance on loans did not spell the end to IMF and World Bank support for Stevens's patrimonial system. What explains the apparent willingness of creditors to overlook practices which their own documents clearly identified as directly undermining the intent of reforms? A Sierra Leone Ministry of Finance official involved in negotiations with the IMF hints that Sierra Leone was peripheral to IMF interests. He said, "getting their arrears is their main motive. Even goodwill payments suffice ... It is not Sierra Leone that they are interested in. They want their money and to show really important countries like Nigeria that everyone has to pay something someday."[35] Another official recalled the prelude to the 1984 agreement in which "they [IMF officials] virtually camped on the steps of the national bank when we fell behind with arrears payments." Another official commented that "the IMF will be flexible on all things. Flexible, that is, on all but arrears."[36]

IMF preoccupation with appearances of successful arrears collections left Stevens with some freedom to adapt IMF intrusion into domestic economic affairs to his advantage. Payments on arrears amounting to about 5 percent of overdue obligations usually enticed the IMF into further negotiations for credit and won access to Paris-Club rescheduling in 1980 and again in 1984. The inflow of official creditor resources and the accumulation of arrears became a major source of state revenue in the early 1980s. Official credits provided 45–55 percent of deficit financing from 1980 to 1983.[37] This external support allowed Stevens to continue using state resources for political purposes, even as domestic revenue sources fell under private control. The inflow of credits also allowed Stevens to limit the government's domestic borrowing. Inflation therefore remained remarkably low, standing at 20 percent in 1982, initially allowing the president to avoid massive economic disruption and provide minimal state services to citizens.

Meanwhile, with creditor support, Stevens, his political associates and their Lebanese business partners profited. Lebanese businessmen increasingly acted as patrons to their politician partner-clients in this expanded Shadow-State-protected market. Access to foreign markets and credits, management of production, and business contacts among Lebanese families and communities all helped them to defend their interests in expanding their economic domination as partners in the elite accommodation. Throughout, the president exercised a (diminishing) capacity to regulate access to markets; to exempt from laws, physically coerce, and threaten the alien Lebanese community and insecure politician partners in his effort to maintain political control.

Economic policy that ostensibly aimed at promoting economic efficiency and stronger bureaucratic capacity in fact became a tool for maintaining Stevens's political control. The president found that he could exploit creditors' own revenue imperatives to balance creditor and client demands without relying too heavily on crumbling state institutions. Lacking the mobilizational capabilities afforded by effective state institutions, Stevens turned to reorienting his political network to extend, web-like, further into the economy and society to institutionalize his alternative Shadow State authority. But as Shadow State domination became more extensive, Stevens increasingly relied upon Lebanese middlemen for services. At the same time Lebanese businessmen extended their own economic interests which undermined the institutions and authority of state power upon which Stevens partially relied to regulate terms of the elite accommodation.

Manipulating "reforms"

Privatizations after 1979 and the flood of contracts attending the OAU conference elevated Jamil and Yazbeck to unprecedented positions in the formal economy. These two men used close personal relations with the president to profit from these ventures. As with diamond exporting, access to credit and foreign exchange gave Lebanese business enterprises advantages that their rivals did not possess. Most of these enterprises included politician partners, expanding Stevens's available resources to distribute to loyal clients. Concentrating the management of contacts with the world economy in the hands of a few Lebanese businessmen facilitated Stevens's direct control over the distribution of resources and enabled him to acquire personal wealth through his own arrangements with Lebanese partners.

At the center of this process of accumulation stood Lebanese mediation of the diamond industry and multilateral lender credits, worth perhaps $300 million a year in the early 1980s. Privatization in the 1980s extended the commercial reach of this network into new areas of the economy such as import–export trades, fisheries, agricultural marketing and banking in a manner reminiscent of the privatization of diamond mining after 1973. That is, accumulation became tightly linked to Stevens's protection and exclusive trading rights not extended to competitors.

For example, the newly privatized International Trading Company, under Jamil's management, used foreign exchange from diamond sales to the Jamil-managed GDO and private joint-venture mining to import goods. State House ensured Jamil and his politician partners of a protected domestic market for their imports by assigning import licenses for certain goods to that company alone. Yazbeck's purchase of National Trading Company included an assumption of exclusive rights to import at least eighty-seven different goods. In this way, the newly privatized enterprises recycled diamond profits through the country's import-trade network, adding another layer of political profit to diamond exploitation.

Seville Trading Company, a private Jamil–Stevens joint venture enjoyed exclusive contract rights to import oil into Sierra Leone as part of a creditor-backed "privatizing" measure. The company bought Iranian oil with foreign exchange generated from diamond sales abroad, already under close Jamil–Stevens control. Jamil's financial support for Iranian-backed groups in Lebanon, along with the government of Sierra Leone's official recognition of an Iranian-backed faction of the Palestine Liberation Organization gave Seville Trading Company access to Iranian oil at concessionary prices.[38] Stevens then ordered the Bank of Sierra Leone to pay for the oil in leones at the black-market rate. These leones were exchanged at the official rate to finance diamond mining and buying in Kono, thus beginning the process again. Transaction records from July 1985 to June 1986 indicate that exchange-rate manipulations for eight oil deliveries produced a net windfall profit of Le 166,972,600 for Seville Trading Company, or $27.7 million after exchange at the official rate at the Bank of Sierra Leone.[39]

Other Shadow State enterprises in sectors of the economy such as construction material and consumer-goods imports produced windfall profits in the Shadow State economy based on political connections. Privatization in Sierra Leone joined Stevens's legal sovereign authority to personal profit akin to what others already saw as "pirate capitalism" in Nigeria or "state banditry" in Zaire.[40] That is, the Shadow State absorbed all attainable resources, now with the help of newly energized non-official collaborators as well as with whatever could be milked from creditors. As this happened, the "state of Sierra Leone" was reduced more thoroughly to Stevens's network and its dependents. In many regards, Stevens's concerns about rivals shadowed colonial fears of independent political activity challenging the Freetown regime's vision of the future for society and the economy. Similarly, both regimes sought greater security in informal arrangements with local collaborators, and especially in agreements with politically emasculated foreign firms.

From politicians' positions, this latest arrangement offered a milchcow reminiscent of "official" chiefs' benefits from colonial and pre-colonial commerce. The alternative, a truly free trade, offered echoes of Nkrumah's fears that "if he permitted African business to grow, it will grow to the extent of becoming a rival to his and the party's prestige."[41] Stevens's Lebanese and politician partners, however, had concerns quite different from their leader. They viewed Stevens's political logic of economic management foremost as an opportunity to advance their own business interests. Stevens was himself becoming deeply involved in business. Thus he possibly experienced in a very personal way the conflict between the pursuit of political authority over purely private interests.

Stevens attempted to impose discipline in a style of rule that emphasized his preeminence as "Pa Shakki," or the wily Old Man. He emphasized his personal control – demonstrating his munificence, distributing money or rice to supplicants. He legitimated his own accumulation of wealth as the personal triumph of an "outsider," a "survivor" over the alien forces of bureaucracy. Some Sierra Leoneans profess to a nostalgia for Stevens's apparent capacity to discipline "citified" ministers, in contrast to his successor, Joseph Saidu Momoh. Stevens crowned his preeminence with the construction of an ostentatious palace high on a Freetown hill – a home which he sold to the government, but was then returned to him as a present.

But for generating political resources, Stevens had little alternative but to rely on Lebanese businessmen to mediate contacts with the world economy and manage enterprises in Sierra Leone. Stevens found that he could tamper with individual politicians' security within this arrangement, but he became dependent upon Lebanese management of the economy to provide resources and economic opportunities that the state could no longer generate. This Shadow State dependence and its incorporation into the world economy would have a profound impact on how other groups came to define their relation to state authority and the "official" private economy. To the extent that Lebanese dealers or politicians could appropriate some of this power, they would be able to challenge Stevens's political primacy.

The political impact of Shadow State expansion becomes more apparent as we consider the "privatization" of trade in agricultural products. Yazbeck took over two Chinese-funded cooperatives and claimed the assets of a North-Korean supported "Juche" agricultural cooperative. Formal exports of cash crops such as cocoa, palm and coffee stagnated or slowly declined, however, especially after European firms fled in the early

1980s.[42] Instead, the privatized agriculture trading firms served the wider aims of Stevens's patrimonial network. The new "Shadow State companies" were more useful to Stevens as conduits of trade and benefits than as agricultural producers. These companies used foreign exchange from diamond-mining operations to finance imports of cheap rice through preexisting trading company channels. Stevens used this national staple, the country's "political food" in the words of one minister,[43] as an instrument to reinforce and broaden his own personal control.

Stevens gave exclusive authorization to the former state-owned enterprises to import rice, which the treasury then bought, often at the high informal-market rate. The president and some politicians directly benefited from these deals, since they were also partners in the importing firms. Lebanese and politician partners could then reinvest profits in diamond mining, thus renewing the cycle of accumulation. Government purchase also ensured that the imported rice – a medium for repatriating profits – fell directly into Stevens's hands. Stevens distributed subsidized rice directly from State House to the military, security forces and police officers.[44] Ironically, the mounting revenue crisis – in part a result of growing government expenditures on imported rice – increased civil servants' reliance on handouts as salaries went unpaid.

From 1982, declining revenue collections forced State House to distribute rice to civil servants as payment-in-kind.[45] This rice supplemented shrinking salaries as inflation reduced the value of pay to 25 percent of the levels of a decade earlier, if they were even paid at all.[46] Even Members of Parliament and high-level civil servants received monthly vouchers for the newly created Rice Purchasing Authority, under the control of Stevens's associate, the Inspector General of Police. These vouchers for high-level officials allowed holders to buy 350 100kg bags of rice at one-seventh the official price in 1982. By 1986, the subsidized price had dropped as low as one-fortieth of market values. Favored MPs reportedly received authorization for access to 500 bags.[47] Some favored government ministers reportedly diverted as many as 1,000 bags for their own purposes.[48]

Politicians now received a valuable resource which they could sell or give to supporters. Politicians' offers of cheap rice to supplicants provided selective exemption from IMF-sponsored austerity programs and plunging official salaries and wages. Rice proved to be the medium through which Stevens could devolve tasks of patrimonial reward to associates while maintaining himself as exclusive head of distribution and securing the discipline necessary to keep state officials at their jobs with little or no cash payment. Since the state employed 70 percent of all salaried workers in the country, even after personnel purges in 1989, the distribution of rice to civil servants still affected a wide segment of the country's elite, totalling perhaps 40,000 workers and their families.[49]

Table 6.3. *Rice production and trade, 1978–84. (1979 = 100)*

	domestic	imports	total trade deficit
1978	112	92	84
1979	100	100	100
1980	97	159	181
1981	91	138	142
1982	85	211	182
1983	80	231	—
1984	72	245	—

Source: Bank of Sierra Leone, *Economic Trends* (Freetown: Government Printer, various issues).

Rice distribution outside Freetown also promoted wider geographical dependence on the president's political networks. For example, in 1990 a former Minister of Finance still held exclusive distribution rights for subsidized rice in the southern province, historically an anti-APC stronghold. He distributed the food from the premises of his business (a hotel) in the provincial capital to loyal district officials and chiefs. Rice distribution provided an alternative tie of obligation to the president and his provincial associates outside the decaying network of local government and regional administration. In this manner, distributions reach favored clients in small towns and extended right up to officials in borderlands distant from Freetown where the bureaucratic state had virtually ceased to exist. Officials there then often smuggled this commodity to less-regulated Guinean or Liberian markets.

The long-term economic impact of this patrimonial reward reinforced client dependence on Freetown. Cheap "political food" undercut locally grown rice and instilled a taste for longer-grain bleached imports. Local commercial agriculture declined. Rice production especially fell as visible imports continued to rise (Table 6.3). In turn, State House had to rely more heavily upon Lebanese businessmen to import rice for Stevens's distribution. Ironically, officials negotiating with the IMF indicated that they could plausibly threaten "political suicides" and promise disruptions of arrears payments if this expensive and unproductive system of distribution were disputed.[50]

Stevens's short-term political gains were clear, however. Access to cheap rice allowed him to offer politicians the opportunity to speculate in the rice markets and reward supporters. By the time rice appeared in markets close to world market prices, politicians and favored traders had reaped considerable profits.[51] Even with high consumer prices, the selective informal subsidy of rice ensured that traders sought out politician supplies before "disengaging" from Stevens's network to become truly private entrepreneurs.

Small-scale ("petty") traders, particularly market women, also depended upon politicians or privatized joint ventures for access to cheap rice. Women sold rice at government prices (set closer to world-market prices at the behest of the IMF), then split the windfall profits with politician-suppliers. Traders and exclusive importers of consumer goods operated in a similar fashion. At first glance, one sees that Freetown contains thousands of petty traders, each competing with one another, selling their wares at tiny profit margins above standard wholesale prices. However, a Freetown observer noted that "Each big time operator has spun a web of small traders in a way that defies any laws or methods of free capitalist enterprise."[52] Privileged access to a supply of cheap rice or consumer goods offered favored traders tied to a politician-headed distribution network a larger profit margin than would be possible among independent traders. For example, in 1990 the privatized National Trading Company still offered imported food items at low prices, but only to favored traders. This absorption of elements of the bureaucratic state at the same time that creditors were attacking these institutions as elements of an "overbearing state" began to give to some a greater independent capability to manipulate Shadow State networks for personal gain.

In return for benefits, some suppliers required that women traders take part in occasional "hardline" APC activities in opposition to Stevens's eventual successor, General Momoh. Activities included visible public displays such as marches or "self-help" volunteer civic projects while wearing APC tee-shirts. Some young men gained access to this distribution network through membership of urban mutual-aid and cultural associations organized around the patronage of prominent local "radical" politicians. Organizations such as the United Indigenous Commercial and Petty Traders Association, originally set up to advance members' interests, also became conduits for the distribution of scarce goods in return for political support. While Stevens and his successor could be fairly confident that their Lebanese associates would not be able to build mass movements out of this influence, the extent to which African politicians could command support was troubling.

Informal trade routes and Shadow State territorial spread

While the Shadow State was becoming somewhat less centralized in Freetown, illicit trade did give Stevens a means to extend his political sway outside Freetown. In this way, Shadow State control again resembled the Freetown–chief–trader accommodations of the nineteenth century. Politi-

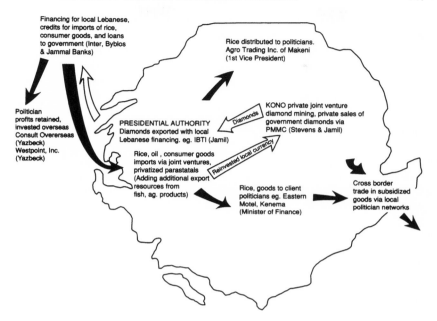

Map 3   Trade and Stevens's patrimonial network

cians with relatively greater access to goods also engaged in cross-border trading, especially in petrol, consumer goods and some agricultural products, to less subsidized or undersupplied regional markets. Koindu, a settlement at the junction of Sierra Leone, Liberia and Guinea, was an entrepôt of this kind (Map 3). Until taken by Liberian ruler Charles Taylor's forces in 1991, Koindu was recognized as one of the busiest of many similar border trading towns. Traders there assert that the town was "busier than Freetown" during the 1980s, due to the extensive trade in formally and informally subsidized goods distributed to politicians.[53] As recently as 1990, Koindu hosted a transit trade that brought vehicles from as far afield as Côte d'Ivoire, Mali, and Senegal.

The local Member of Parliament, Tamba E. Juana, oversaw much of this trade. As an APC politician in this formerly pro-SLPP area, he had personal access to subsidized rice and other goods. One of his constituents and business associates, H.S. Khalil, a long-serving Director of Mines, gave Juana access to a diamond plot. With these additional resources and political connections, Juana acquired more subsidized goods for export. Juana also used opportunities that his government position gave him to "organize" other local exporters. His control of the local police enabled him to sell protection to some traders and block others. Said a former local government official: "Everyone pays Juana his due when he is in, then no one goes there to disturb him."[54]

Even greater reward came through Juana's authority to "subcontract" illicit trade management to Fula traders. Prior to Juana's intervention at the start of the trade in subsidized imports, Mandingo citizens had objected to local Fula immigrants' long-term involvement in illicit trade because Mandingos had customarily conducted that trade. Fulas were better situated to manage trade, however. Links to Freetown politicians and kin ties to Freetown's Sackville Street's illicit currency markets and to regional trade centers in neighboring countries offered Fulas many opportunities for trade.[55] With support from Juana, the Fulas prevailed over Mandingo traders in Koindu as well. This reliance of "strangers" on a politician patron for protection in return for benefits of trade in a part of the country in which Freetown's formal authority existed now as a matter of legal principle mirrored the relationship between Stevens and Lebanese businessmen. Fula ties to this extended Shadow State also reinforced ethnic divisions in the Koindu community. Some non-Fula local residents considered the Fula "cliquish in business." Of Fula prosperity, Mandingo neighbors said: "The president loves the Fula chief too much."[56] Others said that "They [newcomers] believe that they have a political mission to support all politicians when they trade."[57] Local struggles for access to opportunity, however, extended beyond criticism of Fulas. A local Kissi chief noted "more are converting to Islam. They find that it provides them with greater levels of peace and security."[58] Membership in the local Fula mosque also provided access to local trading networks, otherwise organized primarily around kin and political ties.

This broad reach of the patrimonial network recycled money from diamonds and other "official" private exports through many hands, creating a web of opportunity tying diverse social groups to the Shadow State. And like diamonds, illicit trade in subsidized goods followed pre-colonial and clandestine colonial channels of exchange, incorporating local networks, themselves part of larger communities extending across Sierra Leone's borders. Likewise, the president's associates increasingly resembled the pre-colonial "chief at the river's head" or colonial Kono chief struggling to regulate local trade and accumulation as a means of exercising political authority.

Stevens's success in this latest elite accommodation was measurable with respect to the extent that local factional struggles reoriented around the question of who profited within the pervasive context of the extended Shadow State. Despite a shockingly rapid economic decline and falling standards of living, the country remained immune from coups or popular uprisings which some outside observers had long predicted.[59] Stevens understood that "private" exports and patrimonial distribution ensured that goods remained available in the markets, an important factor in limiting popular dissent.[60] But more important was the network's monopolization of opportunity and force as the bureaucratic state capable of managing and resolving social conflicts collapsed.

Stevens avoided the mistake of his erstwhile ally, Guinean leader Sekou Touré, who centralized political distributions in a few "strong" institutions and a narrow group of supporters. When Touré died in 1984, conflict quickly engulfed lines of patrimonial reward that coincided with other social divisions.[61] But in Sierra Leone, repression did not appear to emanate directly from Stevens or the institutions under his control. Instead, for most people, predations of the Shadow State took the form of avaricious Lebanese traders or venal politicians, while Stevens stood above the fray, able to prosecute this politician or denounce that trader. Political conflict in Sierra Leone did not disappear. Rather, it was consistently local. Meanwhile, those condemning the local actions of the Shadow State, such as Mandingo traders lamenting obvious and pervasive corruption and collapsing state services, came to accommodations with other components of it, such as Fula networks and, indirectly, their politician backer. Or as a perceptive student noted, "To get our piece of the national cake requires that we support our oppressors at the same time that we oppose them."[62]

Yet throughout this struggle, Lebanese businessmen exercised exclusive powers to mediate between the world economy and patrimonial accumulation. Their status as "strangers" further removed them from the competition for position that made so insecure their politician partners' pursuits of wealth and power. As in Kono, their necessary services still enabled them to transmit their advantages through kin and ethnic ties. Lebanese autonomy strengthened presidential control over resources to the extent that it deprived others of security, but this autonomy also challenged Stevens's exclusive claim to define the interests of the Shadow State.

Stevens's problems in controlling "private" enterprise

Lebanese businessmen benefited from the rejuvenation of their historic middleman roles. The new "official" private economy built upon preexisting Lebanese business networks. Lebanese businessmen provided the "gateway" for delivering old networks to Shadow State control, a process akin to the colonial imperative to negotiate with chiefs as intermediaries in the establishment of a European alliance with local collaborators. But the key Lebanese role in facilitating this patrimonial expansion rendered these businessmen increasingly autonomous of state interests. Like his colonial predecessors, Stevens's political strategy and fiscal incapacity led to wholesale incorporation of the collaborators' own social networks and networks of exchange, along with all the political dangers to the center inherent in their pursuit of private interests.

Lebanese entrepreneurs, especially Jamil and Yazbeck, but also about fifty other families with lower-profile international contacts, expanded their own business interests through arrangements with politicians and administrators. Some of these families long managed diamond digging and buying operations in Kono on behalf of politician partners. However, the impossibility of ever holding state office prevented Lebanese businessmen from seeking further opportunity through formal politics rather than business. Their status as "strangers" and "exploiters" in the public eye reinforced Lebanese exclusion from full participation in Sierra Leonean society.

Consequently, Lebanese businessmen concentrated on expanding their business activities and protecting their ethnic group interests in all parts of the economy, not just the "official" private economy. In privatizing the Shadow State, Stevens was also exposing his political network to private interests that he did not necessarily share. As one young Lebanese wholesaler explained, "Without us, this government and country would not last a week. We know that most people here look forward to the day that they can kick us out. They would love a Big Man who did that. But as long as these people depend on us to keep this place running, we will stay."[63] The Lebanese business community as a whole occasionally seizes the opportunity to demonstrate their vital role in running the economy. After an airport helicopter shuttle crash killed several Lebanese businessmen in 1990, Freetown's Lebanese businesses shut their doors for two days. By the second day it was impossible to buy much in the city, including fresh food.

Visible displays of dependence show politicians the importance of Lebanese services, but they also heighten popular perceptions of the privileged and isolated position that the "strangers" occupy in the Shadow State. When asked what problems he faced, a housewares distributor in the provinces – himself enjoying favored access to a politician/Lebanese businessman joint venture – replied that:

Our customers do not trust African businessmen. Many people go to the yellow man [Lebanese] because they say that their black brother will treat them like a *bobo* [small, insignificant child]. We have to convince them that they should not always prefer the stranger. But this is difficult when that is what our leaders do.[64]

Such expressions linking opportunity to ethnicity are common among both Lebanese and African businessmen.

The lack of significant African competition and the flight of European

Table 6.4. *Ownership of registered Sierra Leone businesses, 1986*

	Percentage of employees				
	1–11	11–19	20–49	50–99	100+
Lebanese	19	25	56.7	66.5	69.7
African	81	75	43.2	26.5	18.0
European	—	—	0.1	6.9	12.2

Source: Under twenty employees – Freetown tax assessment records, City Hall. Notes for preparation of Sierra Leone Business Advisory Service, *Sierra Leone Business Directory* (Freetown: SLBAS, 1986).

capital also afford opportunities to expand in the formal economy. Lebanese-owned businesses dominate more highly capitalized sectors of the economy (Table 6.4). As in Kono, family connections offer alternative sources of credit outside the collapsing formal banking sector. Just as among Kono Lebanese businesses, family access to foreign exchange facilitates illicit imports of goods, thus giving a further competitive advantage over legitimate African businesses, which are forced to rely upon legal (taxed) imports. This business activity takes place as a spin-off of the "private" economy, but is now virtually the only source of formal state revenue to provide basic services to citizens. Jamil became so confident that he could pursue his own interests that during the course of a dispute with a popular politician, Jamil's private army attacked the official's house with automatic gunfire. This incident underlined the extent to which government capacity to protect even its own officials was in doubt. Such incidents belied the president's claim to exclusive control over the dispensing of favor and punishment as a means of political control. That the president was a personal beneficiary of Jamil's business activities, even where these damaged Stevens politically, began to cause people to wonder whether Stevens was in fact the client of "the White President."

Nor did "privatizing" the Shadow State resolve the state's or its creditors' fiscal crisis. Non-taxable informal-market growth at the expense of formal-sector trade deprived the banking system of the foreign exchange necessary for even minimal state services not directly aiding politicians' or dealers' accumulation of wealth. (Some police and army services would be necessary for the president to convincingly claim that he alone had the capacity to punish and discipline.)

Officials' own estimates indicate that by the mid-1980s, 70 percent of all exports left the country through non-formal channels.[65] Capital investment constituted only 4.7 percent of government spending in 1985.[66]

Deprived of revenue, the State Marketing Board could not offer higher producer prices for agricultural exports, accounting for 50 percent of direct tax revenue in 1979.[67] Coffee prices in 1985 stood at a third of world-market prices and official exports declined more than 90 percent.[68] Stevens and others personally benefited from this illicit trade, to be sure. But precious little revenue found its way into the state treasury. Amidst a disgruntled population and a Shadow State that accumulated authority through manipulating local conflicts, the loss of a monopoly over the use of force presented the danger of breaking down the distinctions between the president and his clients.

Because by 1984 formal state spending collapsed to a quarter of the levels of five years earlier, Stevens continued to maximize his power through building a Shadow State alternative to the "strong" state that creditors envisioned. But as Lebanese businessmen and their politician associates became more central to the provision of Shadow State benefits and occasional payments to creditors, Stevens still needed to devise a way to field a force capable of disciplining wayward clients. At the least, it appeared that Stevens's Shadow State strategy had reached its limits as he confronted the dilemma of building an armed force independent of components of the Shadow State and capable of acting in defense of Stevens's interests alone.

Stevens appeared bound to the core realist proposition that "when the crunch comes, states remake the rules by which others operate,"[69] an awareness that highlights the threat to Stevens of clients' wayward interests. To be sovereign in his own realm, Stevens had to be able to discipline strongmen and maintain order. His attainment of domestic empirical sovereignty required him to possess a stable armed force subject to predictable and habitual obedience. In this regard, maintaining some elements of the inherited bureaucratic state appeared unavoidable. Critics of the Shadow State strategy might point to Stevens's need for a force superior to Shadow State authority, which seemed to fade into societal networks and personal loyalties the farther one moved from the center.[70] And to maintain this force, Stevens faced the same revenue imperative that motivated colonial-era reformers and contemporary creditors.

For the moment, Stevens financed arms purchases and salaries through arrears to creditors, reaching SDR 300 million by his 1985 retirement, ten times the 1979 figures. In 1984, however, the IMF reconsidered their involvement in Sierra Leone. IMF negotiators concluded that Lebanese–politician collaborations were replacing any identification of institutional state interests. The IMF ended credit arrangements in December 1984, noting that "It is clear that trust and confidence have been seriously eroded, in part because of the nature of the relationship between business and

Government"[71] that its own policies had a part in creating. IMF negotiators expressed regret that Freetown had failed to make regular payments on
arrears. Creditor desertion threatened to further expose the population to
the full effects of the accelerating economic decline and bureaucratic chaos.
Lebanese and politician success was becoming a liability to the maintenance of political control which underlay Shadow State intrusion into the
economy.

In the meantime, the IMF promised loans if Freetown showed "an active
demonstration of their intention to cooperate with the Fund by implementing strong adjustment measures in key areas and by making regular and
substantial payments to the Fund."[72] For Stevens to retain access to
overseas credits, IMF officials demanded that he restore some domestic
revenue collection capacity. This conditionality imposed upon Stevens and
his successor a need to look beyond his accommodations with Lebanese
dealers and find a new way to gather resources and at the same time reign-in
unruly members of the elite accommodation. To the extent that creditors'
conditions further undercut state bureaucratic capacity through spending
cuts and further privatizations, Stevens's successor, General Momoh
would look to new accommodations in the Shadow State to resolve these
problems.

Momoh would have to redirect the accumulation of resources that risked
becoming truly private, to service loans to creditors in order to obtain
further loans and restore minimal state services. Rising civil disorder
amidst steady economic decline over the 1980s raised elite fears that the
regime would not survive. Liberian President Tolbert's overthrow and the
subsequent execution of high officials on a Monrovia beach in 1980 under
Sergeant Doe's then-popular regime had frightened many elite Sierra
Leoneans. Popular references to the need for a "Liberian beach party" in
Sierra Leone indicated the extent to which citizens blamed the Shadow
States' head for their predicament. After considerable speculation about his
political future, Stevens eventually retired in 1985. Ostensibly, the octoge-
narian leader retired to live out his days in relaxation. IMF officials were
also making clear their reluctance to negotiate again with the Jamil–Stevens
syndicate.

Stevens chose Brigadier-General Joseph Saidu Momoh as his successor.
This military commander helped to suppress a coup attempt at the start of
APC rule. But lacking his own power-base, Momoh appeared to be one
candidate against whom Stevens and his associates could protect their truly
private interests while Momoh negotiated with creditors. Momoh submit-
ted himself to a referendum – he ran unopposed – which confirmed popular
relief that Stevens was stepping down. Momoh campaigned with a popular
promise of a "New Order" designed to meet demands for political order

and an end to the economic crisis. From the start of his rule, Momoh faced contrary pressures from popular expectations, creditor interests and Stevens's associates. Forced to mediate between these pressures while maintaining his hold on power, Momoh set out to remake the elite accommodation yet again, this time in the context of extensive IMF and World Bank involvement.

7 Foreign firms, economic "reform," and Shadow State power

Do you think that as a minister of government, I want to forgo the luxurious vehicle I am riding in to encourage a multiparty system? Do you think that the policeman who gets a bag of rice at the end of every month can throw away that opportunity for the sake of pluralism?

J.M. Gendemah, Minister of State for Agriculture[1]

Every citizen shall have equality of rights, obligations, and opportunities before the law, and the State shall ensure that every citizen has an equal right and access to all opportunities and benefits based on merit.

The Constitution of Sierra Leone, 1991[2]

President Momoh, Stevens's successor, announced a "New Order" of sweeping reform in 1986.[3] His support for economic reforms led many in the country and abroad to believe that Momoh's "New Order" would attack Sierra Leone's corrupt and inefficient economy. The new president announced plans to eliminate officials' involvement in the informal economy. Policies featured creditor prescriptions to support private enterprise and enhance state revenue capacity. In particular, Momoh took more seriously creditor calls for policies aimed at attracting foreign investors to increase reliable revenue collection. Reform efforts bore fruit. After reaching a tentative agreement with the IMF in 1990, the Sierra Leone government moved closer to access to a promised $280 million in new credits, based on a total projected revenue about 500 percent higher than 1990's revenue collection.[4]

Resources of this magnitude represented significant political and economic capital for Momoh's new regime. This chapter examines the dynamics of reforms aimed at arresting Sierra Leone's economic collapse and its dwindling official revenue capacity, but looks beyond the reforms themselves to see how Momoh used reform conditions to remake his unruly inherited elite accommodation. The process of "reform" highlights the extent to which the political logic of markets in the Shadow State overrode Momoh's interests in an efficient economy. Seen in this light, economic reform emerges as a struggle to control loci of power. Creditors' policies and resources again served as political tools for a Sierra Leone president's

155

efforts to shape an elite accommodation. Momoh used creditor conditions to attract foreign investors to replace unruly Lebanese businessmen and politicians in the elite alliance. IMF demands reinforced Momoh's choice of this Shadow State strategy, since "fiscal responsibility" and budget cutting in this context only hastened the urgency of finding alternative means of ensuring associates' loyalty, thus hastening bureaucratic decay.

This link of economic reform to a political strategy raises an important question. To what extent could Momoh have rejected the logic of his inherited political network and imposed a "strong state" rule envisioned in creditors' "capacity building" rhetoric? Earlier, we saw how Stevens's project of survival and control fell hostage to the shifting contours of the Shadow State, particularly as exchange came under the control of Lebanese–politician collaborations and the changing interests of foreign creditors. It was amidst this internal political struggle that some foreign investors appeared to Momoh to be preferable to Lebanese dealers or Stevens's cronies as partners in rule. Amidst Momoh's struggle for political survival, economic reform served as a weapon to attack threatening wayward elites and to manage creditors' demands.

Placing reform in the context of political struggle offers a broader understanding of how the Shadow State grows in some African countries that are supposedly pursuing reforms as creditors define them. Individual actors, some able to resist the new leader's directives, retain significant powers. Lebanese dealers and some politicians make their own accommodations with foreign investors. Some foreign investors become powerful political actors in their own right, exploiting divisions in the Shadow State for their own, often illicit, business interests. Throughout, this struggle to redefine the terms of elite accommodation extends Shadow State networks of authority at the expense of bureaucratic institutions. Features of the Shadow State become more pronounced, such as the use of private armies. "Reform" thus considered does not produce the conditions of a "strong state" that creditors envision.

Returning to the larger context of this study, the conflicting demands of elite accommodations and creditors' visions of reform continue a long process of adapting the interests of personal political networks, the requirements of state survival and the pressures of the world economy to preserving the Freetown regime. Now, concerned primarily with achieving fiscal balance, creditors offered little help in building bureaucratic institutions that would attract widespread popular support for reform. In fact, creditors' policies achieved the reverse as common people bore the brunt of austerity associated with reform. At the same time, creditor insistence on foreign investment and a further *weakening* of the allegedly "overbearing" state brought officials and foreign businessmen together under the rubric of an expanded Shadow State.

The compatibility of the IMF and Momoh's Shadow State

The new president faced two serious challenges. First, to establish his own authority he had to break the economic stranglehold of the deeply unpopular Lebanese "strangers" and their politician allies, which he had inherited from Stevens's political network. Second, lacking significant internal revenue capabilities, Momoh needed financial support from creditors to defend his own interests independently of Stevens's Shadow State network. For their part, creditors desired increased state revenue capacity to ensure payment of arrears. Creditors' and Momoh's interests coincided on this fiscal imperative. Both saw Lebanese–politician collaborations in the "private" economy as a threat, though for very different reasons. Momoh feared their political capabilities while creditors identified Lebanese dealers as products of "bad policies" and informal-market evasion of state revenue collection.

IMF performance criteria for loans to Sierra Leone directly attacked the economic supports of Stevens's political network. An IMF field report stressed a need for "comprehensive implementation of policies that remove structural bottlenecks in the system of dealing in and exporting diamonds and agricultural products, and the operation of financial institutions."[5] Given Sierra Leone's experience with "privatization," IMF officials now indicated that they believed that foreign firms were far more likely than local businessmen to channel production and profits through the formal economy, to the benefit of the country's treasury.[6] More reliable tax and royalty payments also presented the possibility of bypassing patrimonialized institutions of revenue collection.

IMF officials pointed to the successful operations of Sierra Rutile, a titanium-mining subsidiary of Pittsburgh Paints and Glass. In 1974 Siaka Stevens had granted Sierra Rutile very attractive tax incentives to encourage their investment, and the company expanded its operations in Gbangbama in the Bonthe district, the home area of one of President Stevens's rivals. As one of the few sources of foreign exchange independent of Lebanese–politician businesses, the company received State-House protection and weathered the economic crisis of the 1980s unscathed, functioning as a virtually self-contained enclave operation. The multinational also served another useful purpose. Rutile mining requires expensive excavations of topsoil and underlying clay to uncover the titanium ore. Mining the ore destroys all plant cover, pollutes local water supplies and provides breeding-ponds for malarial mosquitos. But most importantly for State House, this difficult access to the bulky ore ensured that only a foreign firm accountable to State House could gain access to the area's riches. This mining process allegedly destroys villages and farmland, requiring the evacuation and dispersal of the rival's supporters.[7]

This emphasis on foreign investors signalled that State House and creditors did not really view reform as a reengagement of a fugitive informal economy. Instead, coinciding State House–creditor interests focused on reasserting President Momoh's claim on the economic space which Lebanese businessmen and their politician collaborators had appropriated for themselves. Given the bureaucratic state's feeble revenue capabilities, the most effective way to appropriate resources lay in the promotion of an enclave economy. As colonial governors had discovered earlier, foreign investors presented State House with politically safe collaborators who reliably provided revenues that could be distributed later to supporters and service arrears to creditors, while not requiring the construction of autonomous state institutions in this environment of political risk. Momoh's favoritism toward foreign investment would undermine high-profile businessmen such as Jamil and force their politician partners to associate themselves more closely with the presidential entourage to gain access to the new arrangement. Creditors, like the colonial officers before them, could justify foreign investment in political terms as a tool to extend an "official" market that would produce revenues and impose discipline on local entrepreneurs. Momoh could easily adapt these concerns to his own vision of an "official" market devoid of unauthorized interlopers and servicing the resource needs of his Shadow State network.

The case of LIAT finance trade and construction

Momoh found a new political ally in 1986 in the guise of LIAT Construction and Finance Company.[8] This firm, headed by Shaptai Kalmanowitch, an Israeli citizen, promised Momoh that it would boost formal diamond exports if it were given a monopoly over diamond exploitation. If successful, LIAT offered Momoh the possibility of restricting access to diamond resources while receiving the fiscal benefits of a LIAT-dominated diamond trade. Momoh clearly saw that more controlled diamond trading would disrupt disturbingly independent elites whose help Momoh still needed to import rice for distribution to his clients. The President's Office therefore insisted that LIAT import substantial quantities of rice with foreign exchange earned from diamond sales.[9] This strategy allowed Momoh to commercially and politically isolate Lebanese–politician enterprises. Momoh could then use LIAT's intervention to reassert his own control over diamond wealth.

LIAT's intervention into the diamond industry pleased both creditors and the president. Official diamond exports for 1986/87 rose 280 percent over 1985/86 figures,[10] a remarkable increase that took place following LIAT's arrival on the scene.[11] The Bank of Sierra Leone's foreign-reserve holdings rose from a paltry $196,000 after Momoh's November 1985 accession to office, to $7.6 million a year later.[12] Freetown resumed arrears payments to the IMF, which culminated in a November 1986 structural-adjustment agreement for SDR 63.7 million, roughly equal to the year's revenue collection. Meanwhile, LIAT provided additional personal benefits to the first lady, including two buses and office space for her private interests in the state-owned Road Transport Corporation. Kalmanowitch then extended his business operations to include oil imports independent of Stevens's Lebanese–Iranian network.[13]

In return, Momoh provided LIAT with the services of his official position. Kalmanowitch allegedly used Sierra Leone as a base both to buy local diamonds and trans-ship foreign diamonds to Europe. With income from recorded Sierra-Leonean exports, LIAT then imported goods to Sierra Leone. Machinery imports rose more than 300 percent in the 1986/87 fiscal year.[14] Some of these may have been shipped to South Africa (in contravention of existing sanctions) to Kalmanowitch's business interests in Bophuthatswana.[15] State House also provided Kalmanowitch with a diplomatic passport – the Russian emigré became a Sierra Leone cultural attaché – to assist his operations.[16]

LIAT's political services and fiscal performance strengthened the president's hand when it came to pursuing policies designed to win further creditor support at the expense of elements of Stevens's political network. Accordingly, Momoh announced Public Economic Emergency Regulations (PEER) early in 1987. These measures stressed Momoh's commitment to attacking informal markets. PEER promised draconian punishment for informal-market dealings. In reality, PEER was crafted to buttress the process that LIAT had begun; that is, to force accumulation back under the president's control and undercut rivals in the informal economy. IMF officials feared that PEER could hinder legitimate transactions if it became a tool for attacking those businessmen no longer enjoying presidential favor.[17] But they approved of the measure in principle since it appeared to promise greater revenue collection.

Inevitably, politician and Lebanese operators in the diamond industry retaliated against Momoh's attacks on them. Diamond operator and Vice President Francis Minah (Stevens's crony and Momoh's second-in-command), and his partner Jamil arranged for Yasser Arafat to visit Freetown. Rhetorically, the 1986 visit was to "balance" LIAT's Israeli connections. But the visit also included unauthorized negotiations with Arafat to lease a piece of Sierra Leone territory to train PLO fighters, some of whom were already in Sierra Leone to protect Jamil's local diamond operations. These negotiations failed, but tensions rose further with another attack on an official by Jamil's gunmen. This attack injured Daramy Rogers, a politician known for his LIAT connections and his outspoken opposition to Lebanese interests.

Resistance to Momoh's effort to marginalize some elites culminated in a coup attempt in March 1987. Jamil and two-dozen close associates of the retired President Stevens were implicated in the failed coup plot. Jamil fled to London, though he conducted business in Freetown through highly placed associates such as the Speaker of Parliament. Despite Momoh's apparent victory, the incident alerted the president to the dangers of sustained attacks on still-vigorous Lebanese–politician networks. After the coup attempt, enforcement of PEER lapsed. Many politicians resumed their private informal-market activities. When faced with major political opposition, Momoh's relations with creditors took a lower priority than the requirements of his struggle to refashion his inherited accommodations with elites.

Momoh's strategy of asserting political control received a further blow in May 1987 when Kalmanowitch was arrested in London to face charges in North Carolina for fraud and check forgery. Kalmanowitch had allegedly raised money through illegal means in the United States to buy shares in NDMC, a move which creditors supported and which would have weakened the informal diamond market. Kalmanowitch was extradited to Israel to face charges of selling state secrets to South Africa. In any case, LIAT's alliance with Momoh ended.[18]

This setback rendered the president and his associates dependent upon continued collaborations with Lebanese businessmen in the informal economy to distribute benefits to supporters as formal state-revenue capacity diminished. Official diamond exports plunged to only $2 million in the year after LIAT's departure, just 5.3 percent of the previous year. For the first four months of 1989, only twelve carats were exported through formal channels, or 0.0003 percent of the levels common in the mid-1970s.[19] Predictably, payments of arrears to the IMF ceased. As disbursements of loans were blocked, IMF officials "reiterated deep regret over Sierra Leone's continuing failure to fulfill its financial obligations to the Fund."[20] The World Bank followed suit, blocking the distribution of loans in August 1987.[21]

Disappearing creditor and diamond revenues played a major role in a one-year fall of 24 percent in official revenues. Freetown printed money to finance deficits that were larger than total revenues. Inflation soared from an average of 25 percent per annum in the early 1980s to 170 percent by late 1987. Meanwhile, bureaucratic-state and Momoh's Shadow-State demands for credit from local banks drained credit away from the formal sector. Entrepreneurs had to turn to Lebanese–politician enterprises to borrow money or buy foreign exchange, forcing nearly all export financing

into uncontrolled informal channels. Collection of export duties dropped
an incredible 98.3 percent in 1987/88 from the previous year, depriving
Freetown of another major source of revenue. Import duties and excise
taxes aimed to replace some lost revenue but merely encouraged informal-
market trading. In the absence of foreign firms, Momoh now found the
IMF's vision of reform incompatible with his own political imperatives. To
attract IMF support, Momoh had to approve harsh austerity measures that
resulted in an 84.6 percent drop in one year on spending for subsidies,
primarily rice and petrol. A major source of political rewards dwindled.
Socially oriented development expenditures virtually ceased. Presiding
over an economy contracting by 4.6 percent in 1988/89, Momoh's regime
faced grave danger.[22]

Momoh was losing resources to enforce political control. As revenue
shortfalls and IMF austerity measures shut down parts of the state
bureaucracy that had survived earlier Shadow State predations, Momoh's
allies sought other means of supporting themselves as they lost access to
benefits. The pervasive presence of Momoh's rivals, the "private" informal
economy operators offered one of the few alternatives for advancement. As
control of resources shifted further from Momoh, politicians and dealers
had even fewer incentives to obey presidential directives.

The president could no longer control disobedience through a Shadow
State economy of rewards. The reform of "bad policies" neither restored
the president's political control, nor tapped "entrepreneurial energies,"
which were now directed toward evading the president's authority. The
president's collapsing authority was leading to the balkanization of political control. This outcome risked unleashing a deadly warfare of competition for position among groups or individual political entrepreneurs no
longer constrained by a hierarchy of obligation to Momoh in return for
opportunity.[23] Momoh faced political irrelevancy unless he could manage
the crisis and restore his authority to distribute reward or punishment.
"Reengagement" of the economy, in the sense of using state power to
protect private accumulation without political interference was not a
realistic proposition, given that the truly private market in this case
constituted the most serious political threat facing the president.

In fact, creditors did not pursue this unlikely outcome in short-run
practice. Creditors demanded payment. The president remained anxious to
reaffirm his position as the decisive political entity in society. But the
shrinking powers of presidential office offered few viable options to either
party, other than to continue to rely upon foreign investors who would
engage in battle to recapture the informal diamond market. Where the very
means and resources of political control had been "privatized," foreign
investors were seen as the least risky agents for reclaiming control over the

process of accumulation and making arrears payments. This view shared many similarities with the colonial strategy of seeking security and fiscal stability from an enclave economy; as in Kono in the 1930s, one option for controlling renegade networks entailed enlisting foreign investors. This time, however, the introduction of foreign firms was an even more attractive proposition as it also offered a means of gaining access to creditors' resources and creditor support for a vigorous "reform" program of the forcible expulsion of rivals and a presidential reclamation of economic opportunity.

"The Skipper" rescues Momoh and his creditors

President Momoh produced "PEER II" in November 1988 in a renewed bid for creditor support. As with the earlier PEER, this legislation targeted renegade informal-market transactions. This legislation departed from its predecessor in singling out for attack collaborative Lebanese–politician mining and trading in the diamond fields. The legislation empowered the Minister of Mines to "withhold or revoke a mining right at his discretion."[24] Further legislation during the next week brought all diamond-mining areas under the control of the state-owned National Diamond Mining Corporation.[25] These initiatives signalled that State House agreed with IMF advice that the revenue capabilities of export industries would improve if they were dominated by foreign firms.

Momoh now pursued a more vigorous policy of, in IMF words, "institutionalization" of the diamond trade, that is, concentrating it into the hands of a few foreign firms and expelling informal-market enterprises. New regulations announced in January 1989 tied the reissue of private export licenses to a monthly export performance of $500,000, an unrealistic figure for all but perhaps half-a-dozen local enterprises. Reforms raised a further obstacle to indigenous trade in the requirement to post an additional $500,000 bond against that performance.[26] If enforced, these regulations would eliminate hundreds of smaller-scale Lebanese and politician operations that employed several tens of thousands of Sierra Leoneans. These measures secured for Momoh the selective cooperation of some operators, however. Those receiving official favor paid a 2 percent royalty if they imported necessities such as rice. In exchange, they received exemptions from regulations that forced their competitors to surrender foreign exchange from diamond sales. This accommodation with a few local mining operators signaled Momoh's recognition that he needed cooperative big informal market dealers with foreign exchange to import essential commodities.

The Minister of Mines and Kono detachments of the Sierra-Leone Police, who were themselves mining diamonds, ignored the new edicts restricting diamond dealing. The Minister of Mines continued issuing private dealer and export licenses for the 1989 digging season, even though he had no legal right to do so. Despite his official status, President Momoh lacked the crucial element of administrative capacity or coercion to ensure compliance with his edicts.

Opportunity again appeared in the form of an Israeli investor. The N.R. SCIPA Group, under the direction of Nir ("The Skipper") Guaz, arrived in Sierra Leone after failing to break into Zaire's diamond business in 1988.[27] Like Kalmanowitch, Guaz set out to establish favorable relations with politicians who could aid his enterprise. But since, some of the targets of SCIPA's bid for influence, such as the Minister of Mines, still determined developments in the diamond fields, SCIPA's efforts to win local favor did not always coincide with the president's interests. Yet the president could hardly reject SCIPA's promises of much-needed resources.

Since Guaz was interested in the country's diamonds, he reportedly worked directly with some diamond operations in Kono. Local suspicions in Kono held that some politicians were using SCIPA's presence to gain greater independence from their Lebanese partners and Momoh himself to market diamonds. In effect, these politicians would become SCIPA's local middlemen. Smaller-scale tributor overseers reported significant local tensions as miners and local managers were forced to choose between loyalties to established operations and a potentially powerful new patron. For its part, SCIPA allegedly financed legal and illegal exports of locally mined diamonds outside DeBeers channels.[28] "Private" enterprises included in this arrangement became dependent upon links to those controlling access to mining such as the Minister of Mines, Birch Conteh, and SCIPA rather than the president himself. SCIPA played to the interests of politicians and the remnants of the state bureaucracy as demonstrated by Guaz's offer to donate office space for customs and an anti-smuggling unit in Stevens's former Presidential Palace which Guaz controlled.

SCIPA's presence still provided badly needed benefits to Momoh, however. Guaz claimed to import 27,000 tons of rice in 1989 with legal and illicit diamond profits, and promised another 80,000 tons in 1990. These imports provided Momoh with new opportunities to provide cheap rice to presidential clients who speculated in the rice market. New joint ventures with SCIPA in rice importing and fishing – two trades recently "liberalized" from Lebanese–politician involvement in the familiar fashion to attract creditor support – also gave Momoh access to alternative resources outside his rivals' control. These new sources of benefits for members of the presidential clique offered Momoh some protection from the political consequences of direct attacks on his rivals' privilege in the diamond fields that IMF negotiators demanded.

Guaz provided other political services to the beleaguered Momoh. After official accounts were frozen in Britain in the wake of default on a politician's officially guaranteed debt to a British trading company, SCIPA stepped in to privately finance vital imports.[29] Guaz reportedly paid three months' overdue Ministry of Works salaries in return for the use of the Ministry's heavy equipment in the diamond fields. Guaz used these instances of apparent goodwill to mount an extensive public relations campaign. Pictures of his wife and child, along with professions of personal commitment to Sierra Leone in paid newspaper advertisements, appealed to popular hopes that SCIPA would ease the burdens of the country's economic disintegration.[30] Guaz then distributed largesse to private organizations associated with key politicians such as the Senior Policemen's Wives Association, mosques and Islamic educational and religious organizations.

SCIPA's formal-sector exports remained low, however. In 1989, the company exported diamonds worth only $6 million, a figure that some observers considered to represent only about 2 percent of national production, and in any case, far below SCIPA's actual performance.[31] This deviation from Momoh's priorities indicated the extent to which Guaz was building his own political network outside the direct control of the president. Nonetheless, the company rendered valuable assistance in Freetown's April and June 1989 arrears payments of $500,000 to the IMF. Even though these payments, against an SDR 86 million obligation, were very small, IMF officials considered that it "demonstrate[d] actively their intention to cooperate with the Fund ... by making regular and substantial payments."[32] Either through privately financing vital imports or directing foreign exchange through formal channels, SCIPA again proved helpful for meeting mid-December arrears payments of $5 million. IMF officials considered these payments crucial for demonstrating Freetown's credit-worthiness.

However, Guaz's independence in choosing political allies troubled Momoh. Negotiations continued through the fall of 1989 to find more reliable investors interested in long-term commitments in the country. Sunshine Broulle of Dallas Texas, showed interest in deep kimberlite deposits, exploitation of which would require investments of close to $100 million, and would virtually monopolize Kono's resources. Sunshine Broulle, however, registered concern over "the chaotic and insecure environment" that characterized Momoh's inability to regulate the activities of SCIPA and others in Kono's diamond fields.[33]

"The Skipper" was rapidly outliving his usefulness to the president. Momoh now realized that fragmented Shadow State networks offered Guaz the opportunity to pursue commercial interests through independent accommodations with the president's political rivals. SCIPA's diamond buyers paid unusually high prices to miners and politician-overseers as part of an alleged money-laundering scheme.[34] Politicians with mining interests now had easier access to foreign exchange without Momoh's favor. Strongmen still had to be controlled, and the key to this lay in IMF financial support and compliant foreign firms that could control resources on behalf of the president to allow him to marginalize his rivals. Momoh resorted to one of the few direct means of control left to him; he ordered Guaz arrested on Christmas Eve, 1989 for "economic sabotage" under PEER II regulations. Guaz remained under arrest for a month, while his supporters staged mass demonstrations on his behalf. Guaz flouted his ability to build support independent of Momoh. "The people of Sierra Leone are warm and friendly. They love strangers," he said. "That is a gesture we will never misuse as we share the profits with the warm and friendly people of this country."[35]

With Guaz in prison and no foreign-firm allies to take his place, Momoh had no way to finance vital imports. Crude oil sat in ships off-shore in wait for cash payment. Suppliers no longer extended credit to this government, as bills for earlier deliveries had gone unpaid. Commerce halted and transport ceased as petrol prices reached $10 per gallon in the informal market. Within forty-eight hours of Gauz's sudden release from prison, the oil shipment had been paid for and off-loaded. Momoh had been given a severe reminder of the restricted bounds of his autonomy, even with respect to foreigners. While Guaz allowed Momoh to meet his financial obligations and weaken some mining operators in Kono, his independence also demonstrated to Momoh the need to consider more drastic measures to control the distribution of economic opportunity.

In January 1990, the president again announced a policy of forcible exclusion of private diamond dealers from the mining fields, meeting a primary demand of both Sunshine Broulle and Sierra Leone's creditors. This announcement was convincing since it took place through the new Minister of Finance, an appointment that a Freetown banker said "shows the IMF a freshly scrubbed face." The policy's presentation before the Freetown Chamber of Commerce produced audible gasps, but the digging season began in Kono as usual. Indeed, even more activity took place in informal channels since only three major dealers bothered to meet harsh new ($500,000) formal licensing requirements. The January announcement, however, was followed by "Operation Clean Slate" in April, 1990. This military invasion employed loyal Special Security Force and Sierra Leone Army personnel to expel miners. These forces reportedly encountered armed resistance from local police and residents involved in diamond digging.[36] Official reports indicate that in excess of 10,000 out of about 20,000 mine laborers were removed from the area.[37] "Operation Clean

Slate" signalled that violence was to play a larger role in bringing accumulation under direct state control as the president continued to pursue his political objectives amidst collapsing state bureaucracies.

A year later, after repeated military forays into the diamond fields,[38] Sunshine Broulle signed a contract promising an initial $70 million investment to mine kimberlite diamond deposits and rework alluvial operations. Creditors saw a chance to increase arrears payments, even though the firm was to pay a mere 22.5 percent tax on profits, a rate even lower than that SLST had enjoyed in 1933. The real value of Sunshine Broulle to Momoh and creditors, however, lay in the firm's willingness to police mining areas while producing revenues for the state.[39] Momoh and the IMF effectively concluded that if "the state" – differently conceived by both – was the major obstacle to "reform" – also differently conceived – then the most efficient solution was to replace the defective state with reliable subcontractors. The firm's decision to abandon the project in 1991, however, indicated that the political rivalries in the diamond fields did not offer the same attractions to a firm like Sunshine Broulle, which was either unable or unwilling to invest time, effort, and money in manipulating and protecting themselves from elite factions.[40]

Momoh's continuing search for foreign firms

By 1991, the president's search for foreign firms to generate revenues and manage political challengers was desperate. In March, the Revolutionary United Front (RUF), under the command of Foday "Commander" Sankoh, invaded eastern Sierra Leone from Liberia. Backed by *de facto* Liberian leader Charles Taylor, this group attracted support from some who were cut out of, or had never been included in Momoh's refashioned elite accommodation. Creditors continued demanding "reforms" designed to generate income to service loans. Creditor wishes were all the more compelling, since they promised to release loans and grants totalling more than $280 million over several years upon reaching an agreement for further economic "reforms." Momoh desperately needed this money to distribute to loyal clients and to finance his army's battle to retain control over the resources that would attract foreign firms. Momoh also had a lot to gain in terms of greater freedom from the decaying institutional state. Promised disbursements would top 1990/91 formal revenue collection fivefold.[41]

This combination of Momoh's domestic imperative to successfully reconstruct a favorable elite accommodation and continuing creditor demands led to the final expiration of some vital institutional state bureaucracies. Frustrated and impatient, creditors proposed that revenue collection be contracted out to private foreign firms. In return, Sierra Leone was offered a Rights Accumulation Programme (RAP), wherein creditors would approve additional loans and grants if Momoh simply showed that he was making an effort to follow IMF recommendations.[42] The introduction of an RAP indicates that creditors have essentially given up on recovering loans, and are now more concerned about imposing discipline against the "disorganized" tendencies found in some very weak governments. In settings such as Sierra Leone, creditor interest in "capacity building" is synonymous with measures intended to enhance revenue collection. RAP became the mechanism through which creditors continued to exercise influence over the political network, which had largely replaced "the state" as creditors understood it, and was incapable of achieving the long-term changes demanded by earlier loan agreements.

An early case of subcontracted revenue collection involved a joint venture with Britain's McAllister Ellicott Fisheries. Momoh had earlier favored a joint venture with West African Fisheries. "Realizing the difficult position of the Sierra Leone Government in terms of foreign exchange," wrote these investors, "West African Fisheries is prepared to loan Government US $10 million to meet international obligations."[43] This joint venture, under more direct State House control, would have given presidential associates a direct role in the "foreign" firm's management of the "private" fishing industry. IMF officials objected to WAF's close ties to presidential associates. Another firm, Maritime Protection Services of Sierra Leone (MPSSL) received IMF approval instead. Under MPSSL management, fishery royalties collections in 1991 rose 500 percent over 1990 figures.[44] These revenues supposedly remained under direct creditor surveillance to pay official obligations. The MPSSL arrangement also provided $10 million to State House, releasing Momoh from institution-building tasks outside his Shadow State with respect to policing or collecting royalties from the country's fisheries.

Creditors continued to push subcontracting of state operations to private firms to generate revenues. A German firm, Specialist Services International (SSI) took over port operations in 1991 to protect customs receipts from Momoh's officials. SSI quickly detected revenue loss through under-invoicing of exports of the joint-venture Sierra Leone Ore and Metal Co. (SIEROMCO). SSI no doubt saved money, but the arrangement made the bureaucracy of the Sierra Leone Ports Authority largely redundant – not an action likely to promote a "strong state" in the sense of supporting the development of competent state bureaucracies. Nor did SSI officials prove to be above the allures of the Shadow State. A Minister of Transport was later found to have diverted $370,000 from Sierra Leone's freight-levy account with the Bank of Commerce and Credit in Paris in March 1992 with

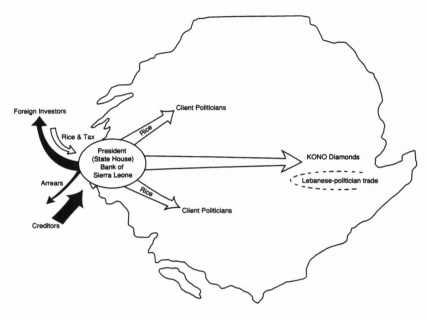

Map 4   Trade and the pruned patrimonial network

alleged SSI connivance.[45] This firm also allegedly paid a percentage on contracts to another official and provided him with a life insurance policy of $100,000.[46]

Joint ventures under minimal bureaucratic state control proliferated. Momoh appeared to be moderately successful in placing himself at the center of a political and economic network based upon collaborating firms' control of exchange (Map 4). The preference of creditors for foreign investors rather than what they perceived to be hopelessly interconnected informal-market and state operations seemed to indicate that they simply wished to disregard those elements of the formal institutional state that they regarded as troublesome, and begin anew with less risky arrangements. These ventures had a very different impact on the Shadow State. They offered Momoh a chance to use creditors' programmes to discipline unruly elites and control resources. Both he and creditors concluded that the country's resources were underutilized and misdirected, though for different reasons. But Momoh could heartily agree with IMF concerns that "Sierra Leone is richly endowed with natural resources, but these resources have not been well developed."[47]

The president continued enlisting foreign firms for IMF approval and to help him battle domestic rivals. Pioneer Resources NL of Australia gained exclusive diamond-prospecting rights to sixty square kilometers of Bo District. Joint ventures with Nigerian investors took advantage of promises of World Bank privatization loans to purchase and refurbish five government-owned rubber estates.[48] State House offered extensive rights in exchange for resources and control in other sectors. Suakoko Wood Corp. bid for twenty years of exclusive rights to log 136,016 ha., a two-year moratorium on rents, an "indefinite tax holiday," and 100 percent foreign-exchange retention for five years. In exchange, the firm would have provided $1.8 million to help pay Sierra Leone's arrears to the International Fund for Agricultural Development. Another firm, Evergreen, received the contract, however. Evergreen offered a direct $900,000 interest-free loan and $520,000 of "social development" in return for a three-year tax holiday.[49]

While destroying incentives to develop anything resembling a bureaucratic "strong state," these joint ventures enabled Momoh to service some international obligations. After paying arrears of $4.8 million to the Africa Development Bank in 1991, Sierra Leone received a $45.8 million "soft loan" to restore electricity to its capital, blacked out more or less continuously since mid-1990. Cynical observers saw a similar exchange in Momoh's decision to send a Sierra Leone Army contingent to the Persian Gulf in 1991. After Kuwait's liberation, the United States provided military assistance in Momoh's battle against rebels and covered the costs of the military excursion to the Persian Gulf. Kuwait's ruler also provided Freetown with a $10 million development grant.[50]

The real challenge to Momoh's Shadow State did not come from creditors, however. Momoh could manage their demands to suit his needs in the short-term. Creditors cannot foreclose on a bankrupt state. In fact, the RAP strategy appears more as a desperate creditor bid to replace the dying bureaucracies of a state with something with which they could continue to negotiate. This required offering Momoh incentives as much as applying pressure. Momoh's most desperate challenge came from a rebel invasion that began in March 1991. His inability to incorporate or eliminate rivals in the diamond fields now haunted him as rebels concluded their own agreements with mine operators. Liberian fighters appeared, with Charles Taylor's backing, to incorporate diamond-producing areas of Sierra Leone for their own enrichment in Taylor's aggressive Shadow State – what Taylor calls "Greater Liberia." The clash of these two rival political networks over the region's resources underlines the important role that violence plays in the Shadow State battle to manage political networks through total control over the distribution of wealth.

Violence and accumulation in the Shadow State

From Momoh's perspective, force was the guarantor of his personal control over accumulation. Direct actions such as "Operation Parasite," the most recent operation in a colonial tradition of military incursions into Kono were risky when pay for soldiers or money to buy weapons was scarce. Foreign firms provided an alternative means of coercion. Ideal collaborators such as Sunshine Broulle might arrive with their own paramilitaries – preferably non-African, and with no possibility of developing local political interests. Momoh need have had no fear that Sunshine Broulle would use its military might to conquer Freetown or unseat himself. On the contrary, it was more likely that he would actively seek out foreign firms to perform the simpler task of driving away local entrepreneurs and politicians. Special treatment from State House, along with the advantages of efficiency and a global reach could bring a crushing level of competition to bear against rivals in the scramble for resources.

As the remnants of state bureaucracies failed to provide any meaningful services to citizens at all, the view from below was of a presidential network that existed only to extract resources and control local strongmen, a new *mise en valeur*, now benefiting the Shadow State and its creditors.[51] Since IMF conditions prohibited subsidies for many basic goods, especially for political uses, and as Momoh was incapable of providing regular salaries for officials in any case, officials intensified their exploitation of their offices. Creditors and Momoh understood that these motivations could actually be harnessed to increase revenues. IMF consultants approved of State House policies encouraging tax farming. In return for superior performance, local officials kept a 10 percent commission on collections above assigned targets.[52] IMF officials further recognized that bureaucracies had ceased to function and that new efforts would need to be directed toward "institutionalizing" elements of the Shadow State that would serve their needs. A foreign advisor to the Ministry of Finance averred that "they have a tradition for this sort of extraction in their social context better than any artificial units of government."[53] Ministry circulars also stressed the centrality of revenue collection to administrative efforts: "If appropriate efforts are applied to revenue collection, a turnaround of Sierra Leone's economy will begin even before the end of this year ... All effort must be made to see that individuals pay their tax ... Let none escape their obligations ... "[54]

But the massive drain of arrears payments on meager official finances, nearly 45 percent of foreign-exchange earnings in 1990, left Momoh with little choice but to jettison efforts to build the "strong state" and a truly private economy that were meant to be the rewards reformers had promised

Table 7.1. *Patrimonial resources from the formal economy, 1984/85–1989–90*

	extra-budget & spending & subsidies ($m)	private sector financing of deficit ($m)	% of private credit
1984/85	73.8	59.8	64.9
1985/86	88.1	126.2	91.0
1986/87	54.2	60.8	85.1
1987/88	15.1	39.7	88.0
1988/89	15.2	35.0	79.7
1989/90	6.6	30.6	—

Note: Figures are converted from leones using an average of the year's official rate for dollars.
Source: Data provided by Bank of Sierra Leone authorities to IMF officials (Ministry of Finance closed file); Bank of Sierra Leone, *Economic Trends* (March–June 1989), for private-sector financing.

would compensate for the pain and sacrifice of austerity. As Momoh struggled to provide for his political network, the needs of the Shadow State continued to be met through short-term state budget financing (Table 7.1).

Formal market credit was unavailable to those without special favor. "Government wants only to work with a few companies," complained a Freetown businessman.[55] Would-be entrepreneurs complained of unfair competition from presidential associates' joint ventures. Women financiers of fishing ventures down the coast from Freetown, for example, complained that cheap MPSSL fish blocked their expansion into the Freetown market.[56]

The contrast between privilege and austerity becomes even more stark as what IMF negotiators called "bold and decisive measures" ended most subsidies to the general public. So while inflation held to a moderate 100 percent in 1989/90, phase-outs of subsidies caused prices of petrol to rise 300 percent and rice to rise 180 percent.[57] Those already outside Momoh's narrowing political network suffered the most from cuts in expenditures. These donor conditions proved easiest for Momoh to follow, since state coffers were largely empty in any case, while the politically significant gained access to the Shadow State's "official" joint ventures.

Earlier, however, as the hand-me-down colonial state collapsed, many citizens had been able to survive through accommodations with the Shadow State. Now, however, creditors' conditions and Momoh's trimming of his political network had reduced the relevance of this alternative

Table 7.2. *Kono auto registrations,
1986–9*

	luxury	compact	motorbikes
1986	15	39	71
1987	13	35	81
1988	17	26	84
1989	13	29	64

Source: Government of Sierra Leone, *Sierra
Leone Gazette* (Freetown: Government
Printer, various issues).

Table 7.3. *Koidu/Sefadu bar and
restaurant license applications,
1986–9*

	Bar	Restaurant
1986	14	10
1987	15	11
1988	10	8
1989	7	4

Source: Government of Sierra Leone, *Sierra
Leone Gazette* (Freetown: Government
Printer, various issues).

political authority in most people's daily struggles to survive. This growing
disparity among those customarily benefiting from the informal market are
reflected in Sierra Leone's auto registration figures, showing a 24 percent
rise in luxury auto registrations in the midst of an overall decline during the
1980s.[58] A similar trend also appeared in Kono (Table 7.2). Declining
opportunities also affected legally registered businesses that depended
upon political or financial support from kin engaged in illicit mining. Kono
bar and restaurant license applications attest to this general decline in
economic opportunity (Table 7.3).

Meanwhile, African traders, who had never benefited in great measure
from Shadow State control of informal markets, and who were supposedly
the targets of efforts to build political support for economic reforms and
governmental efficiency, found themselves in desperate straits. Their
frustration often takes on ethnic overtones as they blame hardships on
wealthier, but struggling Lebanese families in their communities. Said a

Kono businessman: "We are like a sinking ship that has no lifeboats. But the Lebanese, their brothers and cousins are waiting to pick them out of the sea. This arrangement allows them to be saboteurs and strangle any policy they do not like, which only makes the ship sink faster."[59] News reports about "smuggler kingpins" began to appear in Freetown in late 1989.[60] These tenacious elements of Stevens's political network were often portrayed in concrete menacing terms. "A Lebanese government is now formed in Kono," said a Freetown paper, "complete with a president, portfolio and Secretariat!"[61] Still others blamed troubles on "That Vampire Yazbeck."[62]

As "reform" in the Shadow State attacked the middle strata who were supposed to become the constituents of reform, these individuals faced new threats. In his call for support for further austerity measures, Momoh's Minister of Finance explained to a Freetown gathering of primarily Lebanese businessmen how the elite alliance had changed: "When things begin to go wrong, and there will be times when this happens, they will not always have time to look for the Minister or the President or the Permanent Secretary. It is you, who have shops open to them where they see the threats coming from, in the increase in prices. It is you that they are going to fall upon."[63]

Momoh appeared to be capable of confronting powerful political groups and imposing great hardship on Sierra Leone's citizens. He did not appear to be hesitant to impose austerity upon citizens who were deemed marginal to the Shadow State or who were members of rival networks. Thus it was not Momoh's fear of popular rejection of austerity that sabotaged reform, a common explanation for the failure of reform in African countries.[64] The failure of reform in Sierra Leone lay instead in the president's and creditors' lack of commitment to policies that would have rebuilt the institutions of a state that then could protect and serve its citizens' interests.

Given popular disdain for this process of "reform," which appeared to many as a new device to deny them the benefits of even a Shadow State, it is not surprising that some Kono residents initially welcomed invading forces from Liberia in mid-1991. Some of Momoh's jettisoned clients and others long-excluded from elite accommodations welcomed the opportunity to settle old scores. These people tolerated the Revolutionary United Front (RUF), which apparently attracted some popular support for exacting retribution against people who had exploited the local community in the past.[65] Some Sierra Leoneans no doubt believed that they could find greater opportunity in a new collaborative relationship with the rebel incursion. The Sierra Leone Army's tendency to treat young men from the rebel-held areas as collaborators no doubt reinforced this conclusion.

But the threat to Momoh from the rebel invasion was deeper than simply giving voice to regional complaints against State House. Momoh, and Stevens before him, both showed little reluctance to impose harsh austerity upon Sierra Leone's citizens when it suited their political purposes. The greater threat lay in the rebels' capacity to cut Momoh off from the diamonds and other minerals that constituted the lifeblood of his Shadow State and foreign firms' interests in Sierra Leone. Unlike the rebels, Momoh was still attached to the international obligations of the almost-dead bureaucratic state. Creditors would become obstacles in his efforts to use resources to battle the invaders and their local allies.

Momoh could not control creditors' surveillance nor their diversion of foreign firms' taxes from Freetown. These severe constraints, along with a tendency for army officials to divert soldiers' pay into their own pockets, left some troops unpaid. One such soldier, 27-year-old Sierra Leone Army captain Valentine Strasser, and his 23-year-old *aide de camp*, Solomon Musa, marched to Freetown with less than a hundred enlisted men in April 1992 to overthrow President Momoh's government. Momoh fled to exile in Guinea. Citing rampant corruption and officials' lack of concern for the harsh conditions of the fighting troops, Strasser promised extensive reform. Freetown's weary citizens greeted Strasser as "The Redeemer," delivering them from a corrupt and callous government that had treated them just as Strasser described his treatment as a soldier. Amidst popular acclaim, Strasser's National Provisional Ruling Council (NPRC) announced that it would try officials from the Momoh government on charges of corruption.

Sierra Leone's new rulers immediately announced that they were committed to the IMF's conditions; that they would continue to support "private" enterprise, especially foreign investment, and would continue the Momoh government's efforts to negotiate an agreement for an IMF structural-adjustment program. The 1992/93 budget announced that Sierra Leone had prepared a three-year public investment program under World Bank tutelage. In order to receive the estimated $180 million in investments, the NPRC pledged to set up a Public Enterprise Reform and Divestiture Commission. The Minister of Finance, a technocrat from Momoh's regime, made the usual pronouncements that "the government is in the process of evolving a comprehensive framework for their [diamonds'] rational exploitation and final security arrangements to contain the pervasive problem of smuggling."[66]

Once again, one could imagine that a ruler facing utter collapse of state institutions, now of great youth and inexperience and facing an armed invasion of the economically viable parts of the country, would opt for a "strong state" strategy to maximize his chances of survival. Massive IMF support, now amounting to promises of $233 million in aid for social programmes during 1993/97 with promises of additional bilateral aid,[67] seemed to indicate that creditors were willing to actually help finance the bureaucratic "capacity building" initiatives that their literature so heavily touted.[68]

The Shadow State as a war-fighting organization

The real news in Strasser's ascension to power lay not in his commitment to reform, however. Instead, he and his associates concentrated on conquering what they believed their control of State House entitled them to. As the inherited technocrats from the old regime issued promises to the IMF, Strasser's troops were already mining diamonds in Kono for exchange in barter deals for weapons in Belgium and Romania.[69] It was while mining diamonds at Gandohun, near Koidu in Kono, that Strasser's men were overtaken by RUF rebel forces in mid-1992. The invading forces allegedly took advantage of the troops' attention to their mining operations to mount an offensive to take the Kono mining area.[70]

The logic of Strasser's Shadow State strategy lay in the prior destruction of the bureaucratic state and the nature of the inherited fragments of Momoh's Shadow State. Inflexible bureaucratic institutions and a centrally organized military are terribly unsuited for battling the kind of adversaries Strasser now faced. A fragmented collection of old politicians, marginalized factions, disgruntled miners and desperate citizens cooperated with invaders for personal benefit. What in the past would have been political entrepreneurs were now military entrepreneurs, producing an anarchy that would make any organized counter-attack from Freetown difficult to carry out with success. In any case, in the absence of a strong state or centrally organized army, the temptation of individuals to align with disaffected local strongmen would pose unacceptable risks to Strasser.

As this author found in sobering encounters with Liberian National Patriotic Front of Liberia (NPFL) soldiers, those laying claim to the fragments of the Shadow State may delight in opposition to a center of power that has long oppressed them. One observes that armed adolescents may find that warfare offers them liberation from a lack of opportunities, giving them a license to loot, and the chance to wreak revenge on their enemies and settle old scores in ways their parents could only dream of.

The dilemma facing Strasser was not the collapse of a state that had already ceased to exist in any meaningful sense for most people at some point in his early childhood. Unlike Momoh and his associates, these coup leaders had been raised in Freetown's slums. Their experience with political authority involved appeals to officials for favor, or seeing their "unauthorized" attempts to get ahead suppressed and labeled "criminal." It is not surprising then that while the country's new leaders faced the challenges of the Shadow State, they also reflected the values of the slums and their own experiences of the failure of the inherited colonial state to redeem the independence-era promises of justice and social transformation.

Strasser's redefinition of the Shadow State represents a societal revanche of a sort. A monopoly on the exercise of violence, and the capacity to direct and control the exploitation of resources on behalf of new claimants is the primary imperative of Strasser's "government." As before, the ruler engages in private dealings to achieve this control. In Strasser's case, this allegedly involved the private export of 435 carats of diamonds to Sweden in late 1993.[71] Only this time the rewards serve a new Shadow State network devoid of any pretenses of "development" and instead benefits new claimants who can be armed and reliably engaged to battle invaders and rivals. Loyalty is bought more directly through Strasser's permission for access to weapons and the promise of personal benefit from newly conquered areas. And as before, Shadow State control over the access to weapons and the foreign exchange needed to purchase them requires connections to creditors and overseas commercial networks.

Even more so than Momoh's network, Strasser's regime makes nonsense of rigid distinctions between state and society. The "government" in this case is nearly incapable of providing physical protection even for the inhabitants of the capital after dark, a fact to which the proliferation of private security firms attests. On the other hand, a truly "free" market is exceedingly difficult for Strasser to accept, especially after some officials were caught using their unregulated access to foreign exchange to import Ukrainian assault rifles, guided missiles, and grenade launchers to carry out a coup.[72]

This stark vision of political authority is in part a consequence of past Shadow State rule, but it is also shaped by its confrontation with Charles Taylor's NPFL. Taylor's dynamic Shadow State, almost completely divorced from bureaucratic practice while heavily dependent upon foreign commercial networks, offers a more complete vision of Shadow State rule. It is to this expanded analysis of Shadow State succession elsewhere in Africa that we now turn.

8   The changing character of African sovereignty

Throughout their efforts to establish and conserve political authority, Sierra Leone's leaders have reinterpreted the extent of state sovereignty and the exercise of politics. At times, authority from Freetown appeared impotent in the face of societal resistance. This condition historically brought calls for reforms to ensure greater order, peace, and stability. At the same time, reforms strengthened intermediaries and ultimately conflicted with leaders' control over all other organizations and associations. In turn, rulers became concerned about managing these strongmen. The Sierra Leone government's approach toward economic exchange, and particularly informal markets, over the past century, illustrates this intermingling of formal and informal state power and societal authority. This final chapter explains why patrimonial rulers in Sierra Leone and elsewhere have consistently chosen to dominate their potential rivals through these means rather than by mobilizing their citizens through strong bureaucratic institutions. This understanding also illuminates features of state–society relations in many African countries which conflict with expectations that a liberal order will follow recent political and economic "reforms."

Developments in neighboring Liberia illustrate elements of the political economy of a more complete Shadow State ascendancy. Four years after NPFL leader Charles Taylor rules the majority of the country, along with adjacent areas in Sierra Leone and Guinea, from a mobile base. Taylor's "Greater Liberia" demonstrates a relationship of political power and markets remarkably free from the constraints of bureaucracies inherited from his predecessors to the extent that Taylor ignores even the formal borders of the countries upon which he builds his Shadow State. Taylor's confrontation with Strasser's Shadow State in Sierra Leone reinforces this political logic of coercion and control over markets as each leader confronts challenges from the other.

Shadow States in this part of Africa battle other entities and achieve at least a military effectiveness to enforce claims to sovereignty. This development signals a significant departure in the way some African countries are ruled. Taylor cannot lay claim to sovereignty solely in virtue of being a successor to a colonial government. Nor does his state enjoy the post-colonial right of non-intervention. To the extent that Taylor's forces attack them, he imposes on neighbors the same challenges. To survive, Taylor's, and now Strasser's Shadow States must possess the wherewithall to declare and defend a political order both domestically and internationally. Collaboration with external forces such as foreign firms is even more important to Shadow State rulers eager to take advantage of independence.

One ought not, however, to underestimate the weaknesses and fragmentation of Shadow States. Leaders whom the media commonly term "warlords" lack the means to secure significant widespread allegiance and harness the productivity of subjects. But where self-mastery for states has been so lacking, as in many of Africa's externally designed states, the active, self-directive Shadow State shows a possible path for acquiring relatively greater state capabilities than are currently enjoyed by many juridically sovereign states.

The comparison of the Greater Liberia case with Sierra Leone enables one to consider parallels between past and emerging Shadow States in this part of Africa. This brings us back to the basic question of this study: how are alternative forms of political authority institutionalized in the patrimonial setting of collapsing state bureaucracies in Africa?

Greater Liberia – Shadow State warfare and markets

In 1989, at the head of his National Patriotic Front of Liberia, Charles Taylor launched a Christmas Eve invasion of Liberia from Côte d'Ivoire. Since early 1993, his forces have been confined at times to northern and eastern portions of the country. His organization increasingly cooperates and aligns with rival strongmen to maintain influence in other regions. But at his zenith, Taylor, a fugitive from Boston, Massachusetts' Plymouth Corrections Institute,[1] ruled most of Liberia and parts of Guinea and Sierra Leone as "Greater Liberia" from his capital at the former provincial town of Gbarnga. The "Greater Liberia" case illuminates some key features of how the Shadow State ruler abjuring significant bureaucratic institutions expands his authority beyond recognized borders and commands a diverse array of alliances to accumulate wealth and counter internal and external threats.

At its zenith, Taylor's territory boasted its own currency and banking system, television and radio network, international airfield, and deepwater port. In mid-1994, Taylor still presided over a thriving export trade in diamonds, timber, gold and agricultural products.[2] Taylor has used a network of foreign firms to exploit and market these resources, and to finance his military conquest and control of economically useful territory.

Meanwhile, the authority of the Interim Government of National Unity (IGNU) remained confined to the Monrovia area with the crucial backing of ECOMOG, a multinational military force of the sixteen-nation Economic Community of West African States.

Taylor's political authority lies in his ability to manipulate foreign firms to secure foreign exchange, weapons, and political support to further the reach of his political and economic network. Even more than Strasser in Sierra Leone, Taylor inherited an already decrepit and ineffective bureaucracy. Warfare drove most of the remaining bureaucrats out of areas under Taylor's control by late 1990. From the start of his invasion, Taylor has relied upon his personal control of wealth and the use of force to create, protect, discipline, and reward his political network, which includes foreign firms as well as Liberians. Lack of international recognition, ECOMOG hostility, and the need to quickly raise money to pay for weapons reinforced Taylor's preoccupation with establishing personal control and an unhindered exercise of force as the basis of his rule. The general collapse of the Monrovia regime outside the capital also presented Taylor with the task of fending off challenges from rural strongmen who had accumulated weapons and influence as collaborators with the old regime.

Unlike Momoh or Strasser, Taylor found that the absence of internationally recognized sovereignty also removed the constraints on collection and use of revenues that creditors place on debtor states. Meanwhile, the IGNU enclave faced legal entanglements and creditor demands arising from unpaid arrears on a $4 billion debt inherited from a former regime. Ironically, Taylor's freedom from creditors and his access to foreign firms gave him greater capabilities than the Monrovia enclave, with its automatic international recognition, to quickly generate foreign exchange. But to acquire these capabilities, Taylor exercised power almost entirely through non-institutional channels. He hired a United States public relations firm to represent his "movement"; he claimed "warm ties" to former US president Jimmy Carter, interpreting Carter's criticism of ECOMOG during a visit to Liberia as approval for the NPFL;[3] he publicized such messages through *The Patriot*, his "official" newspaper, of such high technical quality that some suspect it was produced by one of his corporate allies. He communicated with publicists and overseas associates through a facsimile and telephone satellite hookup.[4]

To finance these initiatives, Taylor first built his Shadow State with the plunder and sale of mining machinery from the abandoned German-operated Bong Iron Ore Company. Taylor's brother, Gbatu Taylor, oversaw sales of this machinery overseas. This income became the nucleus of the NPFL's "official" financial agency for dealing with overseas associates, the Bong Bank.[5] Charles Taylor later found more reliable sources of income and political benefits in cooperation with Firestone Tire and Rubber, however. This subsidiary of Japanese-owned Bridgestone, long a cornerstone of Liberia's export-oriented economic policies, allegedly reached an accord with Taylor in 1991 to cooperate in rubber production and marketing. Critics accused Taylor of using his "G-2" security force to organize rubber production on the plantation.[6] In return for NPFL protection, Firestone allegedly provided communications facilities and a supply base for "Operation Octopus," the NPFL's October 1992 assault on Monrovia.[7] Travelers to Greater Liberia also report that G-2 enforces regulations requiring that inhabitants use NPFL-issued currency. The security force also restricts inhabitants' movements, allegedly to prevent the development of private long-distance trade that would compete with "official" NPFL trade, a move emphasizing the importance of control as well as the generation of wealth to the Shadow State ruler.

Taylor also arranged arms-for-timber swaps, continuing a former Liberian President Samuel Doe's practice.[8] Taylor organized these sales through a "Forestry Development Authority" with close ties to his brother's Bong Bank to collect cash for timber licenses and tax on rough-log exports.[9] French firms and Lebanese-owned enterprises in neighboring Côte d'Ivoire became heavily involved in this trade,[10] such that "Greater Liberia" became France's third largest source of tropical timber in 1991.[11] NPFL commander, Jessie Gbanue, headed Taylor's "Forestry Development Authority" to collect fees for timber-export licenses. This branch of the NPFL collects $300,000 (cash) for each license and levies a 10 percent tax on exported logs.[12] Reports also indicate that this agency negotiated a $1.5 million logging contract with an American firm in 1991. Weekly shipments allegedly organized by the Liberian Agricultural Cooperative, owned by United States interests, took logs to overseas markets.[13] This access to foreign exchange has enabled Taylor to take advantage of good prices from former Eastern Bloc arms vendors who are eager to sell their wares for hard currency.

Taylor's best prospect for financing his NPFL appeared in a planned joint venture astride the Liberia–Guinea border. Nimba Mining Company (NIMCO), a consortium of North American, European, and Japanese mining firms, had approached the Liberian government in 1989 with plans to dig iron ore in Liberia's Nimba County.[14] This consortium proposed to supply ore to EUROFER, a European Community consortium of iron and steel producers. NIMCO's member firms have shown a willingness to deal directly with Taylor's NPFL since it took over the area in 1990. Liberian American Swedish Minerals Company's (LAMCO) local General Manager returned to "Greater Liberia" to oversee the consortium's interests in former LAMCO assets. Independence-day greetings in the name of some joint-venture participants appeared in Taylor's "official" *Patriot* newspaper.[15]

In turn, Taylor used NIMCO interest in territory he controlled to raise money and limit external interference in his affairs. The British-owned NIMCO partner, African Mining Company of Liberia (AMCL), handled iron-ore shipments in NPFL territory to keep a railroad to the port of Buchanan operational. In return for NPFL iron ore and cooperation, consortium participants allegedly paid Taylor $10 million a month.[16] Meanwhile, Taylor took advantage of the railroad to move timber and stockpiled iron ore to Buchanan for export.[17] Sollac, a French supplier of iron ore to French state-owned Usinor steel mills allegedly organized and purchased ore shipments from Taylor in 1991.[18] This foreign-firm presence complicated the Monrovia enclave's struggle to cut off Taylor's financial and arms networks since foreign commercial interests in Taylor's operations undermined foreign-government support for IGNU's anti-NPFL stance. For example, Taylor exploited concerns in Paris that Nigeria's role in ECOMOG represented Nigerian interference in areas of historic French commercial dominance.[19] French failure to back United Nations' criticism of the environmental consequences of the NIMCO project's potential threat to West Africa's largest remaining stand of tropical rainforest demonstrated French commercial interests' strength in resisting IGNU efforts to scupper Taylor's business deals.[20]

Taylor reaped other benefits from the French–Nigerian regional rivalry. United States diplomatic cables leaked to the press noted that ECOMOG's aggressive military tactics and large Nigerian contingent alienated Liberia's neighbors.[21] The government of "Greater Liberia's" pro-French neighbor, Côte d'Ivoire, shared French reluctance to support ECOMOG's military campaign against Taylor. "The predominant role in determining Liberia's future, Ivorians fear," noted one cable, "now belongs to their longtime rival: Nigeria."[22] Côte d'Ivoire's leader thus tolerated shipments of arms to Taylor from former Warsaw-Pact countries via his and Burkina Faso's territory.[23] Despite State Department information that Taylor stockpiled these weapons "for a serious campaign or protracted lower-level insurgency,"[24] U.S. officials' weak response to these leaks made clear to Taylor and his opponents that the United States had little interest in getting involved in Liberia to directly back the IGNU government.

Taylor exploited these external divisions to protect and extend his range of commercial contacts. For example, Taylor subcontracted Buchanan's port operations and customs collections to the Associated Development Corporation (ADC), a private operation, "because of its expected infusion of investment capital."[25] While ADC brought little investment capital, the firm did attract United States and Lebanese partners interested in Taylor's timber and agricultural products. In this case, contact with one overseas business network led to contact with several other foreign firms that could help market "Greater Liberian" products. The alleged involvement of Lebanese families with ties to the Liberian port city of Buchanan and Côte d'Ivoire as middlemen in these arrangements also suggested that Ivorian state officials possibly shared in the profits of Taylor's operations. Taylor had earlier exploited to his advantage former Ivorian leader Houphouët-Boigny's antipathy for former President Doe for executing Boigny's son-in-law, son of former Liberian President Tolbert. Taylor used logistical and weapons support from another Boigny son-in-law, Burkina Faso President Blaise Compaoré.[26]

All of these private commercial arrangements bolstered Taylor's capacity to exercise political authority. Taylor used his access to foreign exchange and weapons to finance an invasion of eastern Sierra Leone. Naming former Sierra Leone Army Corporal Foday Sankoh "Governor of Sierra Leone," Taylor incorporated the conquered territories into his Shadow State. For a time in 1991 and 1992, the most economically viable parts of Sierra Leone – the diamond fields and export-agriculture lands – became part of the NPFL commercial empire.[27] At various times, Taylor's forces have also cooperated with the United Liberian Movement for Democracy (ULIMO) and the Liberian Peace Council (LPC), both largely consisting of armed bands formerly associated with the Liberian Army.[28] This expansion of NPFL-held territory also provided a means of rewarding fighters. In lieu of cash salaries, NPFL fighters were promised opportunities to loot conquered areas. Taylor's use of force against the deinstitutionalizing Sierra Leonean regime in turn created a more urgent need in Freetown for revenue and weapons, which hastened the process of Shadow State formation there.

Taylor demonstrates how the head of an expansive Shadow State can draw advantages from these diverse networks – ranging from presidential families, foreign firms eager to make a deal, informal-market operators, and various dissidents and small rebel movements eager for a cut in local business – as soon as they pledge their allegiance to him. Taylor places himself in the position of referee and policeman, managing private networks of accumulation to support his personal authority. In the end it is not crucial that foreign firms in Taylor's network engage in productive investments, but rather that they provide the political network with access to hard currency and commercial networks in exchange for minerals and timber. It is through the agency of these firms that Taylor exercises direct control over local trade, and profits from rivalries in Sierra Leone, from control of trade networks dating to pre-colonial times, and from other leaders' family feuds.

The Shadow State creates a central interest out of marriages, commercial contacts, conquests, personal rivalries, and proxy intervention. Private interests and "state" interests become hopelessly intermingled. The two spheres are not simply merged; instead, they shift roles at different times. The notion of "straddling," of one foot in the private sphere, another (at various times) more firmly in the broader political sphere, gets to the heart of the growing interrelation of both within the sphere of domination in the Shadow State.

Naomi Chazan and Janet MacGaffey suspect, however, that such straddling declines as formal state institutions decay. That is, they suspect that officials abandon the realm of the state as it collapses.[29] This is not evident in the Sierra Leone case, nor in Greater Liberia, where the formal state has virtually ceased to exist. Instead, one finds that a position in the alternative institutionalization of the Shadow State, quite distinct from activities in any conceivable "private" economy, serves as the passport to wealth. For instance, one finds that informal diamond-mining networks are the objects of intense attention from Strasser's and Taylor's Shadow States. Private foreign firms solicit for entry into interrelated "state" and private channels of accumulation. Those who attract the ruler's favor receive indulgences of power, to the mutual benefit of themselves and the Shadow State. Private circuits and political circuits of accumulation reinforce each other. Instead of a dichotomous relationship of exclusion, or zero-sum competition, there exists a symbiotic relationship between private and political capital. It is also evident that beneficiaries of this relationship consider the global economy to be their field of accumulation, not the narrow, inherited colonial state boundaries.

These developments have little to do with autonomous class interests of an imagined entrepreneurial "middle strata" upon which creditors' reforms are premised. Nor do these developments have much to offer those who see in state decay the seeds of a civil society that will demand accountability from rulers. They do, however, illustrate the multiple compromises that rulers have made with diverse networks, and that individuals have to make with the Shadow State in order to survive, and how little these accommodations have to do with the spirit of capitalism or the construction of state bureaucratic institutions.

Contradictions of pluralism and the colonial inheritance

Liberia shows that the Shadow State is not exceptional in West Africa. One finds its equivalents in reciprocal elite networks in Senegal, the political role of commercial "barons" in Côte d'Ivoire, and in Nigeria's "Old Brigades'" prominent presence in privatization efforts.[30] In each case, compromises between elites coopt or repress those able to lead a popular mobilization.

The uncertain and contingent nature of compromises exacerbates the hazards of unpredictable economic or political pluralism. In order to conceptualize the challenges of uncontrolled pluralism to elite accommodations, it is useful to return to Carl Schmitt's notion of "political theology" as a response to challenge. Carl Schmitt says of Weber: "when he speaks of differentiation in the categories of legal thought, he equates the word *formal* with the words *rationalized*, professionally *trained*, and, finally, *calculable*. This, he said, "is, from the perspective of sociology, of particular interest in the age of intense commercial activity because commerce is less concerned with a particular content than with a calculable certainty."[31]

In contrast, colonial rulers were haunted by what seemed at one and the same time to be immense administrative and military superiority, and a failure to translate this power into the bureaucratic institutions of a strong state able to see its decisions obeyed. Specialists in colonial juridical and administrative practice recognized that an alternative to Weberian notions of institutionalization could secure colonial competence to rule. "The supervision exercised over them," said Lord Hailey of collaborating elites, "must bring home the lesson that the sanction for their authority is no longer the goodwill of their own people, but the recognition awarded to them by the administration." Hailey hoped that shared power would be "the most effective means for inducing native opinion to accept innovations which it does not actively demand."[32] Lord Lugard regarded this assimilation of elites to the colonial cause as a project to be carried out on British terms, establishing in the eyes of subjects exclusive colonial competence to render decisions. Of India, he confidently noted that "When legislation has to be enacted which is unpopular, there may be a reluctance to accept what will be called 'Babu-made law,' though it would have been accepted without demur as the order of 'the Sirkar' – the British Raj." Through this exercise of colonial competence, "the personal interests of the [local] ruler," said Lugard, "must rapidly become identified with those of the controlling power."[33]

Furthermore, the colonial state's fiscal survival depended upon asserting claims to this competence. Yet as the impact of post-Second-World-War Colonial Office reforms were felt in British Africa, what had been viewed in Freetown as *lèse majesté* became criticism in a democratic polity. Some colonial officers continued to regard political activism as a matter for the police. Others resented the diminution of their (essentially coercive) authority to hold together the colonial elite accommodation. Complained a local administrator just before independence: "Now that we must make cash payments to workers, everybody wants such ... Our word no longer suffices to cause these people to work."[34] Other more forward-looking officials sought to extend their informal ties to new collaborators through targeted development programs such as MADA and the official manipulation of access to private mining in order to influence local political struggles. But as one departing British officer warned, "Chiefs, Tribal Authorities and Village Heads in Kono District would receive annual payments as long as they were 'helpful to Government.'"[35]

Those wrestling with the need to make decisive judgements, faulted liberal reforms for their tendency to divide power, for the "secularization" of sovereignty away from the omnipotent center, and for the provision of refuges from which rivals could mount attacks. As Stevens wrote, for the ruler "it is difficult to draw the line between interfering with proper administration of an organization and expressing legitimate concerns about its progress."[36] These inheritors of the colonial state also shared the colonial tendency to measure political authority less by the degree of institutionalization of rule than by its competence to make decisions. Evenness of practice governed by utility and predictability did not address the ruler's capacity to deal with challenges, especially when rivals threatened the survival of the existing political order.

This notion of sovereignty – of a need to retain the ruler's competence to make decisions and to protect the existing order – dispenses with "legal-rational" limits on the state's capacity to rule. Where legal provisions have threatened regime survival, leaders have chosen other ways to meet an imminent challenge from rivals. Even during "normal times," Stevens and his predecessors placed a premium on the state's ability to engage in exceptional intervention into segments of society from which challenges came. Under conditions of electoral competition, these challenges emerged most forcefully among illicit diamond miners, aggrieved first at their formal, and then their informal exclusion from benefits, but at the same time able to utilize political openings to find forceful spokesmen for their cause. In an effort to adapt to the challenges to their survival unleashed by reforms that empower political entrepreneurs capitalizing on popular grievances, leaders are forced to resort to informal means of control – buying cooperation and punishing disobedience through politically directed MADA funds and other government spending, and by outright violence.

These conflicting views of how the country should be run constituted the major inheritance of colonialism. Central control preserved the integrity of the political system against the challenges of rivals questioning the competence of rulers to rule. Siaka Stevens considered political opposition "as sentinels to the abuse of power ... who take nothing as read, but search assiduously for flaws in the Government machinery and its activities."[37]

When no consensus existed over the "rules of the game," but competition was allowed, what authority could decide upon a definition of political unity? Who defined what forces represented an intolerable threat to unity?

Liberal reform and the increasing "secularization" of authority in which divided power becomes a refuge for rivals, propelled to the fore pressing questions concerning the appropriate nature of state sovereignty. The definition of the ruler's competence to decide what constitutes a challenge and an appropriate response became the ruler's primary concern. That is, survival demanded a return to a more encompassing "theological" politics where the leader remained free to identify and intervene in diverse spheres of interest to offer comprehensive protection to the existing political system from the challenges of rivals.

Stevens's failure to protect state power from private interests reinforced the notion of danger and chaos emanating from society. Political power did not vanish in the weakened state, but instead became attached to groups who sought to exercise power in place of the state. The progressive extension of the ruler's authority became the real political constitution of Sierra Leone. The construction of the political coalition occurred across varied social terrain, often in an *ad hoc*, improvizational manner while facing competitive challenge. Throughout, the leader appeared to be constantly preoccupied with redefining his own sovereignty, particularly with regard to his ability to identify rivals and banish challengers.

To withstand conditions of challenge, President Momoh averred that "What we desire most in this part of the world is discipline ... I can only hope that the rest of the country will be able to keep up with my pace when it comes to displays of discipline."[38] Momoh recognized that he had to keep the exercise of authority fluid enough to coopt, destroy, or appropriate societal structures in any arena in which this power was contested. Creditor-sponsored reforms and efforts to attract foreign investment enforced a new economic hierarchy that placed the state – as creditors understood it with the competent leader at its head – in a position to again monopolize the distribution of benefits. Recapturing resources, along with creditor and foreign-investor aid in marginalizing autonomous elements of informal markets, allowed Momoh to gain some direction over the accumulation and distribution of social reward. For both creditor and ruler, reform returned to the colonial preoccupation of recapturing control over accumulation to enhance the regime's political centrality.

Reforms of this type mock rhetorical commitments to drawing entrepreneurial activity into the formal sector, since there exists little to differentiate state and private spheres of accumulation. This struggle for resources, not the establishment of legalistic "rules of the game" constitutes the building blocks of political authority in the Shadow State leader's eyes. To the extent that creditors' reforms further undermine existing state bureaucratic institutions – either through austerity, or insistence that state functions be taken over by foreign contractors – the pursuit of power takes place in more exclusively Shadow State channels. For Charles Taylor, his lack of international recognition and obligations, coupled with opportunities in the form of conquest and foreign firms, gave him the freedom to abjure bureaucratic institutions and instead maximize his power through a nearly exclusive Shadow State strategy.

But even where creditors do appear to have great leverage, as against the present rulers in Freetown, they collaborate in the ruler's primary task of maintaining a fragile authority to head off the mutually unpalatable alternatives of chaos and anarchy. The ruler fears for his position and life. The creditor fears the day when, as in Somalia, no competent authority exists to acknowledge debts or renegotiate arrears payments. This aversion to the disorder, the potential Somalias in Africa's future, causes many "pragmatists" to argue for continued aid to Shadow State rulers, even though they know that the resources will not be used for the purposes claimed. As among colonial authorities, this elite recognition that existing states are unlikely to obtain sufficient resources to impose strong bureaucratic institutions and their rules on African societies leads to the logical alternative – elite accommodation around coincidental interests in the pursuit of ultimately contradictory goals.

This latest elite accommodation on an international scale makes a mockery of reforms designed to tap the energies of the informal sector, especially when those reforms help to accelerate rulers' shifts from reliance on institutional state power to direct political control of markets. Development of a "middle strata" or civil society capable of rallying behind reform programs is even less likely as society becomes subject to this more pervasive Shadow State inclusion. Ferdnand Braudel recognizes the comprehensive nature of this exercise of power as he describes the relation of political power to exchange in other settings:

The *power apparatus*, the might that pervades and permeates every structure, is something more than the state. It is the sum of the political, social, economic, and cultural hierarchies, a collection of means of coercion where the state's presence is always felt, where it is often the keystone of the whole, but where it is seldom, if ever *solely* in control.[39]

One should recognize, however, that this Shadow State turn to historic networks, elite accommodations, and forms of direct control remains very uncertain. Colonial rule perhaps rendered elite accommodations more or less likely. But the post-colonial era introduces numerous amendments. Already in Sierra Leone and Liberia, troops from Nigeria exercise influence over factional struggles in those places. But more important is the unexpected role of foreign firms and global commercial networks. Their shifting interests and organizations considerably complicate the calculus of Shadow State invasions of societal networks.

The difference in colonial and Shadow State elite accommodations lies in the intensity and comprehensiveness of domination. Elite accommodations remained informally institutionalized in the colonial state, even when they received tacit approval from the Colonial Office or Freetown. Colonial rulers ceded autonomy in some spheres, dispensing it in the name of protecting "native rights" in the interests of reducing demands on limited state resources. Rulers of the post-colonial state, however, respond to internal and external challenges with expanded elite accommodations or outright repression of an increasing range of activities deemed to be a threat to the regime's authority.

The significance of this strategy lies not only in intensified exploitation and repression of society. Its political impact is found in the difficulty of constructing rival political structures in the face of unexpectedly powerful and competent Shadow State powers. This "success" makes it likely that, should the Shadow State fail, the result will not be the flowering of a vibrant civil society. Instead, the more probable heirs to the Shadow State are fragments of elite networks, strongmen striking out on their own. One can imagine that the likely successors to Charles Taylor and Valentine Strasser will be one or several of their current armed collaborators. The more entrepreneurial among them will not lack for supporters since decades of repression and exploitation have led significant numbers to view justice in terms of retribution against their latest oppressors. Entrepreneurs and their supporters will exploit anarchy and anger as an opportunity to rob the countryside on their own behalf. Amidst the collapse of the Shadow State's monopoly on violence, most people will encounter authority in the form of cheap and effective automatic weapons such as the AK–47 and the youths who are adept at using them, rather than the resurgence of a romanticized civil society that will dissolve the immense social damage of patrimonial politics.

Notes

INTRODUCTION

1. Jennifer Whitaker, *How Can Africa Survive?* (New York: Council on Foreign Relations, 1990).
2. For example: Robert Jackson and Carl Rosberg, "Why Africa's Weak States Persist: The Empirical and Juridical in Statehood," *World Politics*, 35,1 (October 1982), 1–24; Crawford Young and Thomas Turner, *The Rise and Decline of the Zairian State* (Madison: University of Wisconsin, 1985); John Frimpong-Ansah, *The Vampire State in Africa* (Trenton: Africa World Press, 1991); and Richard Sandbrook, "Taming the African Leviathan," *World Policy Journal*, 7,4 (Fall 1990), 673–701.
3. Goran Hyden, *No Shortcuts to Progress* (Berkeley: University of California, 1983).
4. Clifford Geertz, *The Interpretation of Culture* (New York: Free Press, 1973), Ch.1.
5. Government of Sierra Leone, Ministry of Finance, *The 1975/76 Budget Speech* (Freetown: Government Printing Department, 1975).
6. Jean-François Bayart, *L'Etat en Afrique* (Paris: Fayard, 1989), 257.

1 INFORMAL MARKETS AND THE SHADOW STATE

1. Thomas Hobbes, *Leviathan* (London: Clarendon, 1909), 251.
2. Larry Diamond, "Introduction: Roots of Failure, Seeds of Hope," in L. Diamond, L. Linz, and S.M. Lipset, eds., *Democracy in Developing Countries: Africa* (Boulder: Lynne Rienner, 1988), 20.
3. Richard Sandbrook, "Taming the African Leviathan," *World Policy Journal*, 7:4 (1990), 677.
4. Richard Joseph, *Democracy and Prebendal Politics in Nigeria* (Lagos: Spectrum Press, 1991), 180–1.
5. Jennifer Whitaker, *How Can Africa Survive?* (New York: Council on Foreign Relations, 1990).
6. Richard Sandbrook, *The Politics of Africa's Economic Recovery* (New York: Cambridge University Press, 1993), 58.
7. World Bank, *Sub-Saharan Africa: From Crisis to Sustainable Growth* (Washington, DC: World Bank, 1989), 55.
8. Ibrahim Babangida, "Nigeria Incorporated: Joint Partnership for Socio-economic Progress," Address to Chief Executives, NICON-Naga Hilton, Abuja, Nigeria, (mimeo), 14 January 1991.

9. Jeffrey Herbst, *The Politics of Reform in Ghana, 1982–1991* (Berkeley: University of California Press, 1993).
10. J. Barry Riddell, "Things Fall Apart Again: Structural Adjustment Programmes in Sub-Saharan Africa," *Journal of Modern African Studies*, 30, 1 (1992), 53–68.
11. Thomas Callaghy, "Lost Between State and Market: The Politics of Structural Adjustment in Ghana, Zambia and Nigeria," in Joan Nelson, ed., *The Politics of Economic Adjustment in the Third World* (Princeton: Princeton University Press, 1990).
12. Jean-François Bayart, *L'Etat en Afrique* (Paris: Fayard, 1989), 241–54.
13. Achille Mbembe, "Pouvoir, violence et accumulation," *Politique Africaine*, 39 (1990), 24.
14. See Marc Augé, "L'organisation du commerce pré-colonial en Basse-Côte d'Ivoire et ses effets sur l'organisation sociale des populations côtières," in Claude Meillassoux, ed., *The Development of Indigenous Markets and Trade in West Africa* (London: Oxford University Press, 1971), 153–67.
15. See Jean Copans, "Du vin de palme nouveau dans les vieilles calebasses? A propos de l'état des marchés, des paysans, des crises et des luttes populaires en Afrique noire," *Genève Afrique*, 27,1 (1989), 7–43.
16. Jean Copans, *Les marabouts d'arachide* (Paris: L'Harmattan, 1988), 203.
17. They include Goran Hyden, *Beyond Ujamaa in Tanzania: Under-development and an Uncaptured Peasantry* (Berkeley: University of California Press, 1980); Naomi Chazan, *An Anatomy of Ghanaian Politics: Managing Political Recession, 1969–1982* (Boulder: Westview, 1983); Naomi Chazan and Victor Azarya, "Disengagement from the State in Africa: Reflections on the Experience of Ghana and Guinea," *Comparative Studies in Society and History*, 29, 1 (1987), 106–31.
18. Angelo Barampama, "Secteur non structuré en Afrique: cacophonie de la survie et leur déspoir," *Genève Afrique*, 22, 1 (1984), 46.
19. Naomi Chazan, "Patterns of State–Society Incorporation and Disengagement in Africa," in D. Rothchild and N. Chazan, eds., *The Precarious Balance: State and Society in Africa* (Boulder: Westview, 1988), 333. See also John Ayoade, "States Without Citizens: An Emerging African Phenomenon," 100–18 in the same volume.
20. Reginald Green, "*Magendo* in the Political Economy of Uganda: Pathology, Parallel System or Dominant Sub-Mode of Production?" Discussion Paper 64 (IDS: University of Sussex, 1981).
21. Nelson Kasfir, "State, *Magendo* and Class Formation in Uganda," *Journal of Commonwealth and Comparative Politics*, 22, 3 (1984), 99.
22. For example, Larry Diamond, et al., *Democracy in Developing Countries: Africa* (Boulder: Lynne Reinner, 1988); Goran Hyden and Michael Bratton, eds., *Governance and Politics in Africa* (Boulder: Lynne Reinner, 1991); Carter Center, Seminars of the African Governance Programme (Atlanta: Carter Center).
23. An early statement is the World Bank, *Sub-Saharan Africa: From Crisis to Sustainable Growth* (Washington, DC: World Bank, 1989).
24. Edward V.K. Jaycox, *The Challenge of African Development* (Washington, DC: World Bank, 1992), 74.

25. William Reno, "Old Brigades, Money Bags, New Breeds and the Ironies of Reform in Nigeria," *Canadian Journal of African Studies*, 27, 1 (March 1993), 66–87.

26. Catherine Boone, *Merchant Capital and the Roots of State Power in Senegal: 1930–1985* (New York: Cambridge University Press, 1992); Christian Coulon and Donal Cruise O'Brien, "Senegal," in D. Cruise O'Brien, R. Rathbone, and J. Dunn, eds., *Contemporary West African States* (New York: Cambridge University Press, 1989), 151–2; and Copans, *Marabouts*.

27. Janet MacGaffey, "Economic Disengagement and Class formation in Zaire," in D. Rothchild and N. Chazan, eds., *The Precarious Balance* (Boulder: Westview, 1988), 171.

28. Muhoya Vwakyanakazi, "African Traders in Butembo, Eastern Zaire (1960–1980)" (Ph.D Dissertation, University of Wisconsin, 1982), 339–40. This approach is characterized by Janet MacGaffey, ed., *The Real Economy of Zaire* (Philadelphia: University of Pennsylvania, 1991).

29. A proposition which Sara Berry rebuts with empirical evidence in her *Fathers Work for Their Sons* (Berkeley: University of California, 1985).

30. Blaine Hardin, "Eye of the Family," in his *Africa: Dispatches from a Fragile Continent* (New York: Norton, 1990), 61–94 illustrates personal dimensions of these claims. Jennifer Whitaker, *How Can Africa*, 94–7, views kinship claims as an obstacle to formal market capital accumulation.

31. Peter Geschiere, "La paysannerie africaine est-elle captive?" *Politique Africaine*, 14(1984), 13–34.

32. Michael Twaddle, "Is Africa Decaying? Notes Towards an Analysis," in H.B. Hansen and Michael Twaddle, eds., *Uganda Now: Between Decay and Development* (Nairobi: Heinemann Kenya, 1988), 334.

33. Janet MacGaffey, *Entrepreneurs and Parasites: The Struggle for Indigenous Capital in Zaire* (New York, Cambridge University Press, 1987).

34. Kasfir, "State, *Magendo* and Class Formation," 95.

35. Alain Morice, "Commerce parallele et troc á Luanda," *Politique Africaine*, 17(1985), 105–20.

36. A notion that Pierre Péan develops in his *L'argent noir: corruption et sous-développement* (Paris: Fayard, 1988).

37. MacGaffey, *Entrepreneurs*, 201.

38. Jean-François Bayart, "Civil Society in Africa," in Patrick Chabal, ed., *Political Domination in Africa* (Cambridge: Cambridge University Press, 1986), 115–16.

39. Crawford Young and Thomas Turner, *The Rise and Decline of the Zairian State* (Madison: University of Wisconsin Press, 1985), 30–1. Earlier reference is found in Henry M. Stanley, *The Congo and the Founding of Its Free State* (New York: Harper & Brothers, 1885), 329–32.

40. Thomas Callaghy, *The State–Society Struggle: Zaire in Comparative Perspective* (New York: Columbia University, 1984), 189, 370–1.

41. Basil Davidson, *The Black Man's Burden* (New York: Times Books, 1992), 258.

42. Young and Turner, *Rise and Decline*, 45, 183.

43. Callaghy, *State–Society Struggle*, 188.

44. David Fieldhouse, *Black Africa 1945–1980: Economic Decolonization and Arrested Development* (London: Allen & Unwin, 1986), 44.

45. Young, *Rise and Decline*, 302–3; Thomas Callaghy, "Africa and the World Economy," in J. Harbeson and D. Rothchild, eds., *Africa in World Politics* (Boulder: Westview, 1991), 39–68.
46. Young, *Rise and Decline*, 405.
47. Janet MacGaffey, "Initiatives from Below: Zaire's Other Path to Social and Economic Restoration," in Goran Hyden and Michael Bratton, eds., *Governance and Politics in Africa* (Boulder: Lynne Reinner, 1991), 251.
48. René Lemarchand, "The Politics of Penury in Rural Zaire," in Guy Grau, ed., *Zaire: The Political Economy of Underdevelopment* (New York: Praeger, 1979), 237–60.
49. MacGaffey, "Economic Disengagement," 183–4.
50. *Ibid.*, 184.
51. Hernando DeSoto, *The Other Path* (New York: Harper & Row, 1989).
52. "Zaire: The Inspirational Master," *Africa Confidential*, 11 January 1991; and "Zaire I: Dual Control," *Africa Confidential*, 16 April 1993.
53. "Zaire: Holding Back the Opposition," *Africa Confidential*, 9 August 1991.
54. Especially Jean Claude Willame, *Zaire: l'épopée d'Inga* (Paris: L'Harmattan, 1986).
55. Emmanuel Dungia, *Mobutu et l'argent du Zaire* (Paris: L'Harmattan, 1992).
56. "Zaire: The Long Goodbye," *Africa Confidential*, 6 March 1992.
57. Jean-François Bayart, "L'énonciation du politique," *Revue français de sciences politique*, 35(1985), 367–9.
58. Michael Schatzberg, *The Dialectics of Oppression in Zaire* (Bloomington: Indiana University Press, 1988), 102–11.
59. *Africa Report*, March/April 1992, 44.
60. Jean-Claude Willame, "Zaire: systéme de survie et fiction d'Etat," *Canadian Journal of African Studies*, 18,1(1984), 83–9.
61. Ayoade, "States without Citizens," 196.
62. Sennen Andriamirado, "Au pays oú les cireurs sont milliardaires," *Jeune Afrique*, 26 November 1992, 34–5.
63. "Zaire II," *Africa Confidential*, 16 April 1993; "Zaire: Les diamants du Mobutu," *Jeune Afrique*, 22 April 1993, 8.
64. Chris Allen, et al., eds., *Benin, the Congo, Burkina Faso* (New York: Pinter, 1989), 134.
65. Schatzberg, *Dialectics of Oppression*, 142.
66. Bayart, *L'Etat en Afrique*, 193–226. See also Christian Coulon, "Une nouvelle exploration du politique en Afrique," *Politique Africaine*, 1(1981), 137–9.
67. Jean-François Bayart, *L'Etat au Cameroun*, 2eme edn. (Paris: Presses de la Fondation Nationale des Sciences Politiques, 1985), 325.
68. J.-L. Domenach, "Pouvoir et société dans la Chine des années soixante-dix," *Bulletin Modes populaires d'action politique*, 1(1983), 29.
69. Bayart, *L'Etat au Cameroun*, 19.
70. Achille Mbembe, "L'argument matériel dans les Eglises catholiques d'Afrique: le cas du Zimbabwe (1975–1987)," *Politique Africaine*, 35(1989), 64.
71. Achille Mbembe, *Afrique Indociles: Christianisme, pouvoir et état en société post-coloniale* (Paris: Karthala, 1988).
72. See also Jan Vansina, "A Past for Africa's Future?" *Dalhousie Review*, 68, 1/2(1988), 8–23; and Edouard Brion, "L'Eglise catholique et la Rebellion au Zaire (1964–1967)," *Cahiers de CEDAF*, 7/8(1986), 61–78.

73. P. M. Hegba, *Emancipation d'Eglises sous tutelle* (Paris: Presence Africain, 1976).
74. Carl Schmitt, *Political Theology* (George Schwab, trans.) (Cambridge: MIT Press, 1985 [1934]), 59.
75. Carl Schmitt, *The Concept of the Political* (George Schwab, trans.) (New Brunswick, NJ: Rutgers University, 1976), 18.
76. *Ibid.*, 14.

2 COLONIAL RULE AND THE FOUNDATIONS OF THE SHADOW STATE

1. Fredrick D. (Lord) Lugard, *The Dual Mandate in British Tropical Africa* (London: William Blackwood & Sons, 1922), 113.
2. DC/RY 42, 1915 "Disaffection in Lei Chiefdom," 25 March 1914. (Official documents from the colonial era to 1954 are located at Sierra Leone National Archives, Fourah Bay College, Freetown.)
3. "Black Colonialism," *The Watchman* (a London-based dissident publication), vol. 1, 1990.
4. Arthur Abraham, *Mende Government and Politics Under Colonial Rule* (Freetown: Sierra Leone University, 1978), 109.
5. Lugard, *Dual Mandate*, 135.
6. *Sierra Leone Times*, 5 December 1898, cited in Christopher Fyfe, *A History of Sierra Leone* (Cambridge: Cambridge University Press, 1962), 581.
7. Most notably, George A. Lethbridge-Banbury, *Sierra Leone; or, The White Man's Grave* (London: S. Sonnenschein, 1888).
8. Lugard, *Dual Mandate*, 133–5.
9. Christopher Fyfe, *History*, 564.
10. Kenneth MacCaullay, *The Colony of Sierra Leone Vindicated* (London: Frank Cass & Co, 1968 [1827]), 74.
11. CSO 3057/17, "Personnel–Reports."
12. Jean-François Bayart, *L'Etat en Afrique* (Paris: Fayard, 1989), 193–226.
13. Fyfe, *History*, 174.
14. Cited in N.A. Cox-George, *Finance and Development in West Africa: The Sierra Leone Experience* (London: Denis Dobson, 1961), 93.
15. Gustav K. Deveneaux, "Public Opinion and Colonial Policy in Nineteenth Century Sierra Leone," *International Journal of African Historical Studies*, 9,1 (1976), 57.
16. Ronald K. Robinson, *Africa and the Victorians* (New York: St. Martin's, 1961), 383.
17. Peter Kup, *Sierra Leone: A Concise History* (London: David & Charles, 1975), 171.
18. Deveneaux, "Public Opinion," 58.
19. Governor's Letter Book (hereafter GLB), 8 November 1891.
20. *West African Reporter* (Freetown), cited in Deveneaux, "Public Opinion," 56.
21. CSO 4186, 7 February 1890.
22. *Report by Her Majesty's Commissioner and Correspondence on the Subject of the Insurrection in the Sierra Leone Protectorate, 1898* (Chalmers Report), Part II: Evidence and Documents (London: HMSO, 1898), 233.

23. GLB, Letter to Commander Denman, 9 August 1893.
24. Robert T. Parsons, *Religion in an African Society* (Leiden: E.M. Brill, 1964), 205.
25. Allen Howard, "Big Men, Traders and Chiefs: Power, Commerce and Spatial Change in the Sierra Leone–Guinea Plain" (Ph.D Dissertation, University of Wisconsin, 1972), found that chiefs associated with traders to gain the power to grant or withhold commercial opportunities which would benefit subjects or harm rivals. See also Robert T. Parsons, *Religion*, esp. pp. 79–80.
26. Despatch to Secretary of State No. 158, 3 October 1889.
27. P.S. d'Orfond, "New Light on the Origin of the Waiima Affair," *Sierra Leone Studies* (n.s.) 11 (1958), 218–35.
28. CSO, 5 April 1894.
29. Sahr Matturi, "A Brief History of the Nimikoro Chiefdom, Kono District," *Africana Research Bulletin* (Freetown), 3,2 (1973), 36.
30. *Ibid.*, 38.
31. Cited in Robinson, *Africa*, 397.
32. Quoted in Martin Kilson, *Political Change in a West African State* (Cambridge, MA: Harvard University Press, 1966), 11.
33. CSO, Governor Cardew, 4 May 1895.
34. Thomas S. Alldridge, *The Sherbro and Its Hinterland* (London: Macmillan, 1901), 342.
35. Chalmers Report, Part II, 189.
36. *Sierra Leone Report for 1897*, Cmd. 9497 (London, 1898).
37. Chalmers Report, Part I, 356.
38. LaRay Denzer and Michael Crowder, "Bai Bureh and the Hut Tax War of 1898," in Robert Rotberg and Ali Mazrui, eds., *Protest and Power in Black Africa* (New York: Oxford University Press, 1970), 178–9.
39. Kilson, *Political Change*, 21.
40. *Laws of Sierra Leone*, Cap. 170, Part II, "Forced Labor," 569.
41. CSO 3147/05 Minute Paper, "Disagreement Between Chief Yema Fodu and Sub-Chief Sera Modu" (1905).
42. CSO 3464/05 Minute Paper, "Tribal Authority Ordinance, 1905."
43. Quoted in Kilson, *Political Change*, 58.
44. DC/RY 37, 1913 "Disaffection in Sandoh Chiefdom," 20 March 1912.
45. DC/RY 52, 1913 "Request for Soapdish," 10 May 1912. The officer notes that this is his second request.
46. Rudolf von Albertini, *European Colonialism, 1880–1940* (Westport, CT: Greenwood, 1982).
47. On the failure of private business to invest in Sierra Leone, see *Private Enterprise in British Tropical Africa* (London: Cmd 2016, 1924), 18–21.
48. DC/RY 90, 1913 "Model Farm" (no date).
49. Cox-George, *Finance and Development*, 158.
50. Government of Sierra Leone, *Blue Book* (Freetown: Government Printer), various issues. The Imperial War Fund assessed Sierra Leone at £50,000 per annum from 1915. The railroad also drained budgets, with operating costs consistently exceeding revenues before closing in the mid-1970s. (World Bank, "Sierra Leone: Prospects for Growth and Equity," Report No. 535256, [Washington, DC: World Bank, March 1985].)

51. *Annual Report on Eastern Province, 1921* (Freetown: Government Printer, 1922), 11.
52. Government of Sierra Leone, *Laws of Sierra Leone*, Cap. 170, "Protectorate Native Law (1905)," Part I, sect. 13, 569–70.
53. Jennifer Whitaker, *How Can Africa Survive?* (New York: Council on Foreign Relations, 1990), 193.
54. Leo Spitzer, *The Creoles of Sierra Leone: Responses to Colonialism, 1870–1945* (Madison: University of Wisconsin Press, 1974), 79.
55. Fyfe, *History*, 615.
56. From a Krio perspective, Akintola Wyse, *The Krio of Sierra Leone* (Freetown: W.O. Okrafo-Smart & Co, 1987), 21–3. Examples of Krio commercial exploits are from this work.
57. Quoted in Cox-George, *Finance and Development*, 149.
58. Lugard, *Dual Mandate*, 481.
59. Official concerns about Krio smuggling in CSO, "Governor's Confidential Despatch to Secretary of State," No. 60, 31 July 1894, and No 89, 15 November 1894.
60. Cox-George, *Finance and Development*, 196–7.
61. CSO, "Control of Prices under Chamber of Commerce," 1919, Bundle A64. Governor's Office reply in same.
62. Thomas N. Goddard, *The Handbook of Sierra Leone* (London: Grant Richards, 1925), 173.
63. CSO Bundle A76, Lt.-Col. E.D. Hammond, "Report of the Management of the Sierra Leone Railroad" (1922).
64. Jimmy Kandeh, "Dynamics of State, Class and Political Ethnicity: A Comparative Study of State–Society Relations in Colonial and Post Colonial Sierra Leone" (Ph.D Dissertation, University of Wisconsin, 1987), 273.
65. CSO 7147, "Judicial Advisor, Protectorate Administration."
66. T.S. Alldridge, *Colony Transformed*, 78–9.
67. *Ibid.*, 184.
68. *Ibid.*, 204.
69. *Laws of Sierra Leone* (1946), "An Ordinance to Regulate the Right to Search for, Mine, and Work Minerals," Cap. 144 [16 December 1927].
70. L.J. Burke, "A Short History of the Discovery of the Major Diamond Deposits," *Sierra Leone Studies*, 12 (1959), 235–8.
71. CF 53/31, "Letter to Colonial Secretary," 9 September 1931.
72. S. Herbert Frankel, *Capital Investment in Africa* (New York: Howard Fertig, 1938), 326–7.
73. The shifting balance of exports as percentage of imports from 84 percent in 1932 to 173 percent in 1936 demonstrates the critical role mining came to play in Sierra Leone's economy. (Cox-George, *Finance and Development*, 66.)
74. CF 47/34, "Diamond Protection Force," 29 May 1934, 2.
75. *Ibid.*, 8.
76. CF17/35, "Concerning SLST, Ltd, Liabilities for Damages," 29 January 1935.
77. See Christopher Fyfe and V.R. Dorjahn, "Landlord and Stranger: Change in Tenancy Relations in Sierra Leone," *Journal of African History*, 3 (1962), 391–7.
78. CSO 99/4/1 (10) "From Commissioner, Protectorate to Colonial Secretary," 16 March 1935.

79. CF/51/35, "Diamond Protection Force – Comments," 3 March 1935.
80. An informant estimated that payoffs from SLST for expelling strangers ranged from £100 to £500 per year by the late 1940s (Interview No. 17, 27 February 1990). Evidence also exists suggesting that SLST directly involved itself in succession struggles within chiefdoms (DP 232/12/46, "Diamond Protection Force to DC Kono," 30 December 1946).
81. Kono Native Authority, "Conduct of PC Kaimachende of Gbense Chiefdom," 16 December 1936.
82. CSO S91/35, "Letter from S.L.S.T. to Provincial Commissioner," 3 January 1935.
83. CSO 99/4/1 (18), "Report of a Trek Through the Gold Areas," March 1935.
84. Details of the Haidara (Idara) Rebellion can be found in Kilson, *Political Change*, 113–17; and B.M. Jusu, "The Haidara Rebellion of 1931," *Sierra Leone Studies*, 7 (1954), 147–9.
85. Cox-George, *Finance and Development*, 243.
86. The *Guardian* (Freetown), 16 August 1939.
87. CSO 7063, "Appointments of Advisors," 4 May 1938.
88. Appendix to *Ibid.*, "District Reports."
89. "Nimikoro Chiefdom Estimates of Revenues and Expenditures, 1949."
90. Informants disagreed over the actual percentage; 65 percent is a more conservative estimate.

3   ELITE HEGEMONY AND THE THREAT OF POLITICAL AND ECONOMIC REFORM

1. Governor's Office, No. 13383/517 (Confidential), 12 February 1959.
2. MD 111/36v (Confidential), "Inspector of Mines, Interim Report on the Alluvial Diamond Mining Scheme," 18 June 1956.
3. Thomas Callaghy, "Africa and the World Economy: Caught Between a Rock and a Hard Place," in John Harbeson and Donald Rothchild, eds., *Africa in World Politics* (Boulder: Westview, 1991), 57.
4. N.A. Cox-George, *Finance and Development in West Africa: The Sierra Leone Experience* (London: Denis Dobson, 1961), 231–4.
5. William M. (Lord) Hailey, *An African Survey* (London: Oxford University Press, 1938), 295.
6. *Ibid.*, 1465.
7. Government of Sierra Leone, *A Scheme for the Reorganization of the Court Messenger Force*, Sessional Paper No.7 of 1939 (Freetown: Government Printer, 1939), 1.
8. Sir Herbert Cox, *Report of the Commission of Inquiry into Disturbances in the Provinces* (Cox Commission) (Freetown: Government Printer, 1956), 149.
9. J.S. Fenton, *Report on a Visit to Nigeria and on the Application of the Principles of Native Administration to the Protectorate of Sierra Leone* (Freetown, 1935), 17.
10. William M. (Lord) Hailey, *Native Administration in the British African Territories* (London: HMSO, 1951), 308.
11. Fenton, *Report on a Visit*, 11.

12. Jean-François Bayart, *L'Etat au Cameroun* (Paris: Foundation Nationale des Sciences Politique, 1979), 257.

13. Sir Andrew Cohen, *British Policy in Changing Africa* (Evanston: Northwestern University Press, 1959), 32.

14. *Ibid.*, 35.

15. Government of Sierra Leone, *Estimates of Revenues and Expenditures, 1952* (Freetown: Government Printer, 1951).

16. Average of Native Authority estimates for Gbense, Tankoro and Nimikoro, 1956.

17. Government of Sierra Leone, *Report on the Administration of the Provinces, 1955* (Freetown: Government Printer, 1956), 16.

18. MP 2/07/2, "Audit Department," 21 May 1958.

19. Cox, *Report of the Commission*, 148.

20. Government of Sierra Leone, *Report on the Administration*, 16.

21. Government of Sierra Leone, *Statement of the Sierra Leone Government on the Report of the Commission of Inquiry into Disturbances in the Province* (Cox Commission) (Freetown: Government Printer, 1956), 3.

22. Government of Sierra Leone, *Report on the Administration*, 4.

23. *Ibid.*, 1.

24. MD 111/36(v) (confidential), "Interim Report, Chief Inspector of Mines," 18 June 1956.

25. KNA 134/56, "Report of Principal Officer, Yengema," 8 November 1956.

26. Compiled for reports in *Sierra Leone Gazette*.

27. No. 13383/517, "RE: Prison Overcrowding," 12 February 1959.

28. MD 113/23 (Confidential), 26 July 1956.

29. MD 111/36(vi), "Chief Inspector of Mines," 18 June 1956.

30. Payments depended on the mining potential of assigned plots. An informant also commented that ADMS legalization led to a steep rise in mining costs. Kono Interview No. 23, 10 March 1990.

31. Kono Interview No. 22, 8 March 1990.

32. *Sierra Leone Gazette*, 16 June 1971.

33. KNA 351/15/9, "To PC Bona, Nimikoro Chiefdom," 7 October 1961.

34. W.E. Minchinton, "The Sierra Leone Diamond Rush," *Sierra Leone Studies*, 19 (1966), 46; and H.L. van der Laan, *The Sierra Leone Diamonds* (London: Oxford University Press, 1965), 65.

35. Kono interview No. 24, 2 April 1990.

36. CMM/72/14 (confidential), "Meeting Between Minister of Mines and Mr DuCane of SLST," 22 October 1958.

37. Government of Sierra Leone, *Report of the Ministry of Mines* (Freetown: Government Printers, 1965), 6.

38. Allegedly, Nimikoro chieftaincy Native Administration received amounts in excess of £1,000 before stranger drives began. Freetown Interview No. 26, 15 April 1990.

39. Minute Paper 954/58/3–58, 18 June 1958. See also "Kono Development Plan," MP 124/25/1/7 No. D 32/1958.

40. CCP 680/8, "Confidential–Minister of Lands, Mines, and Labour," 24 May 1958.

41. S35/58, "Letter to Chief Commissioner for the Protectorate," 15 May 1958.

42. CMM/71/30 No.D: 128/1958, "Kono Development Plan and Distribution of Grants to Diamondiferous Areas," 15 May 1958.
43. Lba. 3/61 (49) (mimeo) Nimikoro Native Authority Files.
44. The item is line 36.6 (discontinued in 1965). Freetown Interview No. 26, 15 April 1990. (Note that DC remained an administrative title until 1964 when it was changed to District officer (DO).)
45. O/3/6/9, "Confidential, Ministry of Interior," 17 January 1965.
46. From Nimikoro and Tankoro Chiefdom Estimates, 1960/61. As informal payments increased, report quality declined. Most chiefdom estimates in the mid-1950s contained four pages. By 1961, most official reports to the Ministry of Interior consisted of a half page, listing "miscellaneous" as the largest category of expense.
47. Gbense Chiefdom Estimates (mimeo), 1958, 1962, 1966.
48. See Fred Hayward, "The Development of a Radical Political Organization in the Bush: A Case Study in Sierra Leone," *Canadian Journal of African Studies*, 6,1 (1972), 1–28, and David Rosen, "Diamonds, Diggers and Chiefs: The Politics of Fragmentation in a West African Society" (Ph.D Dissertation, University of Illinois, 1973).
49. *Daily Mail*, 10 May 1962.
50. *Daily Mail*, 3 April 1962.
51. CMM/71/30, "Mining Areas Development (Gbense and Tankoro)," 30 May 1963.
52. D/2/4, vol. IV (582), 7 September 1963.
53. D/2/4, "Mining Areas Development Grant," 19 December 1963.
54. *Ibid.*, "attached notes," 2 January 1964.
55. 2/7/10A, "Min. of Internal Affairs to Provincial Secretary, Eastern Province," 14 January 1965.
56. 2/7/10B, 15 January 1965. In 1964 the leone was introduced as the national currency at Le2 = £1.
57. Letter from SLST General Director J.P. DuCane to Minister of Lands, Mines and Labour, 12 September 1963.
58. Letter from J.P. DuCane to Chief Bona, cc to Ministry of Lands, Mines and Labour, 13 September 1963.
59. No. 3598/12/182, "Ministry of Lands, Mines and Labour" (Confidential), 14 October 1962.
60. *We Yone* (APC party weekly), 17 July 1965.
61. "Lebanese," as used in Sierra Leone, refers to those of Lebanese or mixed African-Lebanese heritage. Many "Lebanese" families have lived in Sierra Leone for four or five generations.
62. Government of Sierra Leone, *Report on the Survey of Business and Industry, 1966/67* (Freetown: Central Statistics Office, no date).
63. CMM/71/36 (confidential), "Interim Report, Inspector of Mines," 4 June 1957.
64. Government of Sierra Leone, *Report on the Survey*, 21.
65. Government of Sierra Leone, *Report of the Census of 1963* (Freetown: Government Printer, 1964).
66. Bank of Sierra Leone, *Sierra Leone in Statistics* (Freetown: BSL Research Department, 1975).
67. Government of Sierra Leone, *Report on the Survey*.

68. Bank of Sierra Leone, "Trade Reports" (mimeos), Sierra Leone Archives, Bundle A–41.
69. Government of Sierra Leone, *Report of the Wales Commission of Inquiry into the Conduct of the Immigration Quota Committee* (Freetown: Government Printer, 1968), 17.
70. Government of Sierra Leone, *Report of the Forster Commission of Inquiry on Assets of Ex-Ministers and Ex-Deputy Ministers* (Freetown: Government Printer, 1968).
71. *We Yone* (Freetown), "Prime Minister of Kono," 4 September 1966.
72. 2/7/12, "Min. Internal Affairs to Provincial Secretary, Eastern Province," 14 December 1966; Kono Interview No. 24, 2 April, 1990.
73. *Daily Mail*, "Kono Riots," 16 January 1959 and 12 February 1963.
74. Freetown Interview No. 27, 16 April 1990.
75. Freetown Interview No. 26, 15 April 1990.
76. Calculated from interviews conducted in Kono from December 1989 to April 1990.
77. Walter Barrows, *Grassroots Politics in an African State* (New York: Africana Pub. Co., 1976), 258.
78. *Daily Mail*, 4 April 1964, cited in John Cartwright, *Politics in Sierra Leone* (Toronto: Toronto University, 1970), 180.

4   REINING IN THE INFORMAL MARKETS

1. *We Yone* (Freetown), 20 November 1965.
2. Ministry of Information and Broadcasting, *President Stevens Speaks* (Freetown: Publications Division, 1980), 12.
3. Kono Interview No. 8, 10 January 1990 (Kensay area). See also *Dove–Edwin Commission of Inquiry into the Conduct of the 1967 General Elections in Sierra Leone* (Freetown: Government Printer, 1968), 12.
4. Kono District Officer (confidential) 414/3 (276), (To Ministry of Interior), "Report on Development Administration Transfers," 12 June 1968.
5. NRC Decree No. 49, in *Sierra Leone Gazette*, 21 October 1967.
6. Kono District Officer (confidential), 414/3 (272), "Report to Ministry of the Interior," 29 May 1968.
7. Kono Interview No. 21 (Kensay) 7 March 1990.
8. C/S High Court, "Larceny, High Court Case Review, Kono," July 1969 (Kono DO file). This independent-minded businessman also lost his home in a 1986 explosion.
9. Siaka Stevens, *What Life Has Taught Me* (London: Kensal House, 1984), 414, cited in Kelfala Kallon, "The Political Economy of Sierra Leone's Economic Decline," African Studies Association annual meeting, Baltimore, MD, November 1990.
10. Ministry of Mines, *Report of Deputy Inspector of Mines for 1969* (Freetown, 1969).
11. This strategy dates to British and SLPP efforts to shape chief selections – cf. EP 31/58, "Petition of Banta Sesay," 31 May 1957.
12. "Complaint Made by a Delegation Headed by Filie Faboi and Sgt Major Tamba of Tankoro Chiefdom," 13 July 1968 (Kono District Office file).

13. EP 313/4, "Kono DO Memorandum to Ministry of Interior," 12 March 1969.
14. EP 313/3/2, "Kono DO to Provincial Secretary, Eastern Province," 12 December 1969.
15. Kono District Office (confidential), "Intelligence Report, November 1969" (Kono DO file).
16. EP 313/1, no title, 7 February 1969.
17. DO's notes from cross examination, 8 September 1969 (Ministry of Interior Tankoro Chiefdom files).
18. *Laws of Sierra Leone*, Cap. 169, "Protectorate Courts Jurisdiction," sect.7, 2 (a) and (b).
19. Resistance to colonial authority sometimes took the form of claims of supernatural strength outside the control of Europeans. See Martin Kilson, *Political Change in a West African State* (Cambridge, MA: Harvard University Press, 1966), 113–17.
20. EP 313/1 (confidential), 19 December 1968 and EP 1/093/1, 16 February 1969.
21. Freetown Interview No. 14, 14 December 1989.
22. The Friendly Societies Act of 1968 codified government regulations of societies. On the earlier political role of societies, see Michael P. Banton, *West African City* (London: Oxford University Press, 1957), 162–83.

23. Kono Interview No. 8, 10 January 1990.
24. "Commission of Inquiry into the Assets of Former Government Officials – Investigative [File II]," July 1972 (notes in Kono DO file).
25. Freetown Interview No. 28, 19 April 1990.
26. MP 2/03/2, vol. II, "Auditor General: Files on Accounts of Kono District," 27 June 1968.
27. *Ibid.*
28. MP 2/03/2, vol. IV, "Auditor General: Files on Accounts of Kono District," 27 June 1968.
29. MP 2/03/2, vol. I, "Report on Accounts of Kono District Council," 20 July 1968.
30. Government Diamond Office, *Annual Report* (Freetown: Government Printer, 1973), 4.
31. *Africa Confidential*, 23 July 1971. The episode confirms Lonrho director "Tiny" Rowland's dictum that "Even if your man out there is doing a first-class job and he falls foul of the government then he must go," cited in *African Business*, December 1979, 14.
32. On Lonrho's remarkable ability to find profitable investment opportunities in patrimonial settings, see G. Cronje, M. Ling, and S. Cronje, *Lonrho: Portrait of a Multinational* (London: Julian Friedmann Books, 1976).
33. Compiled from Government of Sierra Leone, *Estimates of Revenues and Expenditures* (Freetown: Government Printer, various editions).
34. After 1968, official records omit non-budget expenditures. More accurate deficit figures consider officially guaranteed public and private borrowing. IMF, EBS/85/310, "Staff Report – Consultations" (no date).
35. Others see "disengagement" as political entrepreneurs seizing informal market opportunities. Naomi Chazan and Victor Azarya, "Disengagement from the State: Ghana and Guinea," *Comparative Studies of Society and History*, 29, 1 (1987), 108.

36. *Daily Mail* (Freetown), 23 September 1969.
37. *West Africa*, 20 July 1968, 846.
38. George O. Roberts, *The Anguish of Third World Independence: The Sierra Leone Experience* (Washington, DC: University Press of America, 1982), 56–7.
39. Stevens, *What Life*, 90.
40. MF (Ministry of Finance), 7(1'1), "Negotiations with SLST, Limited," 29 June 1969.
41. John Cartwright discusses motives shaping nationalization decisions in *Political Leadership in Sierra Leone* (Toronto: Toronto University Press, 1978), 252–3.
42. MF 7(2'1)/2, "Negotiations with SLST, Limited," 23 May 1969.
43. Government Diamond Office, *Annual Report* (Freetown, 1974), 5.
44. Peter Greenhalgh, *West African Diamonds, 1919–1983* (Manchester: Manchester University Press, 1985), 219.
45. MF 23(3) vol. 4, "Economic Advisory Committee – Diamond Dealers Taxation – Reassessment," 1974.
46. Arthur Abraham, *Mende Government and Politics Under Colonial Rule* (Freetown: University of Sierra Leone, 1978), 172.
47. MP MI/P/29, "Forster Commission of Inquiry into the Conduct of Chief Kaimachende of Gbense," 1 April 1970.
48. "Petition of Abdulahai Mansaray, et al.," received at Ministry of the Interior, 21 July 1971. The petition gained State House attention in Cabinet Minute Paper, 30/7/71.
49. Freetown Interview No. 12, 12 December 1989.
50. Account confirmed in No. 304/1 (confidential), "From Provincial Secretary to Permanent Secretary, Ministry of Interior," 8 September 1971.
51. PF/NA/405/2/1, "RE: Suspension of Town Chiefs," 1 November 1972, and PF/NA/405/2/1, "Ag. Senior District Officer to P.C. Toli," 16 August 1972.
52. "Petition from Martin Ndapi Torto," 29 September 1972 (Ministry of Interior Chiefdom files – Gbense).
53. Central Statistics Office, *National Accounts for Sierra Leone* (Freetown: Government Printer, 1971), Table 16. The railroad consistently lost money after the First World War. However, a survey of public attitudes in Freetown by the author found that the railroad often appeared in answers to "good things government did but no longer does today."
54. MF 20/30, "3rd Standby Arrangement – Negotiations with IMF," 5 November 1970.
55. NDMC charges in "Petition Against PC Alhaji Sahr Thorlie of Gbense Chiefdom," received, Ministry of Interior, 18 January 1983. A former Kono official accepts these figures as "fairly accurate" (Freetown Interview No. 28, 19 April 1990).
56. James Sorie Conteh, "Diamond Mining and Kono Religious Institutions: A Study in Social Change" (Ph.D Dissertation, Indiana University, 1979). Conteh suspects that locations of sacred bush sites were manipulated to derive maximum compensation from mining companies.
57. This and next item from Chiefdom Treasury payment vouchers P.V. 45/9/73 through P.V. 33/8/74. (Note: figures for 1973 and 1974 only.)
58. Next two items from "Petition Against PC Thorlie, Gbense Chiefdom," received at Ministry of Interior, 16 August 1977.

59. PF/NA/405/1/2 (confidential), "From SDO Kono to Provincial Secretary, Eastern Province," 5 April 1974.

60. Next three items from "Complaint – Unauthorized Market License Levy," received at Ministry of Interior, 20 April 1976.

61. Next two items from Government of Sierra Leone, *Sierra Leone Gazette*, 8 March 1979.

62. See Conteh, "Diamond Mining."

63. Kilson, *Political Change*, 197–202.

64. Sir Herbert Cox, *Report of the Commission of Inquiry into Disturbances in the Provinces* (Cox Commission), (London: Crown Agents, 1956), 152–3.

65. "Chiefdom Treasury Estimates for 1975/76" (Gbense Chiefdom Headquarters files).

66. Capital and operating expenses – see Government of Sierra Leone, *Revenues and Expenditures*, 1971, item 218.

67. *We Yone*, 23 January 1965.

68. All People's Congress, *The Constitution of the All People's Congress* (Freetown: APC Directorate, 1965), Part I, sect. 3.

69. "Petition of Salia Samaru, *et al.*," received at Ministry of Interior, 9 December 1973 (Gbense chiefdom file).

70. The group takes its name from the Public Works Department. "Terminator" is taken from the title of a popular Arnold Schwartzenegger film widely available in Sierra Leone.

71. PF/NA/403/1/1 (confidential), "SDO Kono Intelligence Report – Supplement," 6 May 1973.

72. EP 313/2/1 (confidential), "Intelligence Report," 8 August 1973, Freetown Interview No. 28, 19 April 1990.

73. Freetown Interview No. 17, 7 January 1990.

74. The quote is from Mohamed Jamil in "The Jamil Factor," *West Africa*, 11 March 1985, 452.

75. Kono Interview No. 24, 10 March 1990. See also Abner Cohen, *The Politics of Elite Culture* (Berkeley: University of California Press, 1981), Ch.6 on the role of Freemasons in Freetown politics.

76. Freetown society members with Liberian contacts assert that rebel leader Prince Johnson utilized society links to build support free from Doe government interference in his challenge to Liberian authorities.

77. "Sierra Leone: The Brink of a Republic," *Africa Confidential*, 2 April 1971.

78. Government of Sierra Leone, *Sierra Leone Gazette*, 24 February 1972, 169. Assignment to the Ministry of External Affairs sidelined many a threatening political career.

79. Some Sierra Leoneans confess that the PDG image was not universally positive in the 1970s. To many, Touré's Guinea was the source of many an impoverished refugee.

80. "Sierra Leone: What Sort of Elections?" *Africa Confidential*, 22 September 1972.

81. "Sierra Leone: An Empty Victory?" *Africa Confidential*, 8 June 1973 and "Sierra Leone: Political Pointers," 22 March 1974.

82. John Matthews, *A Voyage to the River Sierra Leone* (London: Frank Cass, 1966 [B. White, 1788]), 142–3.

83. Pre-colonial tenancy is described in Christopher Fyfe and V.R. Dorjahn, "Landlord and Stranger: Change in Tenancy Relations in Sierra Leone," *Journal of African History*, 3(1962), 391–7. The authors note that landlord–stranger relations endure into the colonial era.
84. Stevens, *What Life*, 409.
85. *Ibid.*, 371.
86. *Ibid.*, 325.

5   AN EXCHANGE OF SERVICES

1. "Petition of Mafinda Lebbie, *et al.*, To His Excellency," received at Ministry of Interior, 19 November 1982 (Mafindor Chiefdom file).
2. Freetown Interview No. 26, 15 April 1990.
3. Government Notice No. 648, (Ministry of Mines – Cooperative Contract Mining Scheme folder).
4. Kono Interview No. 24, 2 April 1990.
5. *Daily Mail* (Freetown), 5 January 1974.
6. MF 7(2'2)/1, "Negotiations with SLST, Limited," 23 May 1969.
7. MF 7(2'2)/2 "Negotiations with SLST, Limited," 30 May 1969.
8. Bank of Sierra Leone, *Economic Review* (Freetown: Government Printer, 1987).
9. Calculations are for legal exports only. The figure is derived by subtracting NDMC production from overall exports reported in *ibid.* and calculated at 1980 prices.
10. EP 313/2/2, "Provincial Secretary to DO, Kono," 12 January 1974.
11. Freetown Interview No. 14, 14 December 1989.
12. Government of Sierra Leone, *Laws of Sierra Leone*, Government Notice No. 622, 19 June 1975.
13. Kono Interview No. 23, 10 March 1990.
14. "Koidu-New Sembehun Project Assessment," 14 July 1977 (Ministry of Interior – Gbense Chiefdom file).
15. PF/NA/405/2, vol. II, "To PSEP from Ag. Senior DO, Kono," 12 June 1975.
16. On DeBeers's activity in Sierra Leone, see H.L. van der Laan, *The Sierra Leone Diamonds* (London: Oxford University Press, 1965), 98–103.
17. Jack Lunzar also participated in a failed 1982 attempt to market Zaire's diamonds outside CSO channels. Other contenders for the Sierra Leone position included Maurice Templesman & Sons, another marketer of Zaire's diamonds.
18. Freetown Interview No. 19, 25 January 1990.
19. Government of Sierra Leone, *Laws of Sierra Leone*, 1974 Diamond Corporations Agreement, Sect. 10 (1976 Ratification).
20. On Jamil's background, see *South*, December 1982, 60.
21. "Conversations in an Intercity Taxi" (travel notes).
22. Inclusion of dealer license fees in Government of Sierra Leone, *Budget Speeches*, underscores the high levels of attention this issue receives.
23. *Africa Confidential*, 25 April 1979, draws attention to the domestic market impact of large dealer control.
24. Bank of Sierra Leone, *Annual Report*, 1986.

25. Ministry of Mines, Assorted Dealer Applications, 1981–2.
26. MF 17/82 (Ministry of Finance), "Gold and Diamond Trade Financing – Reassessment."
27. Freetown Interview No. 16, 5 January 1990.
28. Tally taken from posed photos of Hunting Society members.
29. On Hunting Societies, see Michael P. Banton, *West African City* (London: Oxford University Press, 1957).
30. *Africa Confidential*, 20 May 1981.
31. Kono Interview No. 23, 10 March 1990.
32. Paramilitaries and private security forces drew members in disproportionate numbers of non-Konos (see *Africa Confidential*, 17 March 1982).
33. Sierra Leone Producer Marketing Board, "Producer Price Schedule," in Government of Sierra Leone, *Sierra Leone Gazette* (various issues).
34. Kono Interview No. 22, 8 March 1990.
35. Freetown Interview No. 19, 25 January 1990.
36. "Petition of Aiah Korgbende, *et al.*, Suppression of the Rights of Subjects," received at Ministry of Interior, 27 August 1982.
37. *Ibid.* A 1963 law forbade chiefs to sit on chiefdom courts.
38. Personal communication.
39. "Kono Tax Receipts – Ag. DO Kono Reports for 1989" (in Ministry of Interior – Local Government – Kono file).
40. For official recognition of this problem, see Sierra Leone Government, *1989–90 Budget Speech* (Freetown: Government Printer, 1989).
41. Freetown Interview No. 26, 15 April 1990. See also Neil Leighton, "The Lebanese Middlemen in Sierra Leone: The Case of a Non-Indigenous Trading Minority and Their Role in Political Development" (Ph.D Dissertation, Indiana University, 1971).
42. Paul Kennedy, *African Capitalism: The Struggle for Ascendancy* (New York: Cambridge University Press, 1988).
43. Government of Sierra Leone, *Census of Sierra Leone, 1963*, and worksheet of 1986 census (Central Statistics Office, Freetown).
44. Freetown Interview No. 19, 25 January 1990.
45. Government of Sierra Leone, *Sierra Leone Gazette*, 21 June 1988.
46. Freetown Interview No. 17, 7 January 1990.
47. A similar interpretation of competitive elections in Kenya is found in Joel Barkan, "The Electoral Process and Peasant–State Relations in Kenya," in Fred Hayward, ed., *Elections in Independent Africa* (Boulder: Westview Press), 1987, 213–37.
48. Election results can be found in Government of Sierra Leone, *Sierra Leone Gazette*, 9 May 1973, 9 May 1977, 6 May 1982, and 30 June 1986.
49. For more on "Vouchergate," see *West Africa*, 9 April 1982.
50. EP 29/140 (confidential), "Election of Paramount Chief – Tankoro Chiefdom, Kono District," 9 November 1981.
51. "Correspondence of S.H.O. Gborie to HE, the Acting President, Hon. S.I. Koroma," 14 November 1981 (Tankoro Chiefdom file, Ministry of Interior).
52. OP.382/T, "Correspondence from Secretary to the President to Permanent Secretary, Ministry of the Interior," 17 November 1981.
53. Freetown Interview No. 28, 19 April 1990.
54. Kono Interview No. 15, 8 February 1990.

55. "Correspondence from S.H.O. Gborie to H.E. Dr. Siaka P. Stevens," 17 January 1983 (Ministry of Interior – Gbense Chiefdom file).
56. Kono Interview No. 24, 10 March 1990.
57. C/S 140/82, "Hon. Comm. Police vs. Alhaji Sahr Mohamed Thorlie," 23 June 1982.
58. "Correspondence from Minister of Interior to H.E. Siaka Stevens" (Ministry of Interior), 16 June 1982.
59. NA/405/2, vol. 1, "Appointment of a Regent Chief – Gbense Chiefdom," 13 September 1982. The bothersome Provincial Secretary's political career ended in a 1984 corruption investigation. He now operates a successful agricultural export firm.
60. "Correspondence from S.H.O. Gborie to Hon. C.A. Kamara-Taylor, Second Vice President," 18 October 1982.
61. EP 304/8/2, "Suspension from Office of PC S.M. Thorlie," 10 August 1982.
62. Kono Interview No. 26, 26 March 1990.
63. Kono Interview No. 24, 10 March 1990.
64. Freetown Interview No. 23, 29 March 1990.
65. *New Citizen* (Freetown), 6 January 1990.
66. Kono Interview No. 26, 2 March 1990.
67. For a description of a similar process of "totalization" in Guinea, see Alain Morice, "Guinée 1985: Etat, corruption et trafics," *Les Temps Modernes*, 487 (Février 1987), 134–5.
68. "Chief Nabbed in 'Human Deal,'" *Daily Mail* (Freetown), 11 April 1990.
69. "Human Tongue Found in Juju Ritual," *We Yone*, 20 January 1990, and "Le500,000 Contract for Ritual Murder?" *We Yone*, 6 January 1990.
70. See, for example, Robert Price, "Political Culture in Contemporary Ghana: The Big-Man Small-Boy Syndrome," *Journal of African Studies*, 1, 2 (1974), 173–204. Joel Migdal, *Strong Societies and Weak States* (Princeton: Princeton University Press, 1988), 214–37 also stresses "neo-patrimonialism's" adaptation of colonial roots.
71. "Conversation in an Intercity Taxi" (travel notes).
72. Government of Sierra Leone, *Sierra Leone Gazette*, May 1808.

6 THE SHADOW STATE AND INTERNATIONAL COMMERCE

1. Koindu Interview, "Talk with Officials," 14 December 1989.
2. Koindu Interview, "A Traders' Association," 14 December 1989.
3. A.B. Zack-Williams, "Sierra Leone: Crisis and Despair," *Review of African Political Economy*, 49 (1990), 22–33 and Sahr John Kpundeh, "Prospects in Contemporary Sierra Leone," *Corruption and Reform*, 7 (1993), 237–47.
4. Stevens built a considerable fortune while the country was under creditor tutelage. Some estimate that he accumulated up to $1 billion, including London real estate and Caribbean hotels. Freetown Interviews No. 27, 13 April 1990, No. 28, 19 April 1990.
5. René Lemarchand, "The State, the Parallel Economy, and the Changing Structure of Patrimonial Systems," in Donald Rothchild and Naomi Chazan, eds., *The Precarious Balance: State and Society in Africa* (Boulder: Westview Press, 1988), 149–69.

6. Cabinet Minutes, "Deliberations of Foreign Exchange Allocation Committee" (Ministry of Finance closed file No. 5), 10 November 1984.
7. On banking norms governing private loans to governments, see Charles Lipson, *Standing Guard: Protecting Foreign Capital in the Nineteenth and Twentieth Centuries* (Berkeley: University of California, 1985).
8. Alhaji S.H.O. Gborie, 23 April 1983 (Ministry of Interior – Gbense Chiefdom files).
9. From Ministry of Mines, *Annual Reports* (Freetown: Government Printer).
10. Official reports ignore some budget activity. These figures are derived from IMF Article IV Consultation field reports.
11. Sierra Leone Government, *Budget Speech* (Freetown, Government Printer, June 1980).
12. International Monetary Fund, *Balance of Payments*, 7.
13. Bank of Sierra Leone, *Economic Trends* (Freetown: mimeo-graph quarterly memo, 1987).
14. One entrepreneur bought building materials with profits from her transport business, asserting that "real estate is the only reliable bank in Freetown," and was immune from confiscation, unlike her Landrover, diverted from her husband's government office.
15. City of Freetown tax assessment records, City Hall.
16. World Bank, *Debt Tables* (Washington, DC: World Bank, 1981).
17. The exact extent of loans is not known. These figures are estimates from IMF documents EBD/89/234, "Sierra Leone – Staff Report for the 1989 Article IV Consultation," 27 March 1990, and discussed in IMF, SM/88/68, "Staff Report," 20 April 1988.
18. "Sierra Leone: Counting the Cost," *Africa Confidential*, 2 July 1980 and "Sierra Leone: OAU Nightmare," *Africa Confidential*, 9 April 1980.
19. The 1976 figure equaled SDR 9.2 million, 1977 = SDR 11.1 million, 1978 = SDR 21.7 million, 1979 = SDR 33.8 million. International Monetary Fund, *Balance of Payments*. These figures do not include all loans contracted by state agencies on behalf of State House.
20. An additional $30 million in unauthorized loans and debt service was assumed in 1982/83. World Bank, "Review of Public Expenditure in Sierra Leone, Report No. 535256," (Washington, DC: March 1985), 28.
21. For example, "The 'New Order,'" *For Di People* (Freetown), 21 March 1987, "Philips Bros Freezes Accounts in UK," *The Globe* (Freetown), 31 August 1989.
22. Planned expenditures were scaled back from a $450 million proposal from the Yugoslav firm *Energoprojekt*. *Africa Confidential*, 25 April 1979.
23. The OAU story is best chronicled in 1980 issues of *Africa Confidential*. See also *Africa*, June 1980, 29–30, and *Africa Report*, September–October 1980, 42–3.
24. Freetown Interview No. 27, 13 April 1990. See also *Africa*, October 1980, 43.
25. See *Washington Post*, 22 February 1980, and *West Africa*, 25 February 1980.
26. For example, World Bank, *Sierra Leone: Prospects for Growth and Equity* (Washington, DC: World Bank, 1981).
27. World Bank, *Accelerated Development in Sub-Saharan Africa: An Agenda for Action* (Berg Report), (Washington, DC: World Bank, 1981), 65.
28. Ministry of Trade, "Report of Negotiations with IMF," 20 November 1984.

Official tallies vary as the boundaries are blurred between private and state enterprises within the Shadow State.

29. International Monetary Fund, EBS/89/233, "Sierra Leone Staff Report for the Article IV Consultation," 27 March 1990.

30. International Monetary Fund, "Decision No. 5392–(77/63), Surveillance over Exchange Rate Policies," 29 April 1977.

31. See "Death of Sam Bangurah," *West Africa*, 7 January 1980.

32. Official figures only include reported exports but estimate imports from national income statistics which are based on estimates of all transactions. For figures, see Bank of Sierra Leone, *Economic Review*, vol. 20: 1–2 (Freetown: Government Printing Office, 1986), Table 20.

33. Freetown Interview No. 21, 28 February 1990.

34. World Bank, *Sierra Leone*, 6.

35. Freetown Interview No. 15, 4 January 1990.

36. Both Freetown Interview No. 22, 28 March 1990.

37. IMF, *Balance of Payments*.

38. See Stephen Ellis, "Les prolongements du conflit israélo-arabe en Afrique noire: le cas du Sierra Leone," *Politique Africaine*, 30 (Juin 1988), 69–75. Jamil and Stevens used contacts with Amal's Sierra Leone born Nabih Berri and a pro-Iranian faction of the PLO to gain access to Iranian oil.

39. Details of transactions from National Development Bank, Freetown internal documents. Also see May 1987 issues of *For Di People*.

40. Sayre Schatz, *Nigerian Capitalism* (Berkeley: University of California Press, 1977); and Michael Schatzberg, *The Dialectics of Oppression in Zaire* (Bloomington: Indiana University, 1988), 53.

41. Cited in John Illife, *The Emergence of African Capitalism* (Minneapolis: University of Minnesota, 1983), 77.

42. For example, Sierra Leone exported 13,000 tons of coffee through official channels in 1979. Exports fell to 1,900 tons in 1984 (Bank of Sierra Leone, *Economic Review*, vol. 20 (January–June 1986), Table 22).

43. "Momoh Returns," *Globe* (Freetown), 20 October 1988.

44. Fred Hayward observes that Stevens provided rice to supplicants in "Sierra Leone: State Consolidation, Fragmentation and Decay," in D. Cruise O'Brien, R. Rathbone and J. Dunn, eds., *Contemporary West African States* (Cambridge: Cambridge University Press, 1989), 168, fn.12.

45. "Sierra Leone: Salaries in Kind," *Africa Now* (December 1982), 23.

46. Calculated from civil service pay scales reported in Government of Sierra Leone, *Blue Book* (Freetown: Government Printer, various issues).

47. Freetown Interview No. 23, 29 March 1990.

48. "Success Attracts Sabotage," *Spark* (Freetown), 31 January 1990.

49. These are half of state employment figures reported in Government of Sierra Leone, *Blue Book*, 1990.

50. *Globe*, 23 February 1989 observed politicians "extending patronage to and extracting obligations from their retainers depending on kinship, friendship, mood and a nebulous pattern of mutual backscratching."

51. United States PL-480 food aid is distributed in a similar fashion, though since Freetown receives it for free, these imports offer greater opportunities for middleman gain.

52. "Rice Business," *Globe*, 23 February 1989.
53. Koindu Interview, 14 December 1989.
54. Freetown Interview No. 28, 19 April 1990.
55. Alpha Mohammed Bah (Ph.D Dissertation, Wisconsin, 1983).
56. Koindu Interview 16 December 1989, "Self-Help Party."
57. Koindu Interview, 16 December 1989, "An Official's View."
58. *Ibid.*
59. Throughout the early 1980s, *Africa Confidential* reports on Sierra Leone's expected imminent upheaval or coups.
60. From an interview with Stevens, see Hayward,"Sierra Leone," 175.
61. On the political impact of Sekou Touré's alternative to Stevens's control through an "official" private market, see Alain Morice, "Guinée 1985: Etat, corruption et trafics," *Les Temps Modernes*, 487 (Février 1987), 308–36.
62. Freetown, "Discussion with Student," October 30 1989.
63. Freetown Interview No. 18, 24 January 1990.
64. Koindu, "Discussion with Host's Brother," 14 December 1989.
65. Estimate in James Feardon, "International Financial Institutions and Economic Policy Reform in Sub-Saharan Africa," *Journal of Modern African Studies*, 26, 1 (1988), 130; Jeffrey Haynes, Trevor Parfitt and Stephen Riley, "The Local Politics of International Debt: Sub-Saharan Africa," Annual Conference of Political Studies Association, University of Manchester, April 1985, 21.
66. Bank of Sierra Leone, *Annual Report* (Freetown: Government Printer, 1987).
67. Government of Sierra Leone, "Development Strategies and Budget Speech" (Freetown, 26 August 1986), 3–4.
68. Bank of Sierra Leone, *Economic Review*, vol. 20, Table 22.
69. Kenneth Waltz, *Theory of International Politics* (Reading, MA: Addison-Wesley, 1979), 94.
70. Robert Jackson, *Quasi-states: Sovereignty, International Relations and the Third World* (New York: Cambridge University Press, 1990), 50–4, 68.
71. IMF, EBS/89/233, "Sierra Leone."
72. *Ibid.*

7   FOREIGN FIRMS, ECONOMIC "REFORM" AND SHADOW STATE POWER

1. Gendemah is quoted in *Africa Report*, November–December 1990, 26.
2. The Constitution of Sierra Leone, 1991, Part I, Sect. 8 (2)(a).
3. Legislation includes Public Economic Emergency Regulations (1987), Public Economic Emergency (no.2) Regulations (1988), Economic Policy and Control Act (1989), and Currency Control and Economic Sabotage Act (1989).
4. See "1990 Stock Taking," *West Africa*, 4 February 1991; "Power for the People," *West Africa*, 21 January 1991.
5. IMF, EBS/89/233, "Sierra Leone – Staff Report for the 1989 Article IV Consultation" (confidential), 27 March 1990.
6. IMF, SM/88/68, "1988 Article XIV Consultations," 20 April 1988.
7. Ministry of Interior, "Condition of Babu and Bamba Settlements, District Office, Bonthe," 30 May 1988 (Bonthe District file).

8. The name LIAT is derived from the Hebrew character initials of the Israeli owner's daughter.
9. Cabinet Minutes, 2 February 1986.
10. Bank of Sierra Leone, *Economic Trends* (Freetown: mimeo, June 1987).
11. The performance is less remarkable if one believes reports that the diamonds were trans-shipped from South Africa.
12. Bank of Sierra Leone, *Annual Report* (Freetown, Government Printer, 30 June 1987), Table 20.
13. "Sierra Leone: More South Africa Connections," *Africa Confidential*, 7 January 1987.
14. Bank of Sierra Leone, *Annual Report*, Table 22.
15. Stephen Ellis has done considerable research on the LIAT–South Africa connection. See *Africa Confidential*, 17 September 1986, 7 January 1987, 24 June 1987, and "Les prolongements du conflit israélo–arabe en Afrique noire: le cas du Sierra Leone," *Politique Africaine*, 30 (Juin 1988), 69–75. See also 1987 issues of *For Di People* (Freetown).
16. *For Di People*, 18 March 1988.
17. Freetown Interview No. 22, 28 March 1990.
18. See "A Dose too Much," *West Africa*, 6 July 1987.
19. Ministry of Mines, *Report of the Inspector of Mines* (Freetown, July 1989).
20. IMF, EBS/89/233, "Sierra Leone."
21. Sierra Leone was ineligible for further World Bank loans or guaranteed credits until the country resumed loan repayments.
22. Economic statistics are collected from "Notes of IMF Consultation – 'Staff Estimates'" (Ministry of Finance), 19 April 1990.
23. Alain Morice examines such explosive developments in Guinea immediately after Sekou Touré's death in "Guinée 1985: Etat, corruption et trafics," *Les Temps Modernes*, 487 (Février 1987), 112–15.
24. Public Economic Emergency (No.2) Regulations, 1988, sect. 10, Government of Sierra Leone, *Sierra Leone Gazette Extraordinary*, 18 November 1988.
25. The Alluvial Diamond Mining (Declaration of Licensed Diamond Mining Areas) (Amendment) Notice, 1988; Government of Sierra Leone, *Sierra Leone Gazette*, 24 November 1988.
26. See "A Mining Policy for Sierra Leone," *West Africa*, 6 February 1989.
27. See "SCIPA Under Scrutiny," *West Africa*, 14 August 1989.
28. Observation of SCIPA's Kono operations revealed that SCIPA commonly paid 100–105 percent of world market prices for diamonds. Several foreign observers in Sierra Leone alleged that SCIPA laundered money, and hence were more interested in dominating the diamond market and smuggling gems outside traceable channels, than in making a local profit on diamonds.
29. *We Yone* (Freetown), 19 August 1989.
30. After about one week, the wife and child left Sierra Leone. Guaz then traveled only with bodyguards.
31. Freetown Interview No. 19, 25 January 1990.
32. IMF, EBS/89/233, "Sierra Leone."
33. National Diamond Mining Company, correspondence, "Kimberlite Project Negotiations with Sunshine Broulle of Texas, USA," 6 February 1990.
34. Some officials believed that this concern brought visits of United States Drug

Enforcement Agency officials to the country.

35. "SCIPA Will Stay!" *New Shaft* (Freetown), 24 December 1989.
36. *New Citizen* (Freetown), 26 May 1990.
37. *We Yone*, 20 May 1990.
38. Reports following Freetown's request for military aid from Guinea indicate that some Guinean troops were stationed in Kono's diamond fields.
39. National Diamond Mining Company, "Kimberlite Project."
40. "Sunshine Mining Co. Told to Pay Damages," *Wall Street Journal*, 23 January 1992.
41. See "1990 Stock Taking," *West Africa*, 4 February 1991, and "Power for the People," *West Africa*, 21 January 1991.
42. "Recipe for Recovery," *West Africa*, 13 January 1992, 66.
43. Ministry of Agriculture, Natural Resources and Forestry file, "Proposed Joint Venture Agreement for Management and Control of Fishing Rights in Sierra Leone's Territorial Waters," correspondence of 3 January 1990.
44. Economist Intelligence Unit, *Ghana, Sierra Leone, Liberia*, second quarter, 1991.
45. "Ministers Implicated?" *West Africa*, 7 September 1992, 1539. This and the following case related to SSI subjects of the Beccles–Davies Commission of Inquiry into the assets and business interests of former APC officials in 1992.
46. "Sierra Leone: The Redeemer Comes – And Stays," *Africa Confidential*, 9 October 1992.
47. IMF, EBD/89/234, "Delay of Article IV Consultation," 7 December 1989.
48. Economist Intelligence Unit, *Ghana*, second quarter, 1991.
49. *Ibid.*
50. "Things Fall Apart," *West Africa*, 23 March 1992, 494–5.
51. D. Darbon, "L'Etat prédateur," *Politique Africaine*, 39 (1990), 37–9.
52. IMF, EBS/89/233, "Sierra Leone," 9.
53. Freetown Interview No. 20, 28 February 1990.
54. Ministry of Interior, "Precepts – Chiefdom Authorities," circular, no date (mimeo).
55. Freetown Interview No. 17, 7 January 1990.
56. Freetown Interview No. 23, 29 March 1990.
57. Personal observation. Price rises were lower in rural areas where subsidized goods were generally unavailable.
58. Auto registration reports in Government of Sierra Leone, *Sierra Leone Gazette*; "Luxury" autos include Mercedes Benz sedans and the more durable four-wheel-drive Mitsubishi Pajero wagons.
59. Kono Interview No. 23, 10 March 1990.
60. "Kambia," *We Yone*, 15 December 1989.
61. "Alien Government formed in Kono," *Weekend Spark* (Freetown) 8 September 1989. See also "Massive Price Revenge Conspiracy," *Weekend Spark*, 29 September 1989.
62. "Scandalous!" *New Shaft*, 31 September 1990.
63. Minister of Finance, Tommy Taylor-Morgan, Keynote Address, Freetown Chamber of Commerce, Brookfields Hotel, 26 January 1990.
64. For example, John Ravenhill, "Adjustment with Growth: A Fragile Consensus," *Journal of Modern African Studies*, 26, 2 (1988), 179–210.
65. On the invasion, see "Politics of Rebellion," *West Africa*, 21 September 1992,

1608–9.
66. Government of Sierra Leone, *The 1992/93 Budget Speech* (Freetown: Government Printer, 26 June 1992).
67. "Sierra Leone: premier budget du régime militaire," *Marchés Tropicaux*, 23 October 1992, 2818.
68. For example, The World Bank, *Ghana 2000 and Beyond* (Washington, DC: World Bank, February 1993).
69. "Revolution in Crisis?" *West Africa*, 7 December 1992, 2092–3.
70. Critical accounts of events outside Freetown appear in *Eagle*, an irregular Freetown newspaper. Information is more scarce than during Momoh's rule, due to NPRC suppression of the press.
71. See editorials in *New Breed* (Freetown), 13–19 October 1993. The case was first reported in a Swedish journal.
72. *Marchés Tropicaux*, 19 March 1993, 763.

8 THE CHANGING CHARACTER OF AFRICAN SOVEREIGNTY

1. Background on Charles Taylor is found in "Charles Taylor – The True Story," *New African* (London), July 1991, 22–3; "Portrait of a Rebel," *African Concord* (Lagos), 24 February 1992, 26–32; "Rebel's Saga: Mass. Jail to Showdown for Power," *Boston Globe*, 31 July 1990; "Rebels' Roots for Liberian Coup Leaders' Mass. Connections," *Boston Globe*, 8 June 1990.
2. "Liberian Rebel Leader Rules Empire of His Own Design," *New York Times*, 14 April 1992.
3. Charles Taylor, "Letter to the People of America," *Patriot* (Gbarnga, "Greater Liberia" weekly), 12 March 1992.
4. Telephone interview with Taylor associate in Washington, DC, 18 February 1993.
5. "Taylor to ECOMOG – Go to Hell," *Newswatch* (Lagos), 2 November 1992, 38.
6. Economist Intelligence Unit, *Ghana, Sierra Leone, Liberia*, third quarter, 1992, 38; "Charles Taylor fait des affaires," *Jeune Afrique*, 23 April 1992, 12.
7. "La compagnie américaine Firestone accusée d'aider le NPFL," *Marchés Tropicaux*, 19 March 1993, 763.
8. "Ecological Terrorism," *West Africa* (London), 19 November 1990, 2864–5.
9. "Liberia: Sparking Fires in West Africa," *Africa Confidential*, 17 May 1991, 2–4.
10. "Liberia: The Battle for Gbarnga," *Africa Confidential*, 28 May 1993.
11. "Le bois tropical africaine," *Marchés Tropicaux*, 12 February 1993, 436–40.
12. "Liberia: Sparking Fires in West Africa," *Africa Confidential*, 17 May 1991.
13. "Confusion in Gbarnga," *West Africa*, 16 December 1991, 2102.
14. Liberian Iron Ore Limited, "To Shareholders of Liberian Iron Ore Limited," 7 November 1989. Consortium members include Cyprus Minerals (USA), Liberian Iron Ore (Canada), Liberian American Swedish Minerals Company's UK subsidiary, West African Mining Company of Liberia, Sumimoto (Japan), France's state-owned Bureau des Recherches Géologiques et Minières.
15. As advertisements in *Patriot*, 27 July 1992.
16. Economist Intelligence Unit, *Ghana*, fourth quarter, 1992, 32.

17. Environmental Defense Fund, "Update on Mount Nimba Iron Ore Project," 26 August 1992.
18. *Figaro*, 8 January 1992.
19. "Le CEDEAO au chevet du Liberia," *Jeune Afrique*, 25 September 1991, 24–5.
20. United Nations General Assembly, "18.51 Protection of Mount Nimba, Guinea," *New Resolutions* (New York: United Nations General Assembly, 1990), 47.
21. See "Intrigue in Washington," *West Africa*, 18 October 1993, 1871.
22. Confidential Abidjan – 17627, "Info Amembassy Monrovia Ecowas Collective, To Secstate WashDC immediate 2902," 23 October 1992 (from *West Africa*, 16 November 1992).
23. "Liberia: Back to Battle," *Africa Confidential*, 23 October 1992, and "U.S. Recalls Envoy to Burkina Faso," *New York Times*, 6 November 1992.
24. Secret State 347619 "Info Amembassy Windhoen immediate, from SecState WashDC to Amembassy Dakar immediate," 23 October 1992, (from *West Africa*, 16 November 1992).
25. "Takeover Attempt at Buchanan Port?" *Patriot*, 20 April 1992.
26. "U.S. Recalls Envoy to Burkina Faso," *New York Times*, 6 November 1992.
27. "The Politics of Rebellion," *West Africa*, 21 September 1992, 1608; "Charles Taylor to Annex Part of Sierra Leone?" *We Yone* (Freetown), 30 March 1992.
28. "Threat to Peace," *West Africa*, 6 December 1993, 2207–8; Human Rights Watch, "Liberia: Waging the War to Keep the Peace," *Africa Watch*, 5, 6, June 1993.
29. Janet MacGaffey, *Entrepreneurs and Parasites: The Struggle for Indigenous Capital in Zaire* (New York: Cambridge University, 1987); and Naomi Chazan and Victor Azarya, "Disengagement from the State: Ghana and Guinea," *Comparative Studies of Society and History*, 29, 1 (1987), 106–31.
30. C. Coulon and D. Cruise O'Brien, "Senegal," in D. Cruise O'Brien, R. Rathbone, and J. Dunn, eds., *Contemporary West African States* (New York: Cambridge University Press, 1989), 145–64; Y.A. Fauré and J.F. Médard, eds., *Etat et bourgeoisie en Côte d'Ivoire* (Paris: Karthala, 1982); and W. Reno, "Old Brigades, Money Bags, New Breeds and the Ironies of Reform in Nigeria," *Canadian Journal of African Studies*, 27, 1 (1993).
31. Carl Schmitt (trans. George Schwab), *Political Theology* (Cambridge, MA: MIT Press, 1985), 27, 30.
32. William (Lord) Hailey, *An African Survey* (London: Oxford University, 1938), 539, 529.
33. Frederick (Lord) Lugard, *Dual Mandate in British Tropical Africa* (London: William Blackwood, 1922), 196, 210.
34. Letter from DC Sefadu to J.L. Pepys-Cockerell, Kono Development Office, 1 March 1960.
35. CCP 680/8, Chief Commissioner of Mines, "Funds for Kono District Development," 24 May 1958.
36. Siaka Stevens, *What Life Has Taught Me* (London: Kensal House, 1984), 133.
37. *Ibid.*, 222.
38. Interview from *West Africa*, 5 February 1990, 164.
39. Fernand Braudel, *Civilisation matérielle, économie et capitalisme, XVe-XVIIIe siécle*, vol. II (Paris: Arthand, 1981), 555.

Bibliography

BOOKS, ARTICLES, AND PAPERS

Abraham, Arthur. *Mende Government and Politics Under Colonial Rule*. Freetown: University of Sierra Leone, 1978.

Albertini, Rudolf von. *European Colonialism, 1880–1940*. Westport, CT.: Greenwood, 1982.

All Peoples Congress, *The Constitution of the All Peoples Congress*. Freetown: APC Directorate, 1965.

Alldridge, Thomas S. *A Colony Transformed*. London: Seeley and Co., 1910.

The Sherbro and Its Hinterland. London: Macmillan, 1901.

Allen, Chris, Michael S. Radu, Keith Somerville, and Joan Baxter, eds. *Benin, the Congo, Burkina Faso*. New York: Pinter, 1989.

Asch, Susan. *L'église du Prophète Kimbanga et de ses origines à son rôle actuel au Zaire: 1921–1981*. Paris: Karthala, 1983.

Augé, Marc. "L'organisation du commerce pré-colonial en Basse–Côte d'Ivoire et ses effets sur l'organisation sociale des populations côières," in Claude Meillassoux, ed. *The Development of Indigenous Markets and Trade in West Africa*. London: Oxford University Press, 1971, 153–67.

Ayoade, John A.A. "States without Citizens: An Emerging African Phenomenon," in D. Rothchild and N. Chazan, eds. *The Precarious Balance*. Boulder: Westview, 1988, 100–18.

Azarya, Victor. "Reordering State-Society Relations: Incorporation and Disengagement," in D. Rothchild and N. Chazan, eds. *The Precarious Balance*. Boulder: Westview, 1988, 3–21.

Banton, Michael P. *West African City*. London: Oxford University Press, 1957.

Banugire, Firimooni. "The Impact of the Economic Crisis on Fixed Income Earners," in Paul Wiebe and Cole Dodge, eds. *Beyond Crisis: Development Issues in Uganda*. Hillsboro, KS: Multi Business Press, 1987, 313–37.

Barampama, Angelo. "Secteur non structuré en Afrique: cacophonie de la survie et leur déspoirs." *Genève Afrique* 22,1 (1984), 37–54.

Barkan, Joel. "The Electoral Process and Peasant–State Relations in Kenya," in F.M. Hayward, ed. *Elections in Independent Africa*. Boulder: Westview Press, 1987, 213–37.

Barrows, Walter. *Grassroots Politics in an African State*. New York: Africana Publishing Company, 1976.

Bates, Robert. *Markets and States in Tropical Africa: The Political Basis of Agricultural Policies*. Berkeley: University of California, 1981.

Essays on the Political Economy of Rural Africa. Berkeley: University of California, 1983.

Beyond the Miracle of the Market: The Political Economy of Agrarian Development in Kenya. Cambridge: Cambridge University Press, 1989.

Bayart, Jean-François. "Le politique par le bas en Afrique noire." *Politique Africaine* 1(1981), 53–83.

"L'énonciation du politique," *Revue français de sciences politique* 35(1985), 343–73.

L'Etat au Cameroun. Paris: Presses de la Foundation Nationale des Sciences Politique, 1985.

"Civil Society in Africa," in Patrick Chabal, ed. *Political Domination in Africa.* Cambridge: Cambridge University Press, 1986, 109–25.

L'Etat en Afrique. Paris: Fayard, 1989.

Berg, R. and J. Whitaker, eds. *Strategies for African Development.* Berkeley: University of California, 1986.

Berry, Sara. "The Food Crisis and Agrarian Change in Africa: A Review Essay." *African Studies Review* 27,2(1984), 59–112.

Fathers Work for Their Sons. Berkeley: University of California Press, 1985.

Boone, Catherine. "The Making of a Rentier Class: Wealth, Accumulation and Political Control in Senegal." *Journal of Development Studies* 26,3(1990), 425–49.

Merchant Capital and the Roots of State Power in Senegal: 1930–1985. New York: Cambridge University Press, 1992.

Braudel, Fernand. *Civilisation matérielle, économie et capitalisme, XVe–XVIIIe siécle,* vol. II. Paris: Arthand, 1981.

La dynamique du capitalisme. Paris: Arthand, 1985.

Brion, Edouard. "L'Eglise catholique et la Rebellion au Zaire." *Cahiers de CEDAF* 7/8(1986), 61–78.

Burke, L.J. "A Short History of the Discovery of the Major Diamond Deposits." *Sierra Leone Studies* 12(1959), 235–8.

Callaghy, Thomas. "African Debt Crisis." *Journal of International Affairs* 38,1(1984), 21–41.

The State–Society Struggle: Zaire in Comparative Perspective. New York: Columbia University Press, 1984.

"Lost Between State and Market: The Politics of Structural Adjustment in Ghana, Zambia and Nigeria," in Joan Nelson, ed. *The Politics of Economic Adjustment in the Third World.* Princeton: Princeton University Press, 1990.

"Africa and the World Economy: Caught Between a Rock and a Hard Place," in J. Harbeson and D. Rothchild, eds. *Africa in World Politics.* Boulder: Westview, 1991, 39–68.

and E.J. Wilson. "Africa: Policy, Reality or Ritual?" in Raymond Vernon, ed. *The Promise of Privatization.* New York: Council on Foreign Relations, 1988, 179–230.

Carter Center. *Seminars of the African Governance Programme.* Atlanta: Carter Center, published annually.

Cartwright, John. *Political Leadership in Sierra Leone.* Toronto: Toronto University Press, 1978.

Chazan, Naomi. *An Anatomy of Ghanaian Politics: Managing Political Recession, 1969–1982.* Boulder: Westview, 1983.

"Ghana: Problems of Governance and the Emergence of Civil Society," in Larry Diamond, Juan Linz, and Seymour M. Lipset, eds. *Democracy in Developing Countries*. Boulder: Lynne Reinner, 1988, 93–140.

"Patterns of State–Society Incorporation and Disengagement in Africa," in D. Rothchild and N. Chazan, eds. *The Precarious Balance: State and Society in Africa*. Boulder: Westview, 1988.

and Victor Azarya. "Disengagement from the State in Africa: Reflections on the Experience of: Ghana and Guinea." *Comparative Studies of Society and History* 29,1 (1987), 106–31.

Clapham, Christopher. *Private Patronage and Public Power*. New York: St Martin's Press, 1982.

Clarke, John I. *Sierra Leone in Maps*. London: Hodder & Stoughton, 1966.

Cohen, Abner. *The Politics of Elite Culture*. Berkeley: University of California Press, 1981.

Cohen, Sir Andrew, *British Policy in Changing Africa*. Evanston: Northwestern University Press, 1959.

Conteh, James S. "Diamond Mining and Kono Religious Institutions: A Study in Social Change." Ph.D dissertation, University of Indiana, 1979.

Copans, Jean. *Les marabouts d'arachide*. Paris: Harmattan, 1988.

"Du vin de palme nouveau dans les vieilles calebasses?" *Genève Afrique* 27,1 (1989), 7–43.

"La banalisation de l'Etat africain a propos de *L'Etat en Afrique*." *Politique Africaine* 37 (1990), 95–101.

Coulon, Christian. "Elections, factions et ideòlogies au Senegal," in *Aux urnes l'Afrique: Elections et Pouvoir en Afrique noire*. Paris: CEAN, 1978, 145–86.

"Une nouvelle exploration du politique enAfrique." *Politique Africaine* 1 (1981), 137–9.

Coulon, Christian and Donal Cruise O'Brien. "Senegal," in D. Cruise O'Brien, R. Rathbone, and J. Dunn, eds. *Contemporary West African States*. New York: Cambridge University Press, 1989.

Cox-George, N.A. *Finance and Development in West Africa: The Sierra Leone Experience*. London: Denis Dobson, 1961.

Cronje, Gillian, Margaret Ling, and Suzanne Cronje. *Portrait of a Multinational*. London: Julian Friedmann Books, 1976.

Cruise O'Brien, Donal, Richard Rathbone, and John Dunn, eds. *Contemporary West African States*. New York: Cambridge University Press, 1989.

Darbon, D. "L'Etat prédateur." *Politique Africaine* 39 (1990), 37–45.

Davidson, Basil. *The Black Man's Burden*. New York: Times Books, 1992.

Denzer, LaRay and Michael Crowder. "Bai Bureh and the Hut Tax War of 1898," in Robert Rotberg and Ali Mazrui, eds. *Protest and Power in Black Africa*. New York: Oxford University Press, 1970.

DeSoto, Hernando. *The Other Path*. New York: Harper & Row, 1989.

Deveneaux, Gustav K. "Public Opinion and Colonial Policy in Nineteenth Century Sierra Leone." *International Journal of African Historical Studies* 9,1 (1976), 45–67.

Diamond, Larry. "Introduction: Roots of Failure, Seeds of Hope," in L. Diamond, J. Linz, and S.M. Lipset, eds., *Democracy in Developing Countries: Africa*. Boulder: Lynne Rienner, 1988.

Domenach, J.-L. "Pouvoir et société dans la Chine des années soixante-dix."

216   Bibliography

Bulletin Modes populaires d'action politique 1 (1983), 17–31.

d'Orfond, P.S. "New Light on the Origin of the Waiima Affair." *Sierra Leone Studies* (n.s.) 11 (1958), 218–35.

Dungia, Emmanuel. *Mobutu et l'argent du Zaire*. Paris: Harmattan, 1992.

Economist Intelligence Unit. *Ghana, Sierra Leone, Liberia*, third quarter, 1992.

Ellis, Stephen. "Les prolongements du conflit israèlo–arabe en Afrique noire: le cas du Sierra Leone." *Politique Africaine* 30 (1988), 69–75.

Esman, Milton J. and Norman T. Uphoff. *Local Organizations and Intermediaries in Rural Development*. Ithaca: Cornell University Press, 1984.

Fauré, Y.A. and J.F. Médard. *Etat et bourgeoisie en Côte d'Ivoire*. Paris: Karthala, 1982.

Feardon, James. "International Financial Institutions and Economic Policy Reform in Sub-Saharan Africa." *Journal of Modern African Studies* 26,1 (1988), 3–37.

Fieldhouse, David. *Black Africa 1945–1980: Economic Decolonization and Arrested Development*. London: Allen & Unwin, 1986.

Frankel, S. Herbert. *Capital Investment in Africa*. New York: Howard Fertig, 1938.

Frimpong-Ansah, John. *The Vampire State in Africa*. Trenton, NJ: Africa World Press, 1991.

Fyfe, Christopher. *A History of Sierra Leone*. Cambridge: Cambridge University Press, 1962.

Fyfe, Christopher and V.R. Dorjahn. "Landlord and Stranger: Change in Tenancy Relations in Sierra Leone." *Journal of African History* 3 (1962), 391–7.

Geertz, Clifford. *The Interpretation of Culture*. New York: Free Press, 1973.

Gerschenkron, Alexander. *Economic Backwardness in Historical Perspective*. Cambridge, MA: Harvard University, 1962.

Geschiere, Peter. "La paysannerie africaine est-elle captive?" *Politique Africaine* 14 (1984), 13–34.

"Paysans, regime national et recherche hegemonique." *Politique Africaine* 22 (1986), 73–100.

Goddard, Thomas N. *The Handbook of Sierra Leone*. London: Grant Richards, 1925.

Green, Reginald. "*Magendo* in the Political Economy of Uganda: Pathology, Parallel System or Dominant Sub-Mode of Production?" IDS, University of Sussex: Discussion Paper 164, August 1981.

Greenhalgh, Peter. *West African Diamonds, 1919–1983*. Manchester: Manchester University Press, 1985.

Hailey, William M. (Lord). *An African Survey*. London: Oxford University Press, 1938.

Native Administration in the British African Territories. London: HMSO, 1951.

Hardin, Blaine. *Africa: Dispatches from a Fragile Continent*. New York: Norton, 1990.

Hayward, Fred M. "The Development of a Radical Political Organization in the Bush: A Case Study in Sierra Leone." *Canadian Journal of African Studies* 6,1 (1972), 1–28.

"Sierra Leone: State Consolidation, Fragmentation and Decay," in C. Cruise O'Brien, R. Rathbone, and J. Dunn, eds. *Contemporary West African States*. Cambridge: Cambridge University Press, 1989.

Hegba, P.M. *Emancipation d'Eglises sous tutelle*. Paris: Presence Africain, 1976.

Herbst, Jeffrey. *The Politics of Reform in Ghana, 1982–1991*. Berkeley: University of California Press, 1993.

His Majesty's Stationary Office. *Private Enterprise in British Tropical Africa*. London: Cmd 2016, 1924.

Hobbes, Thomas. *Leviathan*. London: Clarendon, 1909.

Howard, Allen. "Big Men, Traders and Chiefs: Power, Commerce and Spatial Change in the Sierra Leone–Guinea Plain." Ph.D Dissertation, University of Wisconsin, 1972.

Hyden, Goran. *Beyond Ujamaa in Tanzania: Underdevelopment and an Uncaptured Peasantry*. Berkeley: University of California Press, 1980.

No Shortcuts to Progress. Berkeley: University of California Press, 1983.

and Michael Bratton, eds. *Governance and Politics in Africa*. Boulder: Lynne Reinner, 1991.

Igué, O.J. "L'officiel, le paralléle et le clandestin." *Politique Africaine* 9 (1983), 29–51.

Ijagbemi, E.A. "The Freetown Colony and the Development of Legitimate Commerce in the Adjoining Territories." *Journal of the Historical Society of Nigeria* 2 (1970), 69–82.

Illife, John. *The Emergence of African Capitalism*. Minneapolis: University of Minnesota Press, 1983.

International Monetary Fund (IMF). *Balance of Payments Statistics Yearbook*. Washington, DC: IMF, 1990.

Jackson, Robert. *Quasi-states: Sovereignty, International Relations and the Third World*. New York: Cambridge University Press, 1990.

and Carl Rosberg. "Why Africa's Weak States Persist: The Empirical and Juridical in Statehood." *World Politics* 35,1 (1982), 1–24.

Jaycox, Edward. *The Challenge of African Development*. Washington, DC: World Bank, 1992.

Joseph, Richard. *Democracy and Prebendal Politics in Nigeria*. Ibadan: Spectrum, 1991.

Jusu, B.M. "The Haidara Rebellion of 1931." *Sierra Leone Studies* 7 (1954), 147–9.

Kallon, Kelfala. "The Political Economy of Sierra Leone's Economic Decline." African Studies Association annual meeting, Baltimore, MD, November 1990.

Kandeh, Jimmy. "Dynamics of State, Class and PoliticalEthnicity: A Comparative Study of State–Society Relations in Colonial and Post Colonial Sierra Leone." Ph.D dissertation, University of Wisconsin, 1987.

Kasfir, Nelson. "State, *Magendo*, and Class Formation in Uganda." *Journal of Commonwealth and Comparative Politics* 22,3 (1984).

Kennedy, Paul. *African Capitalism: The Struggle for Ascendancy*. New York: Cambridge University Press, 1988.

Kilson, Martin. *Political Change in a West African State*. Cambridge, MA: Harvard University Press, 1966.

Kpundeh, Sahr John. "Prospects in Contemporary Sierra Leone." *Corruption and Reform* 7 (1993), 237–47.

Kup, Peter. *Sierra Leone: A Concise History*. London: David & Charles, 1975.

Lemarchand, René. "The Politics of Penury in Rural Zaire," in Guy Grau, ed. *Zaire: The Political Economy of Underdevelopment*. New York: Praeger, 1979, 237–60.

"The State, the Parallel Economy, and the Changing Structure of Patrimonial

Systems." in Donald Rothchild and Naomi Chazan, eds. *The Precarious Balance: State and Society in Africa*. Boulder: Westview, 1988, 149–70.

Lethbridge-Banbury, George A. *Sierra Leone; or, The White Man's Grave*. London: S. Sonnenschein, 1888.

Lipson, Charles. *Standing Guard: Protecting Foreign Capital in the Nineteenth and Twentieth Centuries*. Berkeley: University of California Press, 1985.

Lugard, Fredrick D. (Lord). *The Dual Mandate in British Tropical Africa*. London: William Blackwood & Sons, 1922.

Political Memoranda: Revision of Instructions to Political Officers on Subjects Chiefly Political and Administrative, third edn. London: Frank Cass & Co., 1970.

MacCaullay, Kenneth. *The Colony of Sierra Leone Vindicated*. London: Frank Cass & Co., 1968 [1827].

MacGaffey, Janet. "Economic Disengagement and Class Formation in Zaire," in D. Rothchild and N. Chazan, eds. *The Precarious Balance: State and Society in Africa*. Boulder: Westview, 1988, 171–88.

Entrepreneurs and Parasites: The Struggle for Indigenous Capital in Zaire. New York: Cambridge University Press, 1987.

"How to Survive and Become Rich Amidst Devastation: The Second Economy in Zaire." *African Affairs* 82, 328 (1983), 351–66.

"Initiatives from Below: Zaire's Other Path to Social and Economic Restoration," in G. Hyden and M. Bratton, eds. *Governance and Politics in Africa*. Boulder: Lynne Reinner, 1991.

ed. *The Real Economy of Zaire*. Philadelphia: University of Pennsylvania, 1991.

Matthews. *A Voyage to the River Sierra Leone*. London: Frank Cass & Co., 1966 [1788].

Matturi, Sahr. "A Brief History of the Nimikoro Chiefdom, Kono District." *Africana Research Bulletin* 3,2 (1973), 32–43.

Mbembe, Achille. *Afrique Indociles: Christianisme, pouvoir et état en société postcoloniale*. Paris: Editions Karthala, 1988.

"l'argument matériel dans les Eglises catholiques d'Afrique: le cas du Zimbabwe (1975–87)." *Politique Africain* 35 (1989), 50–65.

"Pouvoir, violence et accumulation." *Politique Africaine* 39 (1990).

"Dèsordres, rèsistances et productivitè." *Politique Africaine* 42 (1991), 2–8.

Meillassoux, Claude. ed. *The Development of Indigenous Markets and Trade in West Africa*. London: Oxford University Press, 1971.

Migdal, Joel. *Strong Societies and Weak States*. Princeton: Princeton University Press, 1988.

Minchinton, W.E. "The Sierra Leone Diamond Rush." *Sierra Leone Studies* 19 (1966), 44–8.

Minikin, Victor. "Local Politics in Kono District." Ph.D dissertation, Birmingham University, 1971.

Miras, Claude de. "De la formation du capital privé á l'économie populaire spontanée." *Politique Africaine* 14 (1984), 92–109.

Mommelson, Wolfgang and Jürgen Osterhammel. *Imperialism and After*. London: Allen & Unwin, 1986.

Morice, Alain. "Commerce parallèle et troc á Luanda." *Politique Africaine* 17 (1985), 105–20.

"Guinée 1985: Etat, corruption et trafics." *Les Temps Modernes* 487 (1987), 97–135.

Naipaul, Shiva. *North of South*. London: Deutsch, 1978.

Nelson, Joan, ed. *Economic Crises and Policy Choice: The Politics of Adjustment in the Third World*. Princeton: Princeton University Press, 1990.

Parfitt, Trevor and Stephen Riley. *The African Debt Crisis*. New York: Routledge, 1989.

Parsons, Robert T. *Religion in an African Society*. Leiden: E.M. Brill, 1964.

Péan, Pierre. *L'argent noir: corruption et sous-développement*. Paris: Fayard, 1988.

Price, Robert. "Political Culture in Contemporary Ghana: The Big-Man Small-Boy Syndrome." *Journal of African Studies* 1,2 (1974), 173–204.

Prunier, G. "Violence et histoire en Afrique." *Politique Africaine* 42 (1991), 9–14.

Ravenhill, John. "Adjustment with Growth: A Fragile Consensus." *Journal of Modern African Studies* 26,2 (1988), 179–210.

Reno, William. "Old Brigades, Money Bags, New Breeds and the Ironies of Reform in Nigeria." *Canadian Journal of African Studies* 27,1 (1993), 66–87.

Riddell, J. Barry. "Things Fall Apart Again: Structural Adjustment Programmes in Sub-Saharan Africa." *Journal of Modern African Studies* 30,1 (1992), 53–68.

Roberts, George O. *The Anguish of Third World Independence: The Sierra Leone Experience*. Washington, DC: University Press of America, 1982.

Robinson, Ronald K. *Africa and the Victorians*. New York: St Martin's Press, 1961.

Roitman, Janet. "The Politics of Informal Markets in Sub-Saharan Africa." *Journal of Modern African Studies* 28,4 (1990), 671–96.

Rosen, David. "Diamonds, Diggers and Chiefs: The Politics of Fragmentation in a West African Society." Ph.D dissertation, University of Illinois, 1973.

Rothchild, Donald. *Ghana: The Political Economy of Recovery*. Boulder: Lynne Rienner, 1991.

Sandbrook, Richard. "Patrons, Clients and Factions: New Dimensions for Conflict in Africa." *Canadian Journal of Political Science* 5,1 (1972), 1–27.

The Politics of Africa's Economic Stagnation. New York: Cambridge University Press, 1985.

"Taming the African Leviathan." *World Policy Journal* 7,4 (1990), 673–701.

The Politics of Africa's Economic Recovery. New York: Cambridge University Press, 1993.

Schatz, Sayre. *Nigerian Capitalism*. Berkeley: University of California, 1977.

"African Capitalism and African Economic Performance," in Harvey Glickman, ed. *The Crisis and Challenge of African Development*. Westport, CT: Greenwood, 1988, 62–85.

Schatzberg, Michael. *The Dialectics of Oppression in Zaire*. Bloomington: Indiana University, 1988.

Schmitt, Carl (George Schwab, trans.). *The Concept of the Political*. New Brunswick, NJ: Rutgers University Press, 1976.

(George Schwab, trans.). *Political Theology*. Cambridge, MA: MIT Press, 1985 [1934].

(George Schwab, trans.). *Political Romanticism*. Cambridge, MA: MIT Press, 1986.

Sierra Leone Business Advisory Service. *Sierra Leone Business Directory*. Freetown: SLBAS, 1986.

Spitzer, Leo. *The Creoles of Sierra Leone: Responses to Colonialism, 1870–1945.* Madison: University of Wisconsin Press, 1974.

Stanley, Henry M. *The Congo and the Founding of Its Free State.* New York: Harper & Brothers, 1885.

Stevens, Siaka. *What Life Has Taught Me.* London: Kensal House, 1984.

Twaddle, Michael. "Is Africa Decaying?: Notes Towards an Analysis." in Holger Bernt Hansen and Michael Twaddle, eds. *Uganda Now: Between Decay and Development.* Nairobi: Heinemann Kenya, 1988, 313–35.

United Nations General Assembly. "18.51 Protection of Mount Nimba, Guinea." *New Resolutions.* New York: United Nations General Assembly, 1990.

van der Laan, H.L. *The Lebanese of Sierra Leone.* The Hague: Mouton, 1975.

The Sierra Leone Diamonds. London: Oxford University Press, 1965.

van de Walle, Nicholas. "Rice Politics in Cameroon: State Commitment, Capability and Urban Bias." *Journal of Modern African Studies* 27,4 (1989), 579–600.

"Political Liberalization and Economic Policy Reform in Africa," in US Agency of International Development. *Economic Reform in Africa's New Era of Political Liberalization.* Washington, DC: USAid, April 1993, 81–98.

Vansina, Jan. "Lignage et idéologie en Afrique centrale." *Enquêtes et documents d'histoire africaine,* 1980.

"A Past for Africa's Future?" *Dalhousie Review* 68,1/2 (1988), 8–23.

Vwakyanakazi, Mukohya. "African Traders in Butembo, Eastern Zaire (1960–1980): a Case Study of Informal Entrepreneurship in a Cultural Context of Central Africa." Ph.D dissertation, University of Wisconsin, 1982.

Waltz, Kenneth. *Theory of International Politics.* Reading, MA: Addison-Wesley, 1979.

Whitaker, Jennifer. *How Can Africa Survive?* New York: Council on Foreign Relations, 1990.

Willame, Jean Claude. *Patrimonialism and Political Change in the Congo.* Stanford: Stanford University Press, 1972.

"Zaire: systéme de survie et fiction d'Etat." *Canadian Journal of African Studies* 18,1 (1984), 113–42.

Zaire: l'épopée d'Inga. Paris: Harmattan, 1986.

World Bank. *Accelerated Development in Sub-Saharan Africa: An Agenda for Action* (Berg Report). Washington, DC: World Bank, 1981.

Debt Tables. Washington, DC: World Bank, 1981.

Sierra Leone: Prospects for Growth and Equity. Washington, DC: World Bank, 1981.

"Sierra Leone: Prospects for Growth and Equity." Report No. 535256. Washington, DC: World Bank, March 1985.

Sub-Saharan Africa: From Crisis to Sustainable Growth. Washington, DC: World Bank, 1989.

Ghana 2000 and Beyond. Washington, DC: World Bank, February 1993.

Wyse, Akintola. *The Krio of Sierra Leone.* Freetown: Okrafo-Smart & Co., 1987.

Young, Crawford and Thomas Turner. *The Rise and Decline of the Zairian State.* Madison: University of Wisconsin Press, 1985.

Zack-Williams, A.B. "Sierra Leone: Crisis and Despair." *Review of African Political Economy* 49 (1990), 22–33.

GOVERNMENT OF SIERRA LEONE PUBLICATIONS

All Peoples Congress. *Constitution of the All Peoples Congress.* Freetown: APC Directorate, 1965.

    Report to the Tenth National Delegates Conference of the All Peoples Congress Party (APC), Makeni, 26–9 January 1989. Freetown: Government Printer, 1989.

Annual Report on Eastern Province, 1921. Freetown: Government Printer, 1922.

Bank of Sierra Leone. *Annual Report.* Freetown, various issues.

    Economic Trends. Freetown, various issues.

    Economic Review. Freetown, various issues.

    Bank of Sierra Leone Research Department. *Sierra Leone in Statistics.* Freetown: BSL Research Department, 1975.

Blue Book. Freetown: Government Printer, published annually.

Brooke, N.J. *Report on the Native Authority System in Sierra Leone.* Freetown: Government Printer, 1953.

Budget Speech. Freetown: Government Printer, various issues.

Central Statistics Office. *National Accounts for Sierra Leone.* Freetown: Government Printer, 1971.

    A Survey of Sierra Leone Businesses. Freetown: Government Printer, 1967.

Consolidated Report of SLPMB. Freetown, 1959.

Dove-Edwin Commission of Inquiry into the Conduct of the 1967 General Elections in Sierra Leone. Freetown: Government Printer, 1968.

Estimates of Revenues and Expenditures. Freetown: Government Printer, various issues.

Fenton, J.S. *Report on a Visit to Nigeria and on the Application of the Principles of Native Administration to the Protectorate of Sierra Leone.* Freetown: Government Printer, 1935.

Further Reports of the Commission of Enquiry into the Conduct of Certain Chiefs. Freetown: Government Printer, 1957.

Government Diamond Office. *Annual Report.* Freetown: Government Printer, 1973.

    Report of the Government Diamond Office. Freetown: Government Printer, 1960, 1965, 1968.

Laws of Sierra Leone. London: Crown Agents, 1925, 1949, 1963.

Marke, R.B. *Report of the Commission of Inquiry into the Issue of Alluvial Diamond Mining Licenses in the Gbambaiadu Area, Kono District.* Freetown: Government Printer, 1957.

Ministry of Information and Broadcasting. *President Stevens Speaks.* Freetown: Publications Division, 1980.

Ministry of Mines. *Report of Deputy Inspector of Mines for 1969.* Freetown: Government Printer.

"Money Supply and Balance of Payments." (mimeo) Freetown: Bank of Sierra Leone, Research Department, April, 1990.

"Precepts-Chiefdom Authorities." (mimeo) Freetown: Ministry of Internal Affairs, no date.

Report by Her Majesty's Commissioner and Correspondence on the Subject of the

Insurrection in the Sierra Leone Protectorate, 1898, Part II: Evidence and Documents (Chalmers Report). London: HMSO, 1898.

Report of the Census of 1963. Freetown: Government Printer, 1964.

Report of the Commission of Inquiry into Disturbances in the Provinces (Cox Commission). London: Crown Agents, 1956.

Report of the Forster Commission of Inquiry of Assets of Ex-Ministers and Ex-Deputy Ministers. Freetown, 1968.

Report of the Inspector of Mines. Freetown: Ministry of Mines. July 1989.

Report of the Ministry of Mines. Freetown: Government Printer, 1965.

Report of the Wales Commission of Inquiry into the Conduct of the Immigration Quota Committee. Freetown, 1968.

Report on the Administration of the Provinces, 1955. Freetown: Government Printer, 1956.

Report on the Survey of Business and Industry, 1966/67. Freetown: Central Statistics Office, n.d.

Sierra Leone Gazette. Freetown, various issues.

Statement of the Sierra Leone Government on the Report of the Commission of Inquiry into Disturbances in the Province. Freetown, 1956.

GOVERNMENT OF SIERRA LEONE – UNPUBLISHED SOURCES

Most pre-1964 official papers are found in the Sierra Leone Archives, University of Sierra Leone, Freetown. Included among these are colonial documents catalogued "CO" (Governor's Council) and "KNA" (Kono Native Authorities) "EP" (Eastern Province).

Many unpublished official papers after 1963, and some Kono District Office papers concerning MADA (Mining Area Development Authority) and ADMS (Alluvial Diamond Mining Scheme) were found in the collections of private individuals.

Official correspondence between the Kono District Officer and the Ministry of the Interior concerning Tankoro and Gbense Chiefdoms (1968–88) were obtained from Ministry of the Interior files. A number of petitions and correspondences between the Provincial Secretary and local Kono authorities were obtained from private sources – the provincial archive was damaged in disturbances in the mid 1980s and some of its contents fell into private hands.

"Fugitive sources," primarily government officials who removed documents when moving to a new position provided other official correspondences. While perhaps intended to conceal activity, more than once requests for private papers were met with "I too have considered writing a book." "Privatized" documents have become one of the many perquisites of office.

Index

Other books in the series

1197397R0

Printed in Great Britain by
Amazon.co.uk, Ltd.,
Marston Gate.